SOCIAL CARICATURE IN THE EIGHTEENTH CENTURY

THE FRENCH COFFEE-HOUSE

FROM THE ORIGINAL WATER-COLOUR DRAWING BY THOMAS ROWLANDSON

GEORGE PASTON

SOCIAL CARICATURE
IN THE
EIGHTEENTH CENTURY

BENJAMIN BLOM
New York

First published London 1905
Reissued 1968,
by Benjamin Blom, Inc. Bx 10452

Library of Congress Catalog Card No. 67-12467

Printed in U.S.A. by
NOBLE OFFSET PRINTERS, INC.
NEW YORK 3, N. Y.

CONTENTS

LIST OF ILLUSTRATIONS

LIST OF ILLUSTRATIONS

LIST OF ILLUSTRATIONS

LIST OF ILLUSTRATIONS

LIST OF ILLUSTRATIONS

PREFACE

IN this book I have attempted, by the aid of the caricaturist, to give a kaleidoscopic view of the lighter side of social life in the eighteenth century. The illustrations, with few exceptions, have been reproduced from prints and engravings at the British Museum. Sixty years ago, when Mr. Thomas Wright was preparing his book on *England under the House of Hanover* (republished as *A Caricature History of the Georges*), he complained that he had received little help from the national collections, which were deplorably poor in English caricature. Since his day the Print Room has received many valuable additions to its stores; and about thirty years ago the satirical prints and drawings (down to *circa* 1770) were mounted, arranged, and catalogued. The Catalogue,[1] prepared by F. G. Stephens, with descriptions by Edward Hawkins, may justly be described as a monument of research and a model of arrangement. I take this opportunity of acknowledging my indebtedness to this work, which, by its innumerable references, has greatly lightened my labours.

It has been impossible, of course, in the space of one volume, to give a representative selection of the works of artists so abnormally prolific as Gillray and Rowlandson. From their output, so far as it was at my disposal, I have drawn such examples as serve to illustrate the phases of social life with which their talent is more especially identified. Hogarth, who can only be called a caricaturist by discourtesy, is here represented by certain of his lighter and more topical designs, the great moral and dramatic series being left untouched. Only brief summaries are here given of the not very interesting or eventful lives of Gillray and Rowlandson. For fuller details readers may

---

[1] Catalogue of Prints and Drawings. Division I. Political and Personal Satires.

PREFACE

be referred to Mr. Grego's valuable monographs, *James Gillray and his Works* and *Thomas Rowlandson, the Caricaturist*. On Hogarth Mr. Austin Dobson has said the last word.

I have to thank Mr. and Mrs. Norman, of Chelmondiston Grange, for placing their collection of Rowlandson drawings and prints at my disposal, and further for their great kindness in sending the following examples to London for the purpose of reproduction : Water-colour drawings—*The French Coffee-house*, *The Return from St. James' after the honour of Knighthood*, and *The Starving Poet and Publisher;* Coloured etchings—*Reconciliation*, *A French Family*, *An Actor Reciting to a Manager*, *The High-mettled Racer* (1), *Going to the Races*, *French Travelling*, and *English Travelling*.

SOCIAL CARICATURE IN THE EIGHTEENTH CENTURY

INTRODUCTION

IT has been said that caricature was born in Italy and nursed in Holland; it might be added that the art attained maturity in England, the land of the free pencil no less than of the free pen. In the wake of William of Orange, chief patron of the famous caricaturist, Romeyn de Hooghe,[1] followed Dutch or Flemish draughtsmen and engravers, who taught the Briton, as yet a neophyte in pictorial satire, the secrets of the craft. The seed thus sown fell on fertile soil, and during some thirty years the Dutch cartoons and emblematical prints, which dealt with the iniquities of the French, and other subjects of interest to both countries, were regularly copied and adapted for the British market, the inscriptions being printed both in Dutch and English. The word "caricature" had not as yet come into general use. Its first appearance in English literature is in the *Christian Morals* of Sir Thomas Browne, who exhorts the reader " not to expose himself by four-footed manners unto monstrous draughts and caricatura representations." It was several decades later that Addison, writing upon " Detractors " in an early number of the *Spectator*, observed, " From all these hands we have such draughts of mankind as are represented in those burlesque pictures which the Italians call Caricaturas, where the art consists in preserving, amidst distorted proportions and aggravated features, some distinguishing likeness of the person, but in such a manner as to transform the most agreeable beauty into the most odious monster." About the same period (1709–10) Steele, in the course of an article in the *Tatler*, states that a burgher of Amsterdam has sent him " several draughts of humourous and satirical pictures by the best hands of the Dutch nation. They are a trading people, and their very minds mechanics. They express their wit in manufacture as we do in manuscript." This, it may be noted in passing, was a peculiarly Philistine view of the province of pictorial satire.

---

[1] Romeyn de Hooghe, born *c.* 1646 at The Hague. He established a school of design at Haarlem, where he died in 1708. He engraved a number of serious as well as emblematical subjects, including The Entry of the Prince of Orange into London, The Marriage of the Prince of Orange, and The Army of William III. on the banks of the Boyne.

B   I

CAPTAIN FRANCIS GROSE
BY HIMSELF

expose him in some absurd or monstrous attitude, than to express the affections of men on canvas. It hath been thought a vast commendation of a painter to say that his figures seem to breathe; but surely it is a much greater and nobler applause that they seem to think."

The instant favour and acceptance accorded to the art of caricature on its introduction into England has been accounted for by M. Filon, one of those French critics who, in their characters of "lookers-on," always seem to know so much more about us than we know about ourselves, on the ground that this grotesque form of art appeals to certain distinctive qualities of the Anglo-Saxon temperament. The English, he explains, have no taste for abstractions, preferring to have ideas presented to them in a concrete form. Again, they combine a love of mockery with a love of preaching, to which predilections may be added a passion for liberty. Now caricature is a most effective weapon in the hand of him who fights against what he believes to be evil in social or political life, the satiric artist being able to throw ridicule upon his opponents at the same time that he seeks to win converts to his own propaganda. Lastly, for the Briton, ugliness is not simply the negation of the beautiful, but an artistic entity to be studied and appreciated for its own sake. Just as, with the exaggerative tendencies of the idealist, he dreams of a beauty and a grandeur that are above nature, so also he conceives of an ugliness and absurdity that are below it.

There is, no doubt, a certain amount of truth in these theories; but perhaps the chief reason for the eagerness with which the English draughtsman pursued the craft of caricature as soon as it had become naturalised in this country may be found in the almost total lack of facilities for art training in the England of the early eighteenth century. There were then no public galleries, no picture exhibitions, and no art-schools worthy of the name. When Thornhill and Kent were the chief British masters, it is hardly surprising that patrons imported their works of art from abroad and neglected native talent. But in caricature untrained ability found and seized its opportunity. The emblematical cartoons and satirical prints were, it is obvious, frequently the production of an amateur or self-taught artist with a gift for catching a likeness or hitting off a foible. Like the child and the savage, he made his meaning plain by exaggerating the characteristics of his models, or by appending a written explanation to his design. Thus in the early "hieroglyphics" the figures are usually numbered with reference to the elucidation which is printed below. To the unlettered patron of these popular prints, with his Saxon love of allegory, it was the pleasant occupation of a winter's evening to solve the meaning of the emblematical cartoon, or, if his education were sufficiently advanced, to spell out the figured key to the puzzle.

The subjects dealt with by the caricaturist during the first half of the century, it is important to note, differ considerably from those which attracted his attention during the latter half, particularly the last thirty years. Down to 1720 the social caricature was practically a negligible quantity, but the picturesque scandals of the South Sea Bubble gave so powerful a stimulus to the graphic satirist, that he was able thenceforward to take up his position as an important factor in the social as well as the political life of the nation. The Bubble agitation brought the young Hogarth into the field with an emblematical print on lines already familiar—a fact of great significance; for though Hogarth was first and foremost a great dramatic artist,[1] he was incidentally a caricaturist, and his methods undoubtedly influenced the work of such of his contemporaries and successors as tried their hands at the grotesque. His genius and his example raised the standard of the art, purged it of many of its puerilities, brought it into repute with persons of cultivated taste, and may be said to have kept it alive until such time as Gillray and Rowlandson rose up to give it new traditions and a fresh impetus.

After the Bubble had been pricked, the caricaturist's chief source of inspiration was the theatre, which was then the people's playhouse, the drama being the one form of art or literature in which the general public took any interest. To all seeming, John Bull had an inexhaustible appetite for cartoons which ridiculed the squabbles of rival managers, the intrigues of the players, and the airs and graces of the Italian singers. The caricaturist at this period was usually a denizen of Lower Bohemia, possessing so slight a knowledge of the great world that he seldom troubled himself to portray their fashions or turn their follies to account. The domestic affairs of those in high places, even of royalty, were made the subject of but few attacks, and this was probably the result rather of ignorance or indifference than of any restraining sense of awe, since with Walpole's rise to power began an era of freedom for tongue, pen, and pencil such as had never been known in England before.

Literature was held in too small account to be worthy of serious attention from draughtsmen who aimed at pleasing the popular taste, though to this rule that bombshell, the *Dunciad*, forms an important exception. Next to the drama, the caricaturist found his best material in the instances of popular credulity, which formed the subject of many a "nine days' wonder" in the first half of the century. Besides the South Sea Bubble, the strange cases of Mary Tofts and Eliza Canning, the hoax of the Bottle Conjurer, the earthquake panic of 1750, and the Cock Lane Ghost, each in its turn contributed a topic for ridicule.

During the last thirty or forty years of the century the status of the caricaturist, and the style of subject treated by him, underwent a gradual change. The comic print gained a footing in fashionable society, prices increased, and print-shops multiplied. The improvement in the art of mezzotint, by which texture could be more faithfully reproduced, led to a great increase in the number of caricatures on contemporary fashions, while the Maccaronies, their modes and follies, eclipsed the theatre as a subject for caricature. Artists like Rowlandson and Bunbury, and the amateurs whose

---

[1] We know, from his own words that, in his famous series, it was Hogarth's aim to produce moral dramas in pictorial form.

designs were frequently engraved by professional craftsmen, knew far more of the social world than their predecessors, and chose their types from a different class. The amours of the Prince of Wales and his brothers, the gambling scandals, the mania for private theatricals, the absurdities of amateur sportsmen, the foibles of professional men, and the minor miseries of life were, together with the perennial extravagance of costume, the raw material from which the satirist drew his inspiration.

Before proceeding to give illustrations of the caricaturist's art, it may be well to inquire into the principles upon which he worked and the characteristics of his models, since by so doing we may be able to clear him in some measure from the reproach of deliberate offensiveness, both in choice of subject and method of treatment, under which he has suffered so long. Of the rules of the craft we have been told something by a member of the profession, Captain Francis Grose, the friend of Burns, who has gained immortality as the "chiel amang us takin' notes," and as the instigator of the poem of *Tam o' Shanter*[1] (Pl. II.). According to Grose, the student begins by learning to draw the human head from one of the drawing-books in which the form constituting human beauty, in accordance with modern ideas, is laid down. As soon as he has acquired facility in drawing heads, he may amuse himself by altering the distance of the principal lines, whereby he will produce a variety of odd faces that will both surprise and please him. But he must be careful not to exaggerate the peculiarities of his subjects, or they will become hideous instead of ridiculous, and excite horror instead of laughter. The several features of the human face are classified by this authority for comic purposes, and include the parrot, bulbous, snub, or broken nose; the blubber, shark, or bone-box mouth; the nut-cracker, double, or cucumber chin. One representative countenance is given, in which the nose is snubbed, the mouth blubbered, the chin double, the eyes goggle, and the brows penthouse. The result is anything but amusing from the modern point of view; it is merely ugly.

It is difficult to lay down any hard and fast rules as to legitimate subjects for comic treatment, since taste in humour changes with each generation. A common cause of laughter, according to Hobbes, is the supposed superiority of the laugher to the person laughed at; while Beattie held that laughter is occasioned by an uncommon mixture of similarity and contrariety exhibited in close relation. This latter theory, as Grose points out, is most frequently put into practice in designs of a ludicrous nature, in which the qualities and employments of the persons depicted are incongruous or incompatible. Thus a cowardly soldier, a deaf musician, a bandy-legged dancing-master, an antiquated fop, a drunken magistrate creating a riot, or a tailor mounted on a

---

[1] Francis Grose (1731 (?)–1791) was the son of an Irish jeweller. He studied art, and in 1766 was elected a member of the Society of Artists. He published *Antiquities of England and Wales*, with illustrations from his own drawings, and in 1789 went to Scotland to collect material for his *Antiquities of Scotland*. It was at this time that he made the acquaintance of Burns, who celebrated him and his travels in "Ken ye ought of Captain Grose?" Grose was a man of varied activities, since he held the post of Richmond Herald for several years, and in 1778 was captain and adjutant of the Surrey Militia.

spirited horse, were all regarded as suitable subjects for the caricaturist; though if the magistrate were represented with a broken head, or the tailor falling into the gutter, the artist was to give the impression that their injuries were only of a trifling nature. National jokes, such as those relating to the Welshman and his leek, or the Scotchman and his scrubbing-post, are also suggested as affording promising material; while anachronistic designs, such as representations of Solomon in a bag-wig and ruffles, the chamber of Cleopatra furnished with a clock and harpsichord, or the Siege of Jerusalem carried on by means of cannon and mortars, have generally found favour with the public.

Incongruity, as we see, was the chief resource of the caricaturist when he desired to supply a design from his own invention. But as a rule, the incidents of the day, the follies or vices of his contemporaries, furnished him with abundant material. The eighteenth-century caricaturist, be it remembered, was professedly a moralist. He held it to be his mission to scourge vice and hold up folly to ridicule, and he was apt to set about his self-appointed task with the intemperate zeal of a hot gospeller. In his political cartoons, more especially, his satire too frequently borders on the ferocious, and it is clear that to him the " other side " is represented solely by idiots or monsters. He tomahawks his victims and tramples on their prostrate bodies with an indecent glee, which would have the effect of alienating modern sympathies from his cause. But he knew his own public, men of strong stomachs and dull brains, whose passions could only be inflamed and their comprehension reached by means of the crudest colours and the most unblushing exaggerations.

But when we turn from the political to the social caricature the case is altered; the touch grows lighter and more genial, the tomahawk and bludgeon are exchanged for fencing foils; at the worst, for fists with the gloves on.[1] The artist is nearly always on the side of the angels, or at any rate upon the side of reason and common sense. But he naturally reflected the tastes and manners of his own time, insomuch that the robust humour of certain of his productions gives offence to those moderns who are shocked at Fielding but delight in Zola. There is a fashion in seemliness as in other social conventions, and it is possible that could some of Gillray's admirers revisit the glimpses of the moon, they might be scandalised at a certain type of picture that appears annually at the Salon, and raise virtuous protest against some of the Gallic farces at which Londoners titter every season. The eighteenth-century satirist was apt to call a spade a spade, but he seldom winked a double meaning.

Against the charge of producing work of unnecessary ugliness it is more difficult to defend the caricaturist, though his worst offences will be found in his political designs. Caricature, of course, implies exaggeration, but exaggeration need not degenerate into monstrosity, though, as we have

---

[1] It must be admitted that the blows were sometimes given below the belt.

seen in the passages quoted from Steele and Fielding, the caricature artist was licensed to produce monstrosities. As a rule, however, it will be found that the most revoltingly ugly designs are those which are most lacking in point, imagination, and humour; while Rowlandson has shown us that a comic cartoon may be a thing of beauty, not unworthy the hand of one of the French "little masters." The worst monstrosities were produced during the most prolific and most "personal" period of the art, from 1770 to 1810, when, as has been said, the caricaturist lived like a caterpillar upon the green leaf of reputation. The saner, more restrained, if less vigorous methods of the earlier half of the century are probably due in a measure to the influence of the foreign craftsmen working in England. Relying frequently upon symbolism for their effects, they were the less inclined to exaggerate the peculiarities of their victims; indeed, their figures are for the most part "conventionalised," and in modern eyes gain a certain picturesqueness and grace from their costume and surroundings.

With regard to the human monstrosities, as we consider them, that disfigure much of the later work, it must not be forgotten that these were regarded as pardonably exaggerated but quite recognisable portraits by the contemporary public, and not as the products of a diseased imagination. Among a semi-civilised people, who, by accepting the material side of civilisation alone, have lost the fine physical condition of the savage without making any marked advance in spiritual development, bodily distortions and weird physiognomies are by no means uncommon. The English of the eighteenth century were in many respects semi-civilised, and their excessive indulgence in eating and drinking, their prejudice against exercise, fresh air, and cold water, to say nothing of the insular eccentricity of character upon which they prided themselves, resulted in unwieldy figures, bloated complexions, and startling developments of dress and demeanour. The reminiscences of the period teem with anecdotes of men of promise and ability who ruined their health or cut short their lives by over-indulgence in the pleasures of the table. John Taylor, for example, mentions two once-popular actors, Ross and Stephen Kemble, who "ate themselves into so unseemly a shape" that they were obliged to quit the stage; while Angelo has many anecdotes relative to the gluttony of his distinguished contemporaries. The deep drinking fashionable throughout the century has been commemorated for all time by Hogarth in his *Modern Midnight Conversation*, and Rowlandson has illustrated the heavy eating with painful realism in a series of etchings representing the attitude and expression of a gourmand before dinner, at dinner, and after dinner.

Though the caricaturist, without doubt, made the most of the flesh and floridity of his subjects, it is to be feared that his portraits were less libellous than we are prone to imagine them. It must be admitted that our great-great-grandfathers had a sense of humour which is apt to strike their descendants as a trifle crude; but to the serious student of a period every manifestation of that period has its interest and value, and probably no development of the eighteenth century is more characteristic than its caricature. The satiric artist was a man who loved to laugh, not always wisely, and seldom too well. Still, from him, as from other frivolous persons, we learn many things that the serious historian leaves untold, and gain illuminating glimpses into the more intimate life of the time.

THE BEAU MONDE

PART I

THE most voluminous, if not the most important, section of a work dealing with social caricatures must necessarily be devoted to a consideration of what was known in eighteenth-century parlance as the " Beau Monde," of its fashions, follies, scandals, and eccentricities. The latter half of the century was by far the most prolific period for caricatures on " high life," partly by reason of the excellent material supplied by the extravagance of the prevailing fashions (1770–1800), but more particularly because society—in the narrow sense of the word—was gradually enlarging its borders, and becoming year by year less of the exclusive coterie that it had been under the first and second Georges. Even the professional caricaturists were able to rub shoulders with the great world, at the Pantheon, Carlisle House, and Ranelagh, instead of merely studying them from a respectful distance in the Mall or Hyde Park ; while in many instances social designs were furnished to engravers by amateurs, who, whatever the defects of their technique, had first-hand knowledge of their subject.

An early specimen of a satire upon fashionable dames may be seen in a quaint little engraving (*circa* 1710) called *The Tea-table*, which heads a copy of verses describing the gossip and scandal-mongering that were supposed even then—only some half-century after the introduction of the Chinese herb —to be the necessary accompaniment of a feminine tea-party. A group of ladies, dressed in the height of the fashion (Pl. III.), are seated round a small table, on which is the tea equipage and a book called *Chit-chat*. An emblematical figure of Envy drives Truth and Justice out of the room, while near the open window are concealed two men, who listen eagerly to the conversation within, the style of which is symbolised by a picture on the wall representing a priest carrying a woman on his back towards a church. Considering the interest taken in the tea-table gossip by the eavesdropping men, there is something slightly illogical about the opening lines of the accompanying verses, with their proud assertion :—

" Here see we Scandal (for our Sex too base)
Seat its dread Empire in the Female Race,
'Mongst Beaux and Women, Fans and Mechlin Lace.
Chief Seat of Slander ! Ever there we see
Thick Scandal circulate with right Bohea ! "

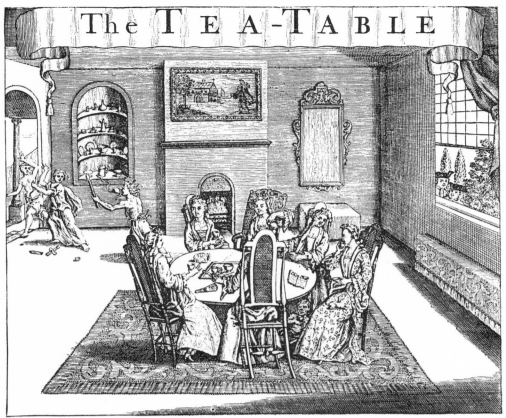

[C. 1710]

THE TEA-TABLE

Sold by Jno. Bowles, Print & Mapseller, at No. 13 in Cornhill

London: Printed for & Sold by CARINGTON BOWLES, No. 69 in St Pauls Church Yard

J. June

[C. 1733]

THE REVIEW

Another attack upon fashionable ladies may be found in a design by J. June[1] called *The Review* (*c.* 1733), a satire upon the hoop petticoat, that favourite topic with the masculine humorist. Some years earlier the hoop was supposed to have been brought to trial before Steele and other writers in the *Tatler*, and its use condemned. In June's design we see a London street in which ladies are walking in large hoops, while one is being let down into her coach through the roof by means of a crane and pulley. On one side a magistrate's court is visible, where a hoopless woman stands between two constables, weeping for the loss of her adornment, which has been condemned and hung up above the entrance to the courthouse (Pl. IV.).

Men and women are jointly satirised in a drawing by L. P. Boitard,[2] called *Taste à la Mode, as in the Year 1735* (Pl. V.). In this the ladies are represented as wearing the flat milkmaid hat, which enjoyed a long period of popularity, low-cut bodices, and moderate-sized hoops under short skirts; while the men wear heavy tie-wigs, fastened with large butterfly bows, full-skirted coats, and cocked hats, which some of them carry, French fashion, under their arms. In the middle of the foreground stands a short, stout footman, dressed in the costume which we are accustomed to associate with a beadle—three-cornered hat, long coat, and official staff. A companion design by the same artist, *Taste à la Mode, as in the year 1745*, shows a change in the fashions, which has taken the direction of longer skirts and larger hoops for the women. The men's coats are somewhat less voluminous; but the alteration is, as might be expected, less perceptible in the masculine than in the feminine attire (Pl. VI.).

The scene in both of the above designs seems to be laid in St. James's Park, the fashionable rallying-place of both sexes, who apparently regarded a stroll under the trees as sufficient exercise for the whole day, in spite of their heavy diet. A detailed account of the life led by a young man of fashion in the early decades of the century is given by J. Macky[3] in his *Journey through England* (1724), from which we learn that he commonly rose at nine, and either attended great men's levees till eleven, or else frequented the tea-tables, the best of which were the "Cocoa Tree" and "White's Chocolate House." "We are carried to these Places in Chairs or Sedans," he explains, writing in the character of a gentleman travelling in England to a friend on the Continent, "which are here very cheap, a Guinea a week, or a Shilling per Hour, and your Chairmen serve you for Porters to run on Errands as your Gondoliers do at Venice. If it be fine Weather we take a Turn in the Park till

---

[1] J. June, an engraver who obtained a good deal of employment as a book-illustrator between 1740 and 1770. He engraved some of his own designs and also a few portraits.

[2] Louis Pierre Boitard was a pupil of La Farges, and came to England, where he married an Englishwoman, in the reign of George I. Besides his caricatures, several of which are directed against his own countrymen, he engraved some portraits and illustrations for books. He died *c.* 1758. Boitard is mentioned in Walpole's *Anecdotes of Painting* as "a very neat workman."

[3] John Macky, a government agent or spy. Date of birth unknown; died in 1726. He was director of the packet-boat service between England and France, but, falling under suspicion of treachery, was imprisoned for some years. He published his *Memoirs of the Secret Services of John Macky*, and the first edition of his *Journey through England* in 1714. An enlarged edition appeared in 1723–4.

Boitard, Inv.

Evan Davis, Sculp.

TASTE À LA MODE AS IN THE YEAR 1735

BEING THE CONTRAST TO THE YEAR 1745

Publish'd Jany. yᵉ 3, 1749, by Robt. Sayer, Map & Printseller, facing Fetter Lane, Fleet Street.   Price 6d.

Boitard, Inv.

F. Patton, Sculp.

TASTE À LA MODE, 1745

Published according to Act, Sept. 12th, 1745. Price 6d.
Sold by C. Moseley, Engraver & Printseller, in Round Court, in the Strand

two, when we go to Dinner, or if it be Dirty, you are entertained at Picket or Bassett at White's, or you may talk Politics at the Smyrna [Coffee-house]. . . . Ordinaries are not so common here as abroad; yet the French have set up two or three pretty good ones for the conveniency of Foreigners in Suffolk Street, where one is tolerably well served; but a general way is to make a Party at the Coffee-house to go and dine at the Tavern, where we sit till Six, when we go to the Play, except you are invited to the Table of some great man, which Strangers are always courted to, and nobly entertained. . . .

"After the Play the best Company generally go to Tom's or Wills' Coffee-houses, where there is playing of Picket and the best of Conversation till Midnight. Here you will see blue and green Ribbons and Stars sitting familiarly with private gentlemen, and talking with the same freedom as if they had left their Quality and Degrees of Distance at home, and a Stranger tastes with Pleasure the universal Liberty of Speech of the English Nation. Or if you like rather the Company of Ladies, there are Assemblies at most People of Quality's houses. And at all the Coffee-houses you have not only the Foreign Prints, but several English ones with the Foreign occurrences, besides Papers of Morality and Party Disputes."

Although there were already various public gardens in London and the surrounding villages, there was as yet no open-air place of entertainment which enjoyed the regular patronage of "persons of quality." In 1732, however, Jonathan Tyers acquired a long lease of Spring Gardens, Vauxhall, and after making considerable improvements in the grounds and pavilions (Hogarth and Hayman were employed to design some of the decorations), he opened a long and prosperous period of management with a Ridotto al Fresco. A few years later an orchestra and grand organ were added to the attractions of the place, the main features of which remained much the same for the best part of half a century.

For the year 1742 there is a satirical view of *Spring Gardens, Vauxhall*, printed and engraved "with authority" by M. Ramus. In this design several well-known persons are represented, including Sir Robert Walpole, Lord Baltimore, Tyers the proprietor, a journalist (probably intended for "Sir" John Hill,[1] editor of the *British Magazine*) who declares that he will "puff and write and puff again," and a clergyman who acted as a sort of honorary chaplain to the gardens. In the artist's opinion prices ruled too high at Vauxhall, for he has introduced burlesque inscriptions into the scene to the effect that "Beef is 12 pence p. oz., Oyl 12 shillings p. Quart, and Horse-radish 12 pence p. Sack." That provisions did not grow cheaper at the gardens seems to be proved by an actual list of prices for the year 1762. A

---

[1] John Hill (*c.* 1716–75), journalist, quack, and Knight of the Swedish Order of Vasa. He is best known for his contribution of daily letters to the *London Advertiser*, under the pseudonym of "The Inspector." These consisted of a scandalous chronicle of the times, and made him many enemies. He wrote some worthless plays, and compiled innumerable works of a pseudo-medical kind, including *The Vegetable System* in twenty-six volumes. He was thrashed by an Irishman at Ranelagh, a fracas that occasioned a number of caricatures. He is now best remembered by Garrick's epigram:—

"For physics and farces his equal there scarce is,
His farces are physic, his physic a farce is."

dish of ham cost a shilling, and it was said to be cut so thin that the guests could read the newspaper through the slices ; a chicken no bigger than a sparrow was half-a-crown, a cheese-cake fourpence, and a tart a shilling. The purchasing power of money, it must be remembered, was then about double what it is at the present time.

In 1742 Hogarth painted his picture of *Taste in High Life* at the request, it is said, of a Miss Edwards, a rich, eccentric old maid, who wished to retaliate upon her contemporaries for the ridicule which they had cast upon her old-fashioned mode of attire. The price paid for the picture was sixty pounds, and the artist refused to allow it to be engraved. Without his knowledge, however, a copy was made, and in May, 1746, an announcement appeared in the *General Advertiser* to the effect that "On Monday next will be published an entertaining new print, called *Taste in High Life* (a companion to *Taste à la Mode*), from an incomparable picture by Mr. Hogarth (designed by a lady lately deceased), proving beyond contradiction that the present polite assemblies of Drums, Routs, etc., are mere exotics, and the supporters of such, and other Divertissements Modernes, a parcel of Insects."

A lady of a certain age and a gentleman (supposed to be intended for Lord Portmore),[1] both dressed in the extreme of the fashion, are here depicted in ectasies over a little china cup and saucer. It may be noted that their attitudes and expressions are very similar to those of the æsthetes who were represented as living up to a teapot, or dining off a lily, in the *Punches* of twenty years ago. A younger woman, probably a *dame de compagnie*, pats a little negro boy under the chin, as he sits on a table playing with a Chinese mandarin. A monkey, wearing the costume of a man of fashion, pretends to read a menu which is written in a mixture of French and English, and shows the Gallic tastes of the lady of the house by containing a "Fricasey of Snails." Packs of playing-cards strew the floor, while the pictures on the walls carry out the satire by showing a foreign dancer in an attitude of artificial grace, and a Venus wearing a hoop and a pair of stays (Pl. VII.).

The rage for old china proved to be no passing fashion, and whatever its affectation, probably had a stimulating effect upon the manufacture of English porcelain. In 1749 Mrs. Montagu observes that the fashionable world, "sick of Grecian elegance and symmetry, or Gothic grandeur and magnificence, must seek the barbarous gaudy goût of the Chinese, and fat-headed Pagodas and shaking mandarins bear the prize from the finest works of antiquity." A dozen years later Goldsmith's "Citizen of the World" visited a lady of quality, who showed him her jars of the right pea-green, which, he said, were paltry enough in the eyes of a Chinese, though useful utensils when filled with an infusion of tea. On hearing that they were empty and intended for ornament only, he informed her that "nothing is truly elegant but what unites use with beauty."

---

[1] The first Earl of Portmore (Sir David Colyear) served under William III. in Ireland and Flanders. He married the Countess of Dorchester, mistress of James II., and died *c.* 1730. The caricatured gentleman must have been the second earl, who died in 1785.

Invented and Painted by Wm. Hogarth

TASTE IN HIGH LIFE

[1746]

THE BEAU MONDE

The fashionable tastes of the period are represented more in detail by Hogarth in the *Toilette Scene* of his series *Marriage à la Mode*, 1745. In this familiar work we see the heroine's little black boy emptying a basketful of objects of art and virtu at his mistress's feet. These, which include ornaments in china and glass, come from the collection of the " Late Sir Timothy Babyhouse." The taste for masquerades is shown by the scenes on the screen, which the Countess and her lover, Lawyer Silvertongue, are examining ; while the rage for foreign singers is illustrated by the group consisting of a fat opera-singer (variously identified as Carestini[1] and Farinelli),[2] who is singing from a music-book to the flute accompaniment of Weidemann, a member of the opera orchestra. Beside the pair sit two or three amateurs in attitudes of affected delight. One of these is supposed to represent Mrs. Lane Fox, afterwards Lady Bingley, and another, a gentleman in curl-papers, has been identified as Herr Michel, the Prussian Envoy.

Towards the close of the forties, the dancing manikins called *pantins* were introduced into English society from France. Lady Luxborough,[3] writing to a friend on the subject of this new mania, observes : " The Duke of New-castle's pantin charms me, and I don't doubt but it made the place. I am in doubt when I hear of this polite fashion whether it is a mark that the world has returned to its infancy (as old people grow childish), or whether it may not be some coquettish invention that Mr. Pantin may say in dumb show what the lady who wears him cannot say for herself. . . . At last I am in the fashion, and have got a Pantin of the newest sort. It has just arrived in England, and is reckoned to make as genteel a curtsey as any M. Pantin in Europe." The new toy is shown in a print called *Pantin à la Mode*, published in September, 1748. A group of ladies and gentlemen are represented in the act of playing with their manikins, a monkey and a kitten being similarly employed. One gentleman holds his snuff-box open, and is apparently instructing a lady how to manage her pantin, so that it may be induced to take a pinch of snuff (Pl. VIII.).

In April and May, 1749, great rejoicings took place in London in consequence of the Peace that had been concluded with Spain, and numerous entertainments were given—masquerades, fireworks, and Venetian fêtes. The fêtes were held at Ranelagh Gardens, which had been opened as a place of public entertainment in 1742, with "long Sir Thomas Robinson"[4] as manager.

---

[1] Carestini, Giovanni (*c.* 1705–60), a famous contralto. He made his first appearance in London in 1733, being engaged by Handel. He is said to have been a good actor as well as a fine singer, and he became one of the fashionable favourites of his period.

[2] Farinelli, Carlo Broschi detto (1705–82). A pupil of Porpora. He came to London in 1734, and sang at the theatre in Lincoln's Inn Fields, then directed by Porpora. Although his salary was only £1,800 a year, his presents from royalty and the nobility brought his income up to £5,000. After three years he retired to Italy, where he built a house which he called " England's Folly." He spent twenty-five years at the Court of Madrid, where he obtained great influence over Philip V. and Ferdinand VI. successively.

[3] Henrietta, half-sister of the first Lord Bolingbroke. She married Robert Knight, afterwards Lord Luxborough, in 1727, and died in 1756. She composed feeble verses, and prided herself on her literary taste. She is best remembered as the friend and correspondent of Shenstone.

[4] Sir Thomas Robinson, first baronet, and brother of the first Lord Rokeby, Governor of Barbados 1742–47. He lived at Rokeby, Yorkshire (immortalised by Scott), but was obliged to sell the place in 1769.

13

Of the " Venetian jubilee masquerade," held on April 26th, that superfine critic, Horace Walpole, writes that though it had nothing Venetian in it, " it was by far the best understood and the prettiest spectacle I ever saw." Mrs. Montagu, as became a learned lady, was more inclined to look with disdain on the new form of entertainment. " People in town," she observes, " had met one another so often at assemblies, they hated each other's faces, and we had masquerades of great expense and show ; these tired too, and we wanted to be transported to another country. A Venetian masquerade was thought of ; it was called a jubilee, and a boat was surnamed a gondola, and all people were transported ; a jubilee at Ranelagh, and a gondola on the canal ! Oh rare ! The conductor of this noble amusement repeats the diversion ; all the people were tired ! "

The great sensation of this season was the appearance of Miss Chudleigh,[1] Maid of Honour to the Princess of Wales, at a masquerade ball in the transparent costume considered appropriate to Iphigenia. Mrs. Montagu declared that the dress, or rather the undress, was so remarkable that the other Maids of Honour (none of the strictest) refused to speak to the wearer, and the Princess is said to have thrown a veil over the indiscreet beauty. But the King was so much impressed by her charms that he gave her a fairing for her watch which cost five-and-thirty guineas, actually disbursed out of his privy purse, and not charged on the Civil List. " Whatever you may think of it," writes Walpole, in his account of the transaction, " this is a far more magnificent present than the cabinet the late King of Poland sent to the fair Countess Königsmarck, replete with all kinds of baubles and ornaments, and ten thousand ducats in one of the drawers. I hope some future Holinshed or Stow will acquaint posterity ' that five-and-thirty guineas was an immense sum in those days.' "

Several caricatures appeared at this time dealing with the fêtes in general, and Miss Chudleigh in particular. One of these was advertised in the public press as "*A Print of the Jubilee Ball, or Masquerade, at Ranelagh, by his Majesty's Command, after the Venetian Manner in the Day-time, April 26th, the Day between the Thanksgiving and the Fireworks for the General Peace, with a perspective view of the Rotunda, Tents, Shops and Gardens ; the Habits which there appeared, particularly the Ladies vying with each other in Dress on that occasion ; in which is introduced Miss ——, in the actual habit she appeared in the character of Iphigenia, the Dress being quite different from any one yet published.*" The fireworks in the Green Park, given by royal command, appear to have met with but little popular approval, judging from a print called *The Grand Whim for Posterity to Laugh at* (Pl. IX.). This gives a representation of some very elaborate set-pieces, one portion of which has caught fire in a manner not intentional, and is being played upon by a very

---

[1] Miss Chudleigh was the daughter of Colonel Chudleigh, of Chelsea Hospital, and her matrimonial adventures are well known. She was married secretly to Captain Hervey (afterwards Lord Bristol), and, in the lifetime of her first husband, she entered into a bigamous union with the Duke of Kingston, for which offence she was tried and convicted in 1776.

PANTIN À LA MODE

Published according to the Act of Parliament, September y^e 7, 1748, for J. Wakelin. Price 6d.

[April 27th, 1749]

THE GRAND WHIM FOR POSTERITY TO LAUGH AT:

BEING THE NIGHT VIEW OF THE ROYAL FIREWORKS, AS EXHIBITED IN THE GREEN PARK, ST. JAMES'S, WITH THE RIGHT WING ON FIRE,
AND THE CUTTING AWAY THE TWO MIDDLE ARCHES TO PREVENT THE WHOLE FABRIC FROM BEING DESTROY'D

L. P., inv. et sculp.   Price 6d.   Publish'd 1749

FOLLY TRIUMPHANT

L. P. Boitard, invt. et sculp.   [C. 1750]

THE BEAU MONDE IN ST. JAMES'S PARK

THE RULING PASSION, BE IT WHAT IT WILL,
THE RULING PASSION CONQUERS REASON STILL

Pope

primitive fire-engine. The legend contains sarcastic references to a disadvantageous peace, and to the amount spent on the rejoicings, which is stated to be nearly equal to the sum (£70,000) claimed from Spain as compensation to the South Sea Company, the original cause, as it was considered, of a long and expensive war.

To the same year, 1749, belongs a caricature by L. P. Boitard called *Folly Triumphant, or an Humourous Epilogue to the Beaux of the Age*. This is, as the title implies, a pictorial summary of the fashionable follies and public blunders of the period. Folly, armed with a pantin, is drawn in a triumphal car by a Butterfly and a Locust, emblems of pride and poverty, under the wheels being the Bible and *The Whole Duty of Man* (Pl. X.). Among the groups portrayed are masqueraders, foreign opera dancers, fribbles, bruisers, rope-dancers, and the Bottle Conjuror; while the Jubilee fireworks, the newly-built Mansion House, the broken arch of Westminster Bridge (opened in 1750, after three years' delay owing to faulty construction), and the west front of Westminster Abbey, whose spireless condition seems to have displeased the satirist, are also represented.

Another design of Boitard's, undated, but probably published in the early fifties, is called *The Beau Monde in St. James' Park*, and has for its motto Pope's couplet :—

" The ruling Passion, be it what it will,
The ruling Passion conquers Reason still."

This is in very much the same style as the pair of prints *Taste à la Mode*, 1735 and 1745, by the same artist. The groups represented are probably composed of persons whose faces were familiar to their contemporaries, though we are no longer able to identify them (Pl. XI.). The men's wigs, it will be observed, are increasing in size, and thus foreshadowing the absurd excrescences worn by the Maccaronies twenty years later; but the ladies still cling to their favourite hats of the small flat milkmaid shape, which with a short skirt and long apron constituted the Englishwoman's morning dress about the middle of the century. A couple of engravings in the same *genre*, though more deliberately caricatured, entitled *Lusus Naturæ, or Carracaturas of the Present Age*, and *A View of the Mall* (L'Agneau *invenit*, J. June *sc.*), were published in March, 1752. Among the personages who figure in the former are the fat Duke of Cumberland, Sir Samuel Prime, one of the " characters" of Twickenhamshire, and Dr. Hill, of the *Inspector*. The figures are purposely ill drawn, with big heads and angular features, as though the caricaturist wished to guard himself against the consequences of too-ready identification (Pl. XII.).

The fashionable taste for foreign productions afforded a perennial subject to the caricaturist, who, whatever his own nationality, found it to his advantage to affect the character and prejudices of a thorough-paced John Bull. In March, 1757, a somewhat elaborate engraving was published under the title of *The Imports of Great Britain from France. Humbly addressed to the*

Laudable Associations of Anti-Gallicans, and the generous promoters of the British Arts and Manufacturies, by their sincere Well-wisher and truly devoted humble servant, L. P. Boitard. This gives a view of the quay at the Custom House, where a French boat is landing her passengers, and the design includes, according to the appended explanation, " Four Tackle Porters Staggering under a mighty chest of Birthday cloathes; behind, several emaciated high-liv'd Epicures, familiarly receiving a French Cook, acquainting him that without his assistance they must have perished of Hunger. A Lady of Distinction offering the Tuition of her Son and Daughter to a cringing French Abbé, disregarding the Corruption of their Religion, so they do but obtain the French Accent; her Frenchified well-bred Spouse readily complying. The English Chaplain regretting his lost Labours; another Woman of Quality in Raptures caressing a French Female Dancer, assuring her that her Arrival is to the Delight and Honour of England. On the Front Ground a Cask overset; the Contents French Cheeses from Normandy bien Raffinie, a Blackguard Boy stopping his nostrils, greatly offended at the Haut Gout. A Chest well-crammed with Tippets, Muffs, Ribands, Flowers for the Hair, and such other Material Bagatelles; underneath, concealed Cambricks and Pomatums, l'eau de Luce, etc., etc., near French Wines and Brandies. At a Distance Landing, swarms of Milliners, Taylors, Mantua-makers, Frisers, disguised Jesuits, Quacks, Valets de Chambres, etc., etc., etc." (Pl. XIII.).

In 1767 Boitard published another of his comprehensive attacks upon contemporary society under the title of *The Present Age. Addressed to the Professors of Driving, Dressing, Ogling, Writing, Playing, Gambling, Racing, Dancing, Duelling, Boxing, Swearing, Humming, Building, etc., etc., etc.* (Pl. XIV.). This gives a view of a crowded street with the sea and shipping at one end. Among the buildings are a theatre, a boxing academy, and houses in a debased style of architecture. There is a numbered explanation, from which we gather that the various groups consist of: British Nobility Disguised (*i.e.* dressed in French fashions); a French valet insulting a brave English soldier reduced to beggary; an industrious Tradesman thrust aside with contempt to make room for a high-born gambler, who is to be paid his debts of honour, while the tradesman's bill is ignored; a Feather of the Turf driving a high phaeton, and a French dancing-master outweighing (in a pair of scales) an honest English shipwright. On the sea is a little vessel called a British Buss, which is described as of more value to the community than ten Italian singers.

L Agneau, invt.

J. June, sc.

LUSUS NATURÆ, OR CARRACATURAS OF THE PRESENT AGE

Published March 5th, 1752.   Sold by B. Dickenson on Ludgate Hill

Published according to Act of Parliament March 7, 1757, by John Bowles, at the Black Horse in Cornhill, London.   Price Sixpence

THE IMPORTS OF GREAT BRITAIN FROM FRANCE

HUMBLY ADDRESS'D TO THE LAUDABLE ASSOCIATIONS OF ANTI-GALLICANS, AND THE GENEROUS PROMOTERS OF THE BRITISH ARTS AND MANUFACTORIES;
BY THEIR SINCERE WELL-WISHER AND TRULY DEVOTED HUMBLE SERVANT, L. P. BOITARD

Invented & Engrav'd by L. P. Boitard

[1767]

THE PRESENT AGE
ADDRESS'D TO THE PROFESSORS OF DRIVING, DRESSING, OGLING, WRITING, PLAYING, GAMBLING, RACING, DANCING, DUELLING, BOXING, SWEARING, HUMMING, BUILDING,
ETC., ETC., ETC.

Printed for John Bowles at the Black Horse in Cornhill, & Carington Bowles in St. Paul's Churchyard, London

THE BEAU MONDE

PART II

IN 1770, or more properly in the years immediately preceding and following this date, several important developments had their rise in that limited area known as the great world, namely, the birth of the Maccaroni, the establishment of the Coterie, or mixed Club, the erection of the Pantheon, and the opening of Carlisle House as a place of entertainment by Mrs. Cornelys. The Maccaroni seems to have been invented in the early sixties, though his golden age was from 1770 to 1772, and by 1776, according to Miss Burney, the word was no longer the *ton*. The type seems to have been originated by a number of young men of fashion, who had made the grand tour and learnt to eat maccaroni at Naples. Having acquired the habit of calling everything that was elegant or uncommon after the national dish of Italy, the young travellers "judged that the title of Maccaroni was very applicable to a clever fellow, and accordingly, to distinguish themselves as such they instituted a coterie under this denomination, the members of which were supposed to be the standards of taste in polite learning, the fine arts, and the genteel sciences, and fashion soon became an object of their attention." As early as 1764 George Williams[1] makes allusion to the clique, observing that he thinks of founding a club for ladies who were divorced or separated from their husbands, since he believes that they might grow as formidable as the Maccaronies, and put domestic felicity out of fashion. In the same year Horace Walpole explains the term to Lord Hertford, and observes, " There are levées and drawing-rooms without end. Not to mention the Maccaroni Club, which has quite abolished Arthur's; for you know old fools will hobble after young ones."

By 1772 the Maccaroni craze was at its height, and a *Maccaroni Magazine* was started, which gave portraits and brief memoirs of some of the more celebrated members of the sect, Lord Villiers figuring as the *Nosegay Maccaroni*, Lord Barrymore as the *Gambling*, Lord Petersham as the *Chapeau*, and the Rev. John Horne (afterwards Horne Tooke) as the *Clerical Maccaroni*. John Bull strongly disapproved of this exotic type, and in the magazines for this year there are numerous satirical articles describing the

---

[1] George Williams, better known as Gilly Williams (1719–1805). The friend and correspondent of Horace Walpole, George Selwyn, and other wits of the period.

appearance and character of the Maccaroni, while the printsellers, Edwards and Darly, published more than one volume dealing almost exclusively with his follies and eccentricities.

A writer in the *Town and Country Magazine* observes that the Maccaronies soon proved that they had very little claim to distinction, save in their personal appearance ; but that, " nevertheless, the infection at St. James' was soon caught in the City, and we have now Maccaronies of every denomination, from the Colonel of the Trained Bands down to the errand boy. They make indeed a most ridiculous figure, with hats of an inch in brim that do not cover the head, with about two pounds of fictitious hair, formed into what is called a club, hanging down their shoulders as white as a barber's sack ; their coat-sleeves are so tight they can with much difficulty get their arms through their cuffs, which are about an inch deep, and their shirt-sleeves, without plaits, are pulled over a piece of Trolly lace. Their legs are at times covered with all the colours of the rainbow; even flesh-coloured and green silk stockings are not excluded. The shoes are scarce slippers, and the buckles within an inch of the toe."

So much for the costume of the Maccaroni. For his character we must turn to an article in the *Universal Magazine*, which informs us that " He is the sworn foe of all learning, and even sets orthography at defiance ;[1] for all learned fellows who can spell or write sense, are either queer dogs or poor rogues. And yet the creature affects some of the fine arts. He attends at auctions, where he picks up the names of painters, and vomits them forth on all occasions. He affects a rapturous taste for music, and is continually humming in a Piano. · If you see him at the theatre, he will scarcely stir without his opera-glass, which he will thrust into a lady's face, and then simper, and be ' pruddigisly entertenn'd ' with her confusion. He laughs at religion, because it is a too rational pleasure for him to conceive. He hates all drinking—except tea and posset—and detests those rude and nasty fellows who drink the generous grape, and swallow punch and the fumes of tobacco."

Among the numerous caricatures of Maccaronies which were published during the early seventies may be mentioned *The Macarony Dressing-room* (Pl. XV.), by Captain Minshull (November, 1772) ; *The Old Beau in an Extasy*, by J. Dixon (July, 1773) ; *How D'ye like Me* (November, 1772), an elderly Maccaroni dressed in all his finery ; *A Maccaroni at a Sale of Pictures* (Brandoin *pinxt*, Grignion[2] *sculp.*, September, 1771) ; *A Gentleman's Toilette* (Pugh *pinxit*,[3] 1770) (Pl. XVI.) ; *English Funn, or Docking the Macaroni* (September, 1774), a butcher attacking a beau who had insulted

---

[1] It will be noted that there is a pleasing variety about the spelling of the word " Maccaroni."

[2] Charles Grignion, or Grignon, line-engraver (1717–1810). Of foreign extraction, but born in Russell Street, Covent Garden. He seems to have had some instruction from H. Gravelot, but at sixteen he went to Paris, where he studied under Le Bas. On returning to London he soon obtained plenty of work in engraving book illustrations after designs by Hayman, Gravelot, Stothard, etc. He was employed by Hogarth on two of his plates. He died in great poverty, having outlived his reputation, and being unable to adapt his style to modern requirements.

[3] This may have been Herbert Pugh, an Irish artist, who was working between 1758 and 1788. Although he practised as a landscape painter, he imitated Hogarth in one or two pictures, which were engraved.

C. White, Sculp.

THE MACARONY DRESSING ROOM
ENGRAV'D FROM THE ORIGINAL PICTURE PAINTED BY CAPTAIN MINSHULL

Printed and Published for T. Bowen, opposite the Haymarket, Piccadilly, as the Act Directs, the 9th Nov., 1772

Pugh pinxt.   *J. Wesson, Excudt.*   *J. Golder, Sculpt.*

A GENTLEMAN'S DRESSING-ROOM.

DONE FROM AN ORIGINAL PICTURE IN THE COLLECTION OF THE RIGHT HONBLE. THE EARL OF GRANARD

Publd. Dec. 17, 1771, by J. Wesson in Litchfield Street, St. Ann's, Soho

him, and cutting away the huge club of false hair which every self-respecting Maccaroni wore at the back of his head ; *The Turf Maccaroni* (Duke of Grafton), *The Eclipse Macarony* ("Count" O'Kelly, owner of the racehorse Eclipse. Drawn by R. St. George Mansergh, May, 1773) ; *The Sleeping Macaroni*, Dreaming for the good of his Country (Stephen Fox, second Lord Holland. By H. Bunbury, June, 1772) ; *The Illiterate Macaroni* (probably Lord Suffolk, Secretary of State) ; *The Macaroni Bricklayer Prior to any other Macaroni* (a gentleman, supposed to be intended for George III., holding a trowel, September, 1772) ; *The Bun Macaroni* (probably intended for a member of the Bunbury family, dressed like a baker, and carrying a tray of buns, October, 1772) ; *A Macaroni in Morning Dress in the Park* (April, 1772), the portrait of a gentleman who is described in Pope's lines——

"Some are bewildered in the maze of Schools,
And some made Coxcombs Nature meant for Fools" ;

The Grub Street Macaroni, a literary man in an ill-fitting wig and badly made clothes (? Dr. Johnson) ; *The Fly-catching Macaroni* (Sir Joseph Banks, the naturalist ; July, 1772) ; *The Simpling Macaroni* (Dr. Solander ; July, 1772) ; *A Female Macaroni* (the portrait of a lady with her hair dressed in the style affected by men of fashion) ; *The Fluttering Macaroni* (Miss Catley, the singer, holding in her hands a tiny gentleman supposed to be Lord Ancrum, afterwards Marquis of Lothian, November, 1772) ; *The Parade Macaroni* (General Fitzpatrick, a leader of the *ton* and one of the authors of the *Rolliad*, February, 1772) ; *The Martial Macaroni* (Ensign Horneck, brother-in-law of H. Bunbury ; November, 1771) ; and *An Old Macaroni Critic at a New Play*, a fastidious-looking elderly gentleman, who is apparently studying a new drama by the aid of a book called "The Critical Quadrant, or Rules for Judging of the Sublime in Tragedy by Benjn. Bombast" (R. St. G. Mansergh *pinx¹*, November, 1772).

The Maccaronies, male and female, were the chief supporters, if not the "onlie begetters" of Almack's, and of the entertainments at Carlisle House and the Pantheon. Mrs. Cornelys, an ex-opera singer, who came to England in 1746 under the name of Pompeati, bought Carlisle House, Soho Square, as early as 1760, and, to quote Horace Walpole's account of her (written in 1771), became the Heidegger of the age, and presided over its diversions. "Her taste and invention in pleasure and decorations are singular. She took Carlisle House, enlarged it, and established assemblies and balls by subscription. At first they scandalised, but soon drew in both righteous and ungodly. She went on building, and made her house a fairy palace for balls, concerts, and masquerades. Her opera, which she called Harmonic Meetings, was splendid and charming. Mr. Hobart[1] [manager of the Italian Opera] began to starve, and the managers of the theatres were alarmed. To avoid the Act she pretended to take no money, and had the assurance to advertise that her

---

[1] Afterwards third Earl of Buckinghamshire (1732–1804).

subscription was to provide coals for the poor. . . . At last Mr. Hobart informed against her, and the Bench of Justices, less soothable by music than Orpheus' beasts, have pronounced against her." Mrs. Cornelys had many vicissitudes of fortune. In her palmy days she had a splendid country-house at Hammersmith, with thirty servants, six carriage-horses, and three secretaries. In 1772 she became bankrupt, owing to the competition of the Pantheon and Almack's, and Carlisle House was sold. In 1775 she was superintending a great fête at Ranelagh at a cost of seven thousand pounds. A few years later she was selling asses' milk at Knightsbridge as plain Mrs. Smith; and in 1797 she died in the Fleet, a prisoner for debt.

Several caricatures appeared on the subject of Mrs. Cornelys' entertainments. In the *Town and Country Magazine* for 1770, is a print called *The Soho Conference, between the Premier and the Journeyman.* The scene is laid at a masquerade in Carlisle House on February 26th of this year, and Lord Shelburne, the Prime Minister, in the costume of a Turk, is listening behind a pillar to a conversation between Lord North and the Duke of Grafton. Among the masqueraders is Captain Watson of the Guards, who "went one better" than Miss Chudleigh by appearing as Adam, and, according to the *Town and Country Magazine*, "personated his part with great propriety and drollery"; but a writer in the *Gentleman's Magazine* declares that "the unavoidable indelicacy of the dress rendered it the contempt of the company."

In the spring of 1770 a coterie or club for both sexes, on the model of that for men only at White's, was started at a tavern or coffee-house, but very soon removed to Almack's. Mrs. Boscawen, one of the blue-stocking set, who describes the new departure in a letter to Mrs. Delany, says that the first fourteen who planned it settled its rules. "There are seventy-five members (the whole number is to be 200). The ladies invite and *choose* the gentlemen, and *vice versâ*, so that no lady can exclude a lady, or gentleman a gentleman. The Duchess of Bedford was at first blackballed, but is since admitted. Lady Rochford and Lady Harrington[1] are blackballed, as is Lord March,[2] Mr. Boothby,[3] and one or two more who think themselves pretty gentlemen *du premièr ordre*, but it is plain that the ladies are not of their opinion. . . . When any of the ladies dine with the society, they are to send word before, but supper comes of course, and is to be served always at eleven. Play will be *deep* and *constant* probably." Mrs. Boscawen must have been misinformed as to the blackballing, for among the original members we find Lord March and Mr. Boothby, besides such leaders of the *ton* as Horace Walpole, Charles Fox, and George Selwyn.

---

[1] Lady Harrington was a daughter of the second Duke of Grafton. She married the second Earl Harrington (then Lord Petersham) in 1746. She was a famous beauty, and one of the most "advanced" members of a very rapid set. There are numerous allusions to her and her daughters in the *Letters of Horace Walpole.*

[2] Lord March was afterwards that notorious Duke of Queensberry who was better known as "Old Q."

[3] Mr. Boothby (1743–1824) was afterwards Sir Brooke Boothby, a very minor poet, who shone in the Lichfield set, and shocked Miss Seward by his extravagances.

T. *Bonner, del. et sculp.*   1770

THE FEMALE COTERIE

WELL, THIS IS CERTAINLY ONE OF THE MOST USEFULL INSTITUTIONS :—

Lame Lover

Chas. White, Delin. et sculp.

[1773]

A MASQUERADE SCENE AT THE PANTHEON

Chas. Brandoin, Inv.t et delin.t　　　　　　　　　*R. Sayer, Excudit*　　　　　　　　　*Rich.d Earlom fecit*

THE INTERIOR OF THE PANTHEON IN OXFORD ROAD
FROM AN ORIGINAL DRAWING IN THE POSSESSION OF ROB.T SAYER

Printed for Rob.t Sayer, No. 53, in Fleet Street, London　　　　　　　　　*30th August, 1772*

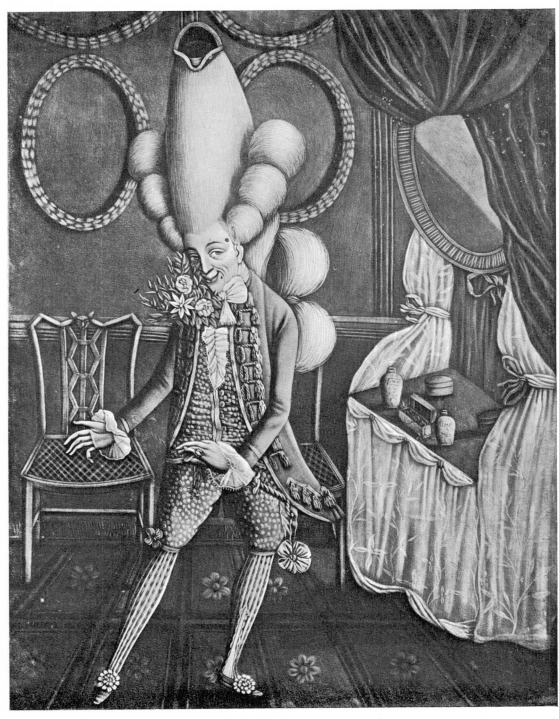

[1782]

PANTHEON MACARONI

THE BEAU MONDE

A somewhat different account was given by Mrs. Harris to her son, afterwards the first Lord Malmesbury, of "a new assembly or meeting called Lloyd's Coffee-room, Miss Lloyd, whom you have seen with Lady Pembroke, being sole inventor. They meet every morning, either to play cards, chat, or do whatsoever else they please. . . . This is a most ingenious thought, for no one ever hit on a scheme that should occupy the fine people all day without inflicting on them the torment of being *some part* of the time in their own houses." Among the rules of the Club, we find that each member had to pay five guineas subscription and eight shillings for dinner, exclusive of wine, for which the gentlemen were to pay, and each party was to pay for its own cards. On a lady being elected, her husband and unmarried daughters also received the freedom of the Club. In the *London Magazine* for 1770 a print was published called *The Female Coterie*, with a motto from *The Lame Lover*, "Well, this is certainly one of the most useful institutions." In this we are shown a number of ladies and gentlemen flirting, drinking, and playing cards in a large, handsome room. It is made tolerably evident that the stakes are high, and the flirting is of a decidedly public character (Pl. XVII.).

The opening of the Pantheon in the Oxford Road seems to have provided the chief social sensation of the season of 1772. The new place of entertainment was inaugurated by one of the most brilliant masquerades ever witnessed in London. "The lighting and the brilliant *éclat* on going in," writes Mrs. Delany, "was beyond description, and the going in and out made so easy by lanes of constables that there was not the least confusion. To balance these delights the High Street robbers give many panics ; but pleasure will conquer all fears, and men on horseback with a pistol at your breast will at last grow so familiar as not to be more regarded than a common turnpike which makes you pay for your passage. Feminine fears, as well as bashfulness, are no more a check upon the female than upon the male Maccaronies ; pleasure is the prize they run for, and then nothing stops their course."

A mezzotint by R. Earlom after a drawing by Charles Brandoin, published in August, 1772, shows *The Inside of the Pantheon, Oxford Road*, with the patrons and patronesses walking or dancing in the splendidly decorated rooms (Pl. XIX.). Another print gives a view of the *Masquerade at the Pantheon* in June, 1773, with a crowd composed of devils, witches, Chinamen, Punches and the like (Pl. XVIII.). That the *Pantheon Maccaroni* was the most fantastic of his type is proved by a portrait of him in a high wig, huge nosegay, tasselled coat, striped hose, and rosetted shoes (Pl. XX.).

In 1776 ladies' headdresses, which had been gradually developing in height during the last few years, seem to have reached a climax, and even the fashion papers were aghast at the monstrous erections crowned with three or five tall ostrich feathers which fashionable women complacently carried on their heads. A writer in *The Lady's Magazine* for March, 1776, remarks on the "copious superfluities" of the new style of hairdressing, and expresses her regret at seeing, during a visit to Ranelagh, " several ladies, very handsome, so disguised, and their features so distorted by the horrid drag of their hair, to a height absolutely half as tall as themselves, and so loaded with gauze, flowers, fruit, herbs, ribbons, pins, etc., that it was hardly to be supposed a living figure." Terrible stories were current of masses of horsehair and pomatum that were only dressed once in three weeks, the wearers being compelled during that period to sleep in one constrained position.

Mrs. Delany, writing to Mrs. Port in March, 1775, reports that "Nothing is talked of now so much as the ladies' *enormous* dresses, more suited to the stage or a *masquerade* than for any *civil* or *sober* societies. The three *most* elevated plumes of feathers are the Duchess of Devonshire, Lady Mary Somerset, and Lady Harriet Stanhope, but some say that Mrs. Hubert's [Hobart ?] exceeds them all. It would be some consolation if their manners did not too much correspond with the lightness of their dress." It was at this period that doors in fashionable houses were carried up nearly to the ceilings, and all lustres were removed. The feathers could no longer be worn in carriages, and therefore were carried in the sword-cases to assemblies, where rooms were set apart for the donning of these lofty adornments.

Numberless are the caricatures on the subject of the " high heads," which remained in fashion, with certain modifications, for several years. As early as 1771 a print called *Ridiculous Taste, or the Ladies' Absurdity*, shows a lady at her toilette with her head being dressed by a hairdresser mounted on a flight of steps, while a gentleman, apparently a naval officer, is " taking an observation " by means of a sextant, to ascertain whether the erection reaches the prescribed proportions. In *The Feathered Fair in a Fright*, by John Collet, we see the fair wearers of the fashionable upstanding plumes being attacked by some ostriches, who are supposed to be enraged at the loss of their natural ornaments (Pl. XXIII.). In *The Preposterous Head-dress* (March, 1776), a lady is having her hair arranged by an artist, who, raised upon a stool, puts in a number of immensely long feathers, while a maid stands by with a large tray laden with fruit and vegetables to serve as further adornments (Pl. XXI.). An even more remarkable design is called *A Hint to the Ladies to take Care of their Heads* (1776), the scene of which is laid in the large assembly room at the Pantheon. A lady's towering feathers have caught fire from the lights in the high roof of the building, and some servants are trying to put out the blaze with a primitive form of hose, while the majority of the company look on in apparent unconcern (Pl. XXII.).

Extravagance in dress was still almost as much a masculine as a feminine foible, though this fact rarely made a man less severe upon the follies of his womenkind. One candid soul, however, in the course of an article upon male fashions, inquires, " Is it not wonderful that we should put forth so many paragraphs concerning Female Fantasticalness as we are prone to do, and

THE PREPOSTEROUS HEAD DRESS

OR THE FEATHERED LADY

Published by Darly, 39, Strand, March 26, 1776

1776

HINTS TO THE LADIES TO TAKE CARE OF THEIR HEADS

Pub. by R. Sayer & Bennett, Fleet Street, London

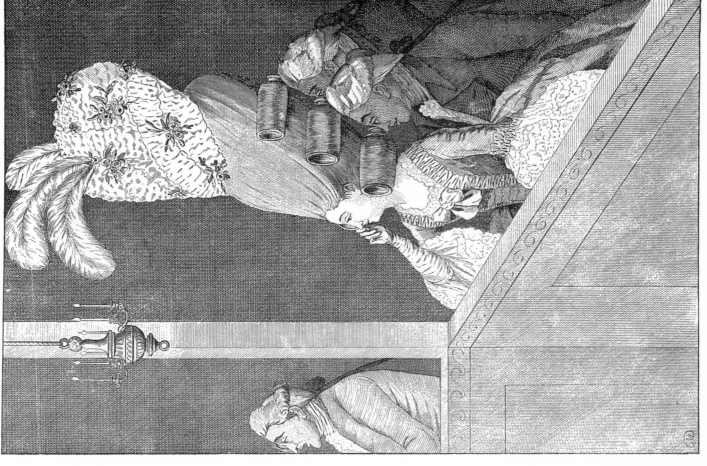

[1772]

THE OPTIC CURLS

1772

THE FEATHER'D FAIR IN A FRIGHT

FROM THE ORIGINAL PICTURE BY JOHN COLLET, IN THE POSSESSION OF CARINGTON BOWLES

Printed for & sold by Carington Bowles at the Map & Print Warehouse, No. 69, in St. Paul's Churchyard. London

STEEL BUTTONS. COUP DE BOUTON

Pub⁴. 29 April, 1777, by H. Humphrey, Gerrard Street, Soho

Pub. by Darly, Feb. 7, 1777

BUCKLES AND BUTTONS

I AM THE THING, DEM-ME

never consider that our own heads are but mere Piece-brokers' shops, full of the remnants of fashion? Do not some of us strut about with walking-sticks as long as leaping-poles, as if we were pioneers to the troop of hickory-cutters; or else with a yard of varnished cane, scraped taper, and bound at one end with a wax-thread, and the other tipped with a neat-turned ivory head, as big as a silver penny, which switch we hug under our arms so jemmy?"

At the period when ladies were piling towers of greased and powdered hair on their heads, men were adorning themselves with immense cut-steel buttons and shoe-buckles. One exquisite thus decorated (1777) exclaims complacently, "*I am the Thing, dem'me*" (Pl. XXV.); while another, walking in the Park, gives a lady a *Coup de Bouton*, which has the same effect as a mild sunstroke (Pl. XXVI.). That these absurd persons resented a parallel absurdity in the other sex may be gathered from a print for the same year called *A Hint to Husbands, or the Dresser properly Dressed*, which represents an irate husband rushing into his wife's room, where she is engaged at her toilette, armed with a huge horsewhip which he seems to have every intention of using both on the lady and her hairdresser. More tolerant and accommodating are a couple of men who figure in a caricature called *The Optic Curls, or the Obliging Head-dress* (1777). Here we see a forerunner of the matinee hat in the shape of an erection of hair which completely blocks the view of some persons in a box at the theatre. With a creditable desire to make the best of their circumstances, two gentlemen are viewing the stage through the long horizontal side-curls of their hostess, in which they have placed their opera-glasses (Pl. XXIV.).

Umbrellas and parasols were now coming into more general use, though they were still regarded by the more conservative as a Frenchified novelty.[1] In 1765 M. Grosley, the French traveller, complained of the ill-effects of the London fogs and rain upon the clothes of those who may be exposed to them, and adds, "Their effect is the more certain and unavoidable as it is the rule with the people of London not to suffer foreigners to use our umbrellas of waxed silk or taffeta. For this reason London swarms with the shops of the scourers, busied in scouring, repairing, and new-furbishing the clothes that are smoked in this manner." In a fashion magazine for 1777, we find an account of "a small silk umbrella fastened to the head of a long cane, which French ladies call a parasol," supplemented by a careful explanation of the manner in which the new invention may be opened or shut by pressing a spring. According to the same authority, broad hats were coming into fashion in order to save the trouble of carrying little sun-umbrellas in the pocket. It seems to have been in this, or the following year, that the Duchess of Bedford invented the calash, a sort of whale-boned hood, which could be drawn down over the eyes for protection from sun or wind. This invention, which is illustrated in

---

[1] Gay mentions umbrellas in his *Trivia*, but only as used by milliners, who were obliged to be out in rough weather. Jonas Hanway, the philanthropist, is said to have carried an umbrella thirty years earlier than any other man in London.

a contemporary print called *Miss Calash* (1788), was revived in early Victorian times under the appropriate name of an " ugly " (Pl. XXVII.).

In 1777 several caricatures were published dealing with the appearance and management of the new shield against the weather. For example, *Le Ton at Greenwich* is a representation of a lady, probably sketched from life, walking in the park, attired in a short skirt, an apron, and a large calash. Behind her stalks a man-servant carrying an umbrella (Pl. XXVIII.). In *This is Something New* we see a lady armed with an umbrella and wearing a huge " dress improver," upon which a little monkeyish-looking beau has seated himself without her knowledge, and thus gains protection from the rain. In Gillray's *Meeting of the Umbrellas* (1782), three men, each holding a wide-spreading " gamp," have met upon a narrow pavement, and become interested in some discussion, oblivious of the fact that they are obstructing the footway to other passengers (Pl. XXIX.).

The Westminster election afforded the great sensation of the year 1784, and comparatively few caricatures were published which did not deal in one form or another with the fight between Charles Fox, Sir Cecil Wray, and Lord Hood. The subject would hardly come within the scope of this work if it were not that a number of great ladies threw themselves into the fray and canvassed for the rival candidates. Fox, friend of the people though he was, counted three duchesses among his supporters, their Graces of Devonshire, Portland, and Gordon, to say nothing of that leader of fashion, Lady Archer.

Many and malicious were the reports circulated about the methods adopted by the great ladies to gain a vote. These find illustration in Rowlandson's etching *The Two Patriotic Duchesses on their Canvass ; requesting the Favour of an early Poll* (Pl. XXX.). The Duchess of Devonshire is represented in the act of kissing a butcher, and at the same time slipping a well-filled purse into his pocket. Her companion, the Duchess of Portland, is trying her blandishments on the butcher's apprentice, who receives them with the coldness of one who has been sated with the attentions of ladies of quality. An anonymous caricature shows the chairing of Charles Fox after his election. He is borne aloft by three ladies, the two Duchesses and Lady Archer. A cap of liberty is hung upon a pole at the back of the chair, and Fox holds a paper inscribed, " The Rights of England." The *Morning Post*, *The World*, and other papers which dealt in society scandals, libelled the Duchess of Devonshire after the manner of their kind ; but that there was at least one chivalrous spirit among the caricaturists is proved by a design called *The Apotheosis of the Duchess of Devonshire*, in which the lady is portrayed holding Truth by one hand and Virtue by the other, while her foot is placed on Scandal, who grasps a copy of the *Morning Post* (Pl. XXXI.).

At this period we obtain from the pencils of Bunbury and Rowlandson one or two comprehensive glimpses of the *Beau Monde*, as it took its pleasure in a public park or at Vauxhall. A drawing by Bunbury called *St. James'*

THE TON AT GREENWICH

A LA FESTOON DANS LE PARK A GREENWICH

[1777]

XXVII

MISS CALASH

DRAWN BY MISS CALASH, 1778

Pub. Octr. 14, by W. Richardson, No. 68, High Holborn

Pub'd by W Humphrey. 227. Strand.

3 Ap., 1784. *Rowlandson*

THE TWO PATRIOTIC DUCHESSES ON THEIR CANVASS REQUESTING THE FAVOUR OF AN EARLY POLL

A MEETING OF UMBRELLAS

Pub,d Jan 25 1782 by H. Humphrey, 227, Strand

Pub. 25 May, 1784, by H. Humphry, No. 227, Strand

THE APOTHEOSIS OF THE DUCHESS OF DEVONSHIRE

Bunbury Del.

ST. JAMES PARK

London, Publish'd Nov. 30th, 1783, by J. Wallis, No. 16, Ludgate Street, & E. Hedges, No. 92, under the Roy^l Exchange, Cornhill. S. D. *Price 2 6 plain*

H. Repton inv.   T. Rowlandson fecit.

1784, OR THE FASHIONS OF THE DAY

Pub. 24 July, 1784, by E. Bull, Ludgate Hill

Park (1783) gives rather an attractive picture of the groups of fashionable people and bourgeoisie, who are strolling or sitting under the trees on a summer's day (Pl. XXXII.). In the foreground are two pretty women, evidently drawn from life, who are followed by a little black boy carrying a dog. An old beau bows low before them, and several other men (one of whom is vigorously reproved by his elderly wife) stare admiringly at the attractive pair. On a shady bench an elderly citizen slumbers peacefully, while his pretty wife, with two children on her lap, exchanges tender glances with a good-looking youth. Repton's design, etched by Rowlandson, called *1784, or the Fashions of the day*, gives another view of the great world airing itself in one of the parks, the men ogling the women through their glasses in a manner more suggestive of French than English breeding (Pl. XXXIII.).

Rowlandson's celebrated design, *Vauxhall Gardens* (1785), is a much more elaborate study. In this we see the famous Rotunda, with Madame Weichsel (mother of Mrs. Billington) singing, and Bartlemon[1] leading the band. Conspicuous among the listening groups are two fashionable dames who have been identified as the Duchess of Devonshire and her sister, Lady Duncannon. Near by is a pretty youth making love to a charming little lady, supposed to be none other than "Perdita" Robinson, listening to the persuasive flatteries of Prince Florizel. Near Lady Duncannon stands the notorious fighting parson, Sir Henry Bate Dudley,[2] editor of the scandal-mongering *Morning Post*, accompanied by a brother of James Perry,[3] editor of the *Morning Chronicle*, who is wearing his favourite Highland costume. Another journalistic celebrity here represented is Captain Topham,[4] the editor and proprietor of *The World*, who is looking at the ladies through his spy-glass. In a supper-box is a group of unattractive looking persons who have been labelled Dr. Johnson, Boswell, Mrs. Thrale, and Oliver Goldsmith (Pl. XXXIV.).

In 1786–7 we note a change in the fashions, or rather a development of the protuberant style of dress, said to have been introduced by Mrs. Fitz-

---

[1] F. H. Bartlemon (1741–1808). Born at Bordeaux, and began his career as an officer in the Irish Brigade. He soon exchanged the military profession for that of a musician, and, coming to London in 1765, he was engaged as leader of the Opera orchestra. In 1770 he was appointed leader of the band at Vauxhall Gardens. Bartlemon, who married a niece of Dr. Arne, is best remembered as the composer of the tune to "Awake, my soul, and with the sun."

[2] The Rev. Sir H. Bate Dudley (1745–1824) was more notorious as a journalist and man about town than distinguished as a parson. He edited the then scurrilous *Morning Post* and founded the *Morning Herald*. He was imprisoned for libelling the Duke of Richmond, and his various affrays at Ranelagh earned for him the name of the Fighting Parson. Later he seems to have "ranged himself," or possibly his friendship with the Prince of Wales stood him in good stead, for he was created a baronet in 1813, and in 1817 was made a Prebendary of Ely.

[3] James Perry (1756–1821) was another rowdy journalist. Besides editing the *Morning Chronicle* he founded the *European Magazine*.

[4] Edward Topham (1751–1820) belonged to the same clique as the above. He started *The World* as a daily paper in 1787, and became well known as a man of fashion, and the friend of Wilkes and Sheridan. His paper was notorious for its scandalous personalities, and Topham was tried for libelling Lord Cowper, but acquitted. He wrote a few plays, but his most popular work was the *Life of John Elwes, the Miser*. He figures in a good many of the caricatures of the period.

herbert to conceal her own natural embonpoint.   From Gillray's plate, *Such Things Are* (April, 1787), with the motto—

"That such things are, we must allow,
But such things never were till now,"

we gain some idea of the huge muffs, the still towering feathers, and the padding with which ladies loaded themselves at this period (Pl. XLVI.). That they felt the inconvenience may be gathered from a design of Miss Aynscombe's, called *Les Incommodités de Janvier*, 1786, which depicts an unfortunate lady nearly extinguished by her hat and muff.

VAUXHALL GARDENS

[June 28, 1795]

THE PORTLAND PLACE A——R. DRIVING WITHOUT A BEAU TO R——D'S PERFUME WAREHOUSE, P—LL M—LL

Pub.ᵈ June 18th, 1782, by C. Clarke, No. 6, Princes Street

THE BEAU MONDE

PART III

AT the period we have now reached there were four or five ladies, leaders of fashion, whose personalities and propensities rendered them the object of rather unflattering attentions from the caricaturists in general, and from Gillray in particular. These were Lady Cecilia Johnstone, Lady Archer, Lady Mount Edgcumbe, and Mrs. Hobart, afterwards Lady Buckinghamshire. During the last ten or fifteen years of the century these ladies are continually held up to ridicule or reprobation, on account of their indulgence in gambling, flirting, and private theatricals. For some unknown reason Lady Cecilia Johnstone, a daughter of Lord Delawarr, and married to General Johnstone, reputed the handsomest man and best swordsman in the army, was one of Gillray's *bêtes noires*, and he seldom lost the chance of a fling at her. Yet that arch-gossip, Horace Walpole, whose friend and neighbour she was, found nothing to say against her, and in August, 1777, sent her a rhymed invitation to dinner to meet Garrick, Mrs. Clive, and Le Texier. After describing the other guests in facetious fashion he concludes :—

> " Oh, would divine Cecilia deign
> With her brave warrior to augment the train,
> From every castle famed in days of yore,
> From which or poets or romancers tell—
> For wit, or cheerfulness, or humour store—
> My Strawberry, my Strawberry, shall bear away the bell."

One *mot* of Lady Cecilia's has come down to us, which shows that she was accustomed to speak her mind with a certain *brusquerie*. Having remonstrated on one occasion with her married daughter for consorting with a fast and frivolous set, she found it necessary some years later to comment disapprovingly upon her child's preference for the society of authors and journalists. "But, mamma," expostulated the culprit, "I should have thought you would be pleased that I should associate with people of literature." " Litera—pudding ! " was Lady Cecilia's retort, which naturally put an end to the argument.

The notorious Lady Archer was presumably the wife of Lord Archer, Baron of Umberslade, and the daughter of Mr. West, sometime President of the Royal Society. Lady Archer, who died in 1801, attracted some public attention by her skill as a whip, and the pains which she bestowed upon her complexion. Rowlandson portrayed her in his series, *Six Stages of Mending a Face*, and an anonymous artist sketched her as *The Portland Place Archer, Driving without a Beau to R——d's Perfume Warehouse, Pall Mall* (Pl. XXXV.). In this design Lady Archer is seen driving four grey horses in a high phaeton with another lady as sole companion. As an example of the outspokenness of the Press at this period, it may be noted that in June, 1795, the *Morning Post*, announcing the death of another Lady Archer, observes : " This is not the celebrated character whose *cosmetic powers* have long been held in public estimation."

Of the Lady Mount Edgcumbe of that period we know little, except that she was the daughter of John Gilbert, Archbishop of York, and that she married Lord Mount Edgcumbe in 1761. But she was connected with a much more notorious person—Albinia, daughter of Lord Vere Bertie, who married in 1757 the Hon. George Hobart, son of the Earl of Buckinghamshire. Mrs. Hobart has been represented by her contemporaries, both with pen and pencil, as a roundabout little lady, with a passion for gambling, dancing, and acting, and a sanguine spirit, which inspired her to give rustic fêtes on Ham Common. Her neighbour, Horace Walpole, writing to Lady Ossory in July, 1781, says, " Mrs. Hobart did not invite me to her Sans Souci last week, though she had all my other juvenile contemporaries. Perhaps you do not know that the lady of the fête, having made as many conquests as the King of Prussia, has borrowed the name of that hero's villa for her hut on Ham Common, where she has built two large rooms of timber under a cabbage."

Ten years later Mrs. Hobart was still giving abortive fêtes, as we learn from a letter to Miss Berry, dated June 14th, 1791, in which the Lord of Strawberry Hill describes himself as cowering over a fire (" summer having set in with its usual severity ") and continues, " Mrs. Hobart had announced a rural *breakfast* at Sans Souci last Saturday ; nothing being so pastoral as a fat grandmother in a row of houses on Ham Common. It rained early in the morning ; she despatched post-boys for want of cupids and zephyrs to stop the nymphs and shepherds who tend their flocks in Pall Mall and St. James', but half of them missed the couriers and arrived."

Mrs. Hobart, being a woman of spirit and resource, introduced the fiasco of her pastoral fête, when the rain turned all the creams into milk and water, into a little piece called *Le Poulet*, which was acted at Brandenburgh House. The Margravine of Anspach (late Lady Craven)[1] had built a private theatre, and Mrs. Hobart was one of the most brilliant members of her troupe. In spite of the fact that she resembled a " spangle-pudding," the little lady

---

[1] Lady Craven was *née* Lady Elizabeth Berkeley (1750–1828), and married Lord Craven in 1767. She separated from him, and after some adventures on the Continent, married the Margrave of Anspach immediately after her husband's death in 1791. The pair settled at Brandenburgh House, where they gave theatricals, in which the Margravine and her son Keppel Craven took prominent parts. She wrote some feeble plays, and published her Travels and Memoirs.

J^s G^y.

Pub. May 12, 1787, by H. Humphrey, New Bond Street

LA BELLE ASSEMBLÉE

"HERE LOVE HIS GOLDEN SHAFTS EMPLOYS; HERE LIGHTS
HIS CONSTANT LAMP: AND WAVES HIS PURPLE WINGS
REIGNS HERE AND REVELS."
Milton.

J^s G^y des^t et fec^t.   Pub^d June 13th 1795, by H.Humphrey N°.37. New Bond Street

ENTER COWSLIP WITH A BOWL OF CREAM

AS A CEDAR TALL AND SLENDER   IS HER NOM'TIVE CASE
SWEET COWSLIPS GRACE   AND SHE'S OF THE FEMININE GENDER

Vide Brundenbury Theatricals

London Pub^d by W. Holland, N° 50. Oxford Street. Sep^t 23 1789

THE SCOTCH WEDDING

In Holland's Exhibition Rooms may be seen the largest Collection in Europe of Humorous Prints.   Admittance, one shilling

acted so well and danced so lightly that one wit declared that her activity could only be accounted for on the ground that she was *hollow*. Gillray has left a portrait of her in one of her favourite parts under the title of *Enter Cowslip with a Bowl of Cream. Vide Brandenburgh House Theatricals*, 1795 (Pl. XXXVII.). Below the sketch of the stout, rubicund little lady are engraved the following lines from the piece in question :—

> " As a cedar tall and slender ;
> Sweet Cowslip's grace
> Is her nom'tive case,
> And she's of the feminine gender."

The four ladies described in the foregoing pages are all introduced into Gillray's effective etching *La Belle Assemblée* (May, 1787), being represented as offering oblations in the Temple of Venus (Pl. XXXVI.). Lady Cecilia Johnstone plays the lyre, Lady Archer, dressed in a riding habit, leads a lamb to the altar by a garland of flowers, Lady Mount Edgcumbe offers a pair of turtle-doves, while Mrs. Hobart throws incense upon the flames.[1]

The Duchess of Gordon[2] and her match-making efforts on behalf of her four pretty daughters supplied some excellent material to the caricaturists about this period. That the Duchess was a woman of untiring energy is sufficiently proved by the journal of her movements during a couple of days in May, 1791, furnished by Horace Walpole. " She first went to Handel's music in the Abbey ; she then clambered over the benches, and went to Hastings' trial in the Hall ; after dinner to the play ; then to Lady Lucan's assembly ; after that to Ranelagh, and returned to Mrs. Hobart's faro-table ; gave a ball herself in the evening of that morning, into which she must have got a good way ; and set out for Scotland next day." It was small wonder that a lady blessed with such powers of activity and endurance should have succeeded in marrying three of her daughters to dukes, and the fourth to a marquis.

In September, 1789, Gillray published a caricature called *The Scotch Wedding*, in which the Duke of Richmond and Lady Anne Gordon are seen jumping over a broomstick, while the bride's mother plays a triumphal tune upon the bagpipes (Pl. XXXIII.). In April, 1797, the same artist produced a more elaborate design called *The Gordon Knot, or the Bonny Duchess Hunting the Bedfordshire Bull*. The Duke of Bedford, in the guise of a bull, has taken fright at a noose of ribbon inscribed " Matrimony," with which the Duchess is endeavouring to snare him. The would-be mother-in-law cries in broad Scotch, " Ye overgrown fule, what are ye kicking at ? Are we not ganging to lead ye to graze on the banks of the Tweed, and to mak' ye free o' the mountains of the north ? " Lady Georgiana, the daughter on whose behalf the chase has been started, cries, " Run, mither, run ; how I long to lead the sweet bonny creature in a string." In the background the Duchess's other daughters are dancing as the Three Graces, namely, Lady

---

[1] Gillray also caricatured Lady Mount Edgcumbe as *A Witch upon Mount Edge* (*vide* Fuseli) and Lady Archer in *The Finishing Touch*.

[2] Jane, daughter of Sir William Maxwell. She married the fourth Duke of Gordon in 1767, and died in 1812.

Charlotte, Duchess of Richmond, who leads a King Charles' spaniel, Lady Susan, Duchess of Manchester, and Lady Louisa, afterwards Lady Cornwallis. The Duke of Bedford temporarily escaped the noose, but a few years later the Duchess ran him to earth in Paris, with the result that he was married to Lady Georgiana in 1803.

In Rowlandson's etching *A Squall in Hyde Park* (1791) we have a spirited representation of the flurry and agitation of a smart crowd caught in a sudden thunder-shower (Pl. XXXIX.). The little French umbrellas are blown inside out, the tall feathers hang limply out of curl, and the gauze or muslin dresses cling forlornly to their wearers' forms. The Prince of Wales on horseback is making a dash for Carlton House, and the sporting Lord Barrymore[1] is steering his high phaeton and spirited horses with some difficulty through the throng. One elderly gentleman has slipped down in the mud, and serves as a stumbling-block for the crowds that follow him, whose movements are hastened by the attentions of a zealous bulldog, troubled by suspicions as to the reason for this sudden flight. Another glimpse of social life is afforded us by Rowlandson in his water-colour drawing *The Return from St. James', after receiving the honour of knighthood*, a humorous sketch of a newly-knighted gentleman being welcomed home by his remarkably plain womenkind (Pl. XLI.).

During the early nineties some rather startling changes took place in the fashions, the costume of the men being affected no less than that of the women. The sword-cane, wig, and elaborate toilette of the Maccaronies had given way to the almost barbaric simplicity of cropped heads, skirtless coats, and heavy bludgeon sticks. The dandy who clung to the old effeminate fashions was designated a "Jessamy," and in Rowlandson's. *Series from Proverbs* (1790) we see a youth of this type, who illustrates the text, "A wise Son maketh a glad Father ; but a foolish Son is the Heaviness of his Mother." In *A Spencer and a Thread-paper* (1792) Gillray portrays the new garment invented by Lord Spencer, who declared that if he cut off the skirts of his coat, in less than a week the whole world would be following the fashion (Pl. XL.).

By the spring of 1794 the ladies had discarded not only their pads, but their hoops and their long-waisted stays, the sash being tied under the armpits in what is now called Empire fashion. The bodice, both for day and evening wear, was exceedingly *décolleté*, while the skirts were thin and scanty, showing every line of the figure. For a sketch of the out-door fashions we may turn to a design of Miss Aynscombe's, engraved by Gillray under the title *And Catch the Living Manners as they Rise* (Pl. XLII.). Here we see a fashionable couple, supposed to be members of the Rutland family, the lady wearing the newly introduced turban, from which rise three immense feathers, as well as a high stiff ornament of the brush variety. Her companion appears to be simply

---

[1] This was Richard, second earl (1769–93). Of him Sir Egerton Brydges writes : "With talents to shine in a course of honourable ambition, with wit, good nature and engaging manners, he shone a meteor of temporary wonder and regret, by freaks which would have disgraced Buckingham or Rochester, until the accidental discharge of his musket . . . put an end to his troubles and his follies."

Drawn & Etch'd by T. Rowlandson   *Acquatinta by T. Malton*

A SUDDEN SQUALL IN HYDE PARK

[1791]

J⁰ G⁹

A SPENCER AND A THREADPAPER

THE RETURN FROM S⠀ JAMES'

AFTER THE HONOUR OF KNIGHTHOOD

From the Water-colour Drawing by Thomas Rowlandson

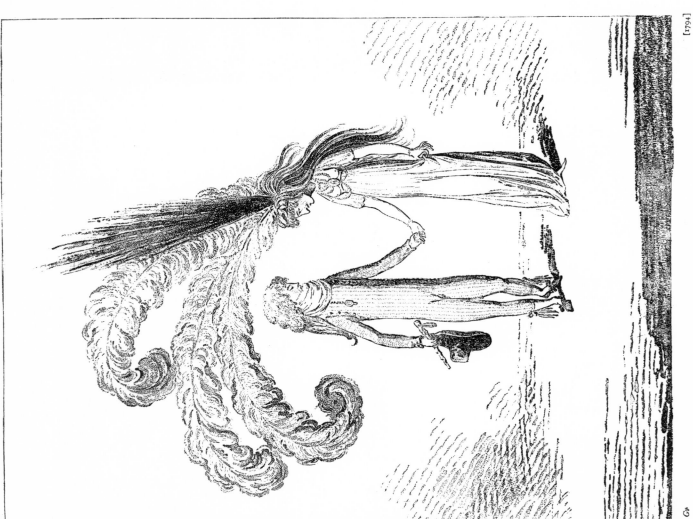

XLIII

Pub^d June 15, 1795, by H. Humphrey
No 37, New Bond Street

PARASOLS FOR 1795

XLII

[1794]

AND CATCH THE LIVING MANNERS AS THEY RISE

R. NEWTON del et fecit.

London. Pub. by Willm Holland, No 60, Oxford S^t
Novem^r 12, 1795

SHEPHERDS, I HAVE LOST MY WAIST!
HAVE YOU SEEN MY BODY?
SACRIFICED TO MODERN TASTE
I'M QUITE A HODDY DODDY!

COMFORTS OF BATH

Rowlandson fecit

Pub^d Januay 6. 1798 by S. W. Fores, No 50 Piccadilly, corner of Sackville Street
Repub^d June 16th 1857 by Robt. Walker, Harley Street, Bath

Publish'd April 6th 1787 by
H. Humphrey, No 51, New Bond Street

SUCH THINGS ARE

THAT SUCH THINGS ARE WE MUST ALLOW,
BUT SUCH THINGS NEVER WERE TILL NOW.

XLVII

O'Keefe inv' et sculp.

Nov 15, 1794, Pub. by H. Humphrey
No 37, New Bond Street

PEOPLE OF CONSEQUENCE

attired in striped pyjamas and a huge cravat which covers both his chest and his chin.

Gillray, who paid a good deal of attention to the vagaries of costume about this period, published in the course of the year four etchings dealing with the fashions, entitled respectively *The Graces of 1794*, a caricature of a smart crowd in Kensington Gardens; *The Rage, or Shepherds I have Lost my Waist*, designed by R. Newton,[1] in which an unfortunate lady is refusing all refreshments at a party because she has been left no space "for cheese-cake, tart or jelly" (Pl. XLIV.); *People of Consequence* (Pl. XLVII.); and *Following the Fashions*, a plate divided into two compartments, the one called *St. James' giving the Ton—a Soul without a Body*, the other *Cheapside aping the Mode—a Body without a Soul*.

To the year 1794 is also due *The Long Minuet as Danced at Bath*, one of the most popular designs of Henry Bunbury. This consists of several couples, most of them unattractive in appearance, in various attitudes appropriate to the dance. It may be noted that in Bunbury's portrait he is represented at work upon the *Long Minuet*, so that it was evidently regarded as his masterpiece. While on the subject of life at the West-country watering-place, we may glance at Rowlandson's series *The Comforts of Bath* (1798), which was suggested by Anstey's[2] *New Bath Guide*, first published in 1766. This is written in rhymed epistles, and deals with the adventures of the B—r—d Family at Bath, with the Consultation of Physicians, the Gaming-Rooms, the Balls, the Bathing, and the Public Breakfasts. Young "B—r—d," who "commences Man of Taste and Spirit," describes his costume in the following lines :—

> "I ride in a Chair with my Hands in a Muff,
> And have bought a silk Coat, and embroidered the Cuff.
> But the Weather was cold, and the Coat it was thin,
> So the Taylor advised me to line it with Skin.
> But what with my Nivernois Hat can compare,
> Bag-wig and laced Ruffles, and black Solitaire?
> And what can a Man of true Fashion denote,
> Like an Ell of good Ribbon tyed under the Throat.
> My Buckles and Box are in excellent Taste,
> The one is of paper, the other of Paste,
> And sure no Camayer was ever yet seen,
> Like that which I purchased at Wickstead's machine.
> My Stockings of Silk are just come from the Hozier,
> For to-night I'm to dine with the charming Miss Tozer."

Among the best of Rowlandson's Bath sketches are *The Concert*, a *Tea-party*, the *Guests drinking the Waters*, and *The Assembly* (Pl. XLV.).

The year 1795 is scarcely less rich than 1794 in caricatures relating to the extravagances of costume, the most important being from the indefatigable pencil of Gillray. In *Modern Elegance* he portrays the beautiful Lady

---

[1] Richard Newton (1777–98). In his short career he executed a few caricatures, and also painted some portraits in miniature.

[2] Christopher Anstey (1724–1805). He distinguished himself at Cambridge by his facility in writing verse. He translated Gray's *Elegy* into Latin verse, and published his *New Bath Guide* (much admired by H. Walpole) in 1766. The last thirty years of his life were spent at Bath.

Charlotte Campbell[1] (afterwards Bury), who in later years rendered herself somewhat too notorious by her book on the Court of George IV. (Pl. XLVIII.). Another great lady, and one of the most famous beauties of her time, the Duchess of Rutland, figures in the same artist's design, *Characters in High Life, Sketched in the New Rooms, Opera House* (Pl. L.). The Duchess, whose charming face is familiar to us from Reynolds' portrait, is leading her sister-in-law, Lady Gertrude Manners, who wears five high-standing feathers in her hair. The motto chosen to illustrate the picture is " Delightful task, to teach the young idea how to shoot."

More satirical in intention, though not less graceful in design, is the etching entitled *A Lady putting on her Cap* (Pl. LII.). A fashionable dame has just begun what promises to be the lengthy task of donning her turban. Although two maids are supporting the countless yards of drapery, a lap-dog plays unobserved with one end, while his mistress twines the other round her head. A grotesque couple appear in a print called *Parasols for 1796* (Pl. XLIV.). Straw had lately come into fashion for the decoration of hats and dresses, and in this design the lady, who carries a tiny parasol, wears three huge tufts of straw upon her little beaver hat. Her hair is hanging down her back in a compact mass, the ends alone being plaited. Her companion, a very attenuated gentleman, wears a hat of much the same shape as the lady's, but so large that it serves as a complete protection against the sun. In *Waggoners' Frocks, or No Bodys of 1795*, some ladies are portrayed in short, loose smocks, with large bunches of straw in their hair (Pl. XLIX.).

During the last twenty years of the century play was the passion of all classes, the E.O. tables being patronised by the middle and lower orders, while faro, hazard, and unlimited loo were the amusements of the " quality." In 1781 Rowlandson, himself an ardent gambler, published his *E.O., or the Fashionable Vowels*, the representation of a party of players grouped round a table on which is a revolving board, marked with the letters E and O, and worked on much the same principle as a roulette wheel. A year later an attempt was made by the Justices of Westminster to put down the public tables, of which there were three hundred in the parish of St. James alone. Gillray, resenting this interference with the liberty of the subject, issued (in 1782) his etching, *The Westminster Jackasses a' Braying, or the Downfall of the E.O. Tables. N.B. The Jackasses are to be indemnified for all the mischief they do by the Bulls and Bears in the City.* The magistrates in the guise of asses are here depicted in the act of destroying the obnoxious tables with heavy mallets.

Some years later great scandal was caused by the establishment of private faro-banks in the houses of certain great ladies, by means of which many young men were ruined. Chief among the offenders were our old friends Mrs. Hobart, now transformed into Lady Buckinghamshire, Lady Archer, and

---

[1] Lady Charlotte (1775–1861) was the daughter of the fifth Duke of Argyll. In 1796 she married Colonel John Campbell, and in 1818 the Rev. Edward Bury. She was appointed Lady-in-Waiting to Caroline, Princess of Wales, and published several novels, as well as her *Diary Illustrative of the Times of George IV*.

XLIX

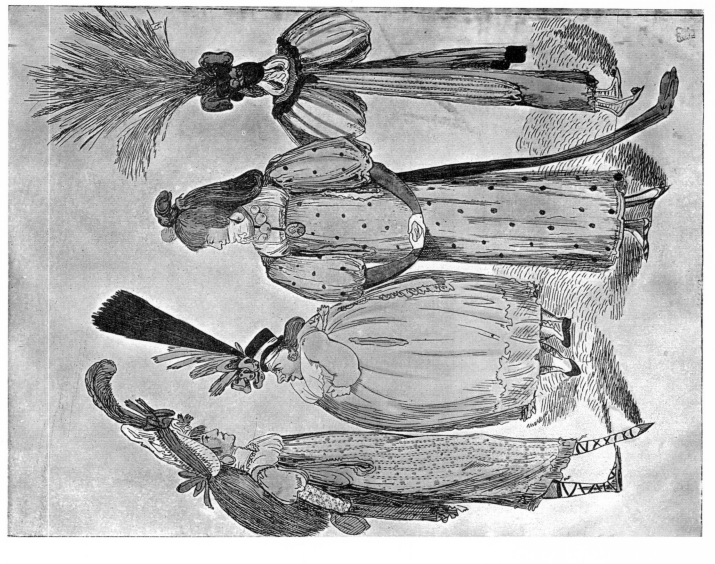

WAGGONERS FROCKS OR NO BODYS OF 1795

Publd. Aug 4th 1795 by S. W. Fores, No. 50, Piccadilly, the corner of Sackville Street
Folios of Caracatures Lent out for the Evening

XLVIII

MODERN ELEGANCE
A PORTRAIT

Publd. May 22d 1796, by H. Humphrey No 37 New Bond Street

Jˢ G⁹ del. et fect.

Pub. June 20ᵗʰ 1795, by H. Humphrey
No 37, New Bond Street

CHARACTERS IN HIGH LIFE

SKETCH'D AT THE NEW ROOMS, OPERA HOUSE

" Delightful Task! to teach the young idea how to shoot ! "

Pub.d May 12th 1796, by H. Humphrey, New Bond Street

EXALTATION OF FARO'S DAUGHTERS

J^s G^y   *Pub^d June 30th 1795, by H. Humphrev, No 37, New Bond Street*

A LADY PUTTING ON HER CAP,—JUNE 1795

Lady Mount Edgcumbe, who became known as "Faro's Daughters." On the 9th of May, 1796, Lord Kenyon,[1] summing up in a case that had been brought to recover a gambling debt, strongly denounced the vice that permeated all classes of society, and particularly inveighed against the bad example set by those in high places, adding, "They think they are too great for the law; I wish they could be punished. If any prosecutions of this nature are fairly brought before me, and the parties are justly convicted, whatever be their rank or station in the country—though they be the first ladies in the land—they shall certainly exhibit themselves on the pillory." Gillray seized upon the suggestion with malicious glee, and on May 12th published his famous plate, *The Exaltation of Faro's Daughters*, in which Lady Buckinghamshire and Lady Archer are portrayed in the pillory (Pl. LI.). In another design of the same subject, Lord Kenyon, in the character of town-crier, exclaims: "Oh yes! Oh yes! this is to give notice that several silly women in the parishes of St. Giles', St. James', and St. George, have caused much uneasiness and distress in families by keeping bad houses, late hours, and by shuffling and cutting have detained divers valuable articles: Whoever will bring before me," etc. etc.

A year later, in March, 1797, information was actually laid against Lady Buckinghamshire, Lady E. Luttrell, Mrs. Sturt, Mrs. Concannon and Mr. Martindale for having played faro at the first-named lady's house in St. James' Square. Mr. Martindale, as proprietor of the table, was fined £200 and the ladies £50 each. Lord Kenyon had evidently reconsidered his threat about the pillory, but Gillray engraved a plate depicting the punishment as he thought it ought to have been under the title of *Discipline à la Kenyon*, wherein we see Lady Buckinghamshire being flogged at the cart's tail, while Lady Archer and Mrs. Concannon stand in the pillory. Another design, *The Loss of the Faro-bank*, was suggested to the artist by the fact that Lady Buckinghamshire's faro-bank was stolen one evening while she and her guests were absorbed in their play. The party, as represented in Gillray's caricature, includes the usual notorious ladies, whose male companions are Fox, Sheridan, and Colonel Hanger. Lord Buckinghamshire, who has been sent to fetch the banker's cash-box, returns exclaiming in dismay, "The bank's stole! We're ruined, my lady! But I'll run to Bow Street, and fix the saddle on the right horse." "The bank stole, my lord," cries his wife; "why I secured it in the housekeeper's room myself! This comes of admitting Jacobins into the house. Seven hundred gone smack without a single cock of the cards." "Bank stole," puts in Mrs. Concannon; "why I had a gold snuff-box stole last night from my table in Grafton Street." "Stole! bless me!" comments Lady Archer. "Why, a lady had her pocket picked at my house last Monday." "Zounds! I hope they don't smoke me," mutters Fox guiltily; while Sheridan echoes, "Nor me."

The mischief wrought by the keepers of private faro or hazard tables was

---

[1] Lloyd, first Baron Kenyon (1732–1802), Lord Chief Justice from 1788 to 1802.

the subject of frequent comment in the public Press. There was enormous profusion at the entertainments of the gambling ladies when the faro mania was at its height, thousands being spent annually upon dinners, and hot suppers being served regularly at one and three a.m. After the French Revolution, however, the tables were surrounded by French *émigrés*, who " punted " with crowns instead of dashing on guineas, and the profits would barely allow of bread and cheese and porter, while the stakes were frequently in kind. By 1796 the ladies were reduced to desperate expedients to obtain pigeons, if we may judge from an article in the *Carlton House Magazine*, which was published professedly in the interests of the most fashionable set. " All young heirs," explains the writer, " or others who possess money or estates, are regularly invited by the public newspapers to those scenes of dissipation and destruction, under the title of *Arrangements of haut ton, the fashionable parties of the week.* Her grace gives a public dinner such a day ; the marchioness a supper and ball ; the countess tea and cards ; the viscountess a conversazione ; my lady a concert ; Mrs. Gobblefat the delectable game of all-fours, or any other pleasing pastime as best suits the inclination of the parties. It is really astonishing to behold the motley groups which compose these parties ; they are of all descriptions, from royalty to the meanest blackleg. . . . Ten or twenty thousand pounds is paying very high for the bewitching smiles or enchanting looks of her ladyship or her grace ; we believe, however, it might be very easily proved that such a high price has been paid for those allurements in the manner above alluded to."

The fashions for 1796 may be seen in Gillray's etching *High Change in Bond Street, or la Politesse du grand Monde* (Pl. LIII.). The Scaramouch style, as it was called, was now the *ton* for the young men of the day, whose manners were as unconstrained as their dress, judging from the nonchalance with which they elbow the ladies off the pavement. The cropped heads had come in the previous year in consequence of the imposition of a tax upon hair-powder, the unpopular measure of a Tory Government. Gillray, in his caricature *Leaving off Powder*, has shown a whole family in consternation at their appearance without their floured wigs. " The following noblemen and gentlemen," to quote a paragraph of fashionable intelligence from a daily paper (June, 1795), " were of the party with the Duke and Duchess of Bedford at Woburn Abbey, when a general cropping and combing out of powder took place, Lord Wm. Russell, Lord Villiers, Lord Paget, etc., etc. They entered into an engagement to forfeit a sum of money if any of them wore their hair tied and powdered within a certain period." Those who paid the guinea tax were called guinea pigs, those who did not were pigs without a guinea.

The new fashions found but small favour in the sight of elderly persons who cherished the ideals of the past. Lady Hesketh, writing to her young cousin, Cowper's " Johnny of Norfolk," says, " As I mentioned *dress*, let me *entreat* you not to give way to the *blackguardism of the Times*. For Heaven's

Pub⁴. March 27, 1796, by H. Humphrey, New Bond Street

HIGH CHANGE IN BOND STREET—OU—LA POLITESSE DU GRANDE MONDE

sake, if not for mine, do not go without powder! nor wear *checked Shirts!* nor a coloured handkerchief about your neck like a sailor out of employ— nor your hair dirty and ill-combed, as if you had just come out of a dungeon. Many of the young men I see affect this abomination of all abominations, and look like so many hang-dogs."

This account of the golden youth of the period is borne out by George Woodward in his little book *An Olio of Good Breeding*, in which a typical "well-bred man" is represented as standing in a *dégagé* attitude in front of the fire, his coat-tails under his arm and his hat cocked over one eye. With the women of breeding also carelessness in dress seems to have been the order of the day, since, to quote from the same authority, "Who in times like these would pay the smallest regard to feminine attire? Downright masculine Amazonian decorations are infinitely preferable: the dirty dashing half-boot, beaver hat and stylish spencer can alone command respect and consequence."

The fashions for the closing year of the century may be seen in Gillray's *Monstrosities of 1799—see Kensington Gardens*. This plate was published in June, when the weather may have justified to some extent the low-cut bodices and the thin transparent gauze gowns. A large poke bonnet was worn on the head, almost concealing the features, while the hair was drawn down over the eyebrows. The men are attired in hideous "Jean de Bry" coats, heavily padded on the shoulders, high Hessian boots, and huge bandages swathing both chin and throat. The ladies clung to their scanty gauze robes even after winter had set in, as is proved by a couple of caricatures for this season, *Transparencies* and *Ladies in their Winter Fashions for 1799*. In the former, a rather graceful design, three girls are portrayed, all attired in the airiest garments, which contrast oddly with their immense fur muffs. A cold January, however, put an end to this absurd fashion, and the return to a more appropriate style of dress was illustrated by Gillray in a caricature entitled *Boreas effecting what health and modesty could not do* (January 5th, 1800), which shows a party of ladies hastily exchanging their transparent robes for thick petticoats and other warm undergarments.

DRAMATIC AND MUSICAL

PART I

THE first quarter of the eighteenth century saw the almost total eclipse of the legitimate drama in England, and the growth in public favour of those exotic entertainments—operas, pantomimes, and masquerades—which were denounced by the more conservative among the critics as childish, immoral, and degrading. The adoration lavished on foreign singers, and the enormous sums paid to them, aroused the envious ire of the native performer, while the neglect of Shakespeare and other classic playwrights was a favourite subject for the scourge of the satirist. A brief statement of the position of the theatrical world at this period must necessarily preface an account of the caricatures that were levelled against the profession. In 1682 the two existing theatrical companies, the King's and the Duke's, had been united under one patent at Drury Lane, where in 1690 Christopher Rich[1] became the predominant partner. In 1695, however, Betterton[2] obtained a patent for a theatre in Lincoln's Inn Fields, whence in 1705 he transferred the company to a new house in the Haymarket, planned by Vanbrugh for Italian opera. Ill success followed the venture, and the Haymarket was let a year later to an agent of Rich's, who recruited his company from Drury Lane, and thus for a time the two theatres were practically under one management.

This monopoly did not answer long. Rich's avarice and tyrannical ways disgusted his *employés*, and there were incessant squabbles over contracts and salaries. Appeal was made to the Lord Chamberlain, Rich lost control of the Haymarket, and for a short time Drury Lane was closed. In 1709 a lawyer named Collier obtained the lease and licence of this theatre, but Rich acquired the patent of the little house in Lincoln's Inn Fields, which he rebuilt in what was then considered splendid style. Christopher died just before the new building was finished, but it was opened in December, 1714, by his son, John Rich, better known as "Lun" the Harlequin, with a company con-

---

[1] Christopher Rich (*d.* 1714) began his career as an attorney, but acquired a share in Drury Lane about 1688, and later obtained practical control of the three London theatres.

[2] Thomas Betterton (*c.* 1635–1710). Actor-manager. He was associated with Sir Charles Davenant at the theatre in Lincoln's Inn Fields, and later with Congreve. He joined the company at Drury Lane in 1682.

sisting chiefly of seceders from Drury Lane. In April a pantomime was produced with such amazing success that an entertainment of the same kind was given every year down to 1760, and Drury Lane, now under the triple rule of Cibber, Wilkes, and Doggett, was compelled to follow suit. As a harlequin, Rich is said to have been unrivalled, even the severer critics waxing enthusiastic over the wit and coherence of his pantomime.

Meanwhile Italian opera had become firmly established at the Haymarket under Heidegger, and masquerade had also been introduced, greatly to the consternation of the "unco guid." As early as 1710–11 the "absurdity" of opera, as exemplified in Handel's *Rinaldo*, had been attacked in the *Spectator* by Addison, who pointed out the puerility of the libretto translations, which always brought the wrong word on the wrong note, the folly of giving performances partly in Italian and partly in English, and the error of attempting to mix shadows with realities in the same piece, such as real singing-birds in painted groves, real cascades in artificial landscapes, and enchanted chariots drawn by Flanders mares. He complained that native music was quite rooted out, and declared that historians of the future would state that "in the beginning of the eighteenth century the Italian tongue was so well understood in England that operas were acted upon the stage in that language."

Steele had written in much the same vein in the *Tatler* (1709), but had put forward the curious theory that rational pleasure might again be expected from dramatic performances on condition that only one playhouse was supported by the public. "It has been within the observation of the youngest among us," he remarks, "that while there were two houses they did not outvie each other by such representations as tended to the instruction and ornament of life, but by introducing mimical dances and fulsome buffooneries. . . . To please the people two houses must entertain them with what they can understand, and not with things which are designed to improve their understandings, and the readiest way to gain good audiences must be to offer such things as are most relished by the crowd; that is to say, by empty shows, immodest action, or impertinent activity. In short, two houses cannot hope to subsist but by means which are contradictory to the very institution of a theatre in a well-governed kingdom."

At this time Nicolini,[1] allowed on all hands to be a superb singer and accomplished actor, was the star contralto at the Opera. A few years later, in 1720, the arrogant Senesino,[2] the idol of the "Smart Set," made his appear-

---

[1] Nicolini, Grimaldi, born *c.* 1673 at Naples. He first appeared in London in 1708, and at once obtained such popularity that the Opera prices were raised. He was the first great Italian singer who performed in Opera in this country, and in spite of their British prejudices he won the admiration of both Steele and Addison. The operatic arrangements were remodelled in accordance with his advice and suggestions. He returned to Italy in 1717, but the date of his death is unknown.

[2] Senesino, Francesco Bernardi, detto (1680–*c.* 1750). Handel engaged him for London in 1720, when he appeared in Buononcini's *Astarte*, and made a prodigious sensation. His departure in 1726, and failure to return for the winter season, seems to have been regarded as a public calamity. However, he reappeared in 1727. His success seems to have turned his head, and he had many quarrels with Handel and with his fellow-singers. He retired upon the then large fortune of £15,000.

ance in London, where he was afterwards joined by the rival songstresses Faustina[1] and Cuzzoni, who divided the town on the subject of their charms. A print undated, but published probably about 1725, is called *The Landing of Senesino*, and shows the great man standing on a quay, with ships in the background, being rapturously welcomed by the Faustina, the Cuzzoni, and some members of the musical public (Pl. LIV.). "Two rough uncouth Fellows," to quote from the figured explanation, "are showing by their action their contempt for the Polite Arts and those Illustrious Performers, whose coming into this Country has proved so beneficial and advantageous to the Publick." Senesino, after singing in several of Handel's operas with great success, quarrelled with the composer, and seceded to Lincoln's Inn Fields, where Italian opera was established by Handel's rival, Porpora, in 1733. Here he sang in company with Farinelli and Cuzzoni until 1735, when he retired to Italy upon his fortune.

Another engraving, attributed to Hogarth, but neither signed nor dated, shows the gigantic Senesino as Marc Antony and the dumpy Cuzzoni as Cleopatra singing a duet in Handel's opera "Julius Cæsar," while Berenstadt, another idol of the public, displays in the character of Cæsar the most superb indifference to the performance of his two colleagues (Pl. LVI.). The same design reappears on a show-cloth in Hogarth's little plate *Masquerades and Operas*, published in 1724 (Pl. LV.). This contains in small compass a fierce attack upon the various fashionable entertainments that had almost ousted the legitimate drama from the boards. On one side of a space in front of Burlington House a crowd of persons are rushing into a theatre to witness a performance of the pantomime "Dr. Faustus," lately given at both theatres, while on the other a figure of Folly and a demon are leading a number of people enclosed in a rope into a colonnade inscribed "Masquerade." In the foreground a woman is carting away in a wheelbarrow the dramatic works of Shakespeare, Ben Jonson, Dryden, and Congreve. On the gate of Burlington House is a statue of Kent,[2] the artist-architect (the rival of Sir Thomas Thornhill, Hogarth's father-in-law), between the reclining figures of Michael Angelo and Raphael.

This plate in all probability suggested, or was suggested by, an anonymous print which contains an attack upon Heidegger, the promoter of operas and masquerades. The punning title is "Hei! Degeror, O! I am undone!" and the design shows Heidegger lying on the ground and begging for mercy from Hercules, who holds an upraised club in one hand and in the other a chain enclosing a group of masqueraders who have their hands tied behind them. Heidegger's money is falling out of his pockets, his wealth being

---

[1] Faustina Bordoni (1700–83) made her début at Venice in 1716, and was engaged by Handel for the London season of 1726, at a salary of £2,000 a year. She is described as a beautiful woman of charming manners, and she became very popular in society. Later she went to Venice, where she married Hasse, the composer and Director of the Dresden Opera. The latter part of her life was spent between Dresden, Venice, and Vienna.

[2] William Kent, painter, sculptor, and architect (1684–1748). He was a protégé of Lord Burlington, with whom he lived. Kent built Devonshire House and the Treasury Buildings, and is responsible for the statue of Shakespeare in Poets' Corner.

*Sold by J. Clark Engraver & Printseller
in Grays Inn, Pr. 1 shill.*

THE LANDING OF SENESINO

Wm. Hogarth Invt et sculpt.

Price 1 Shilling [1724]

MASQUERADES AND OPERAS

[*By Hogarth*]

[1725]

BERENSTAT, CUZZOIN AND SENESINO

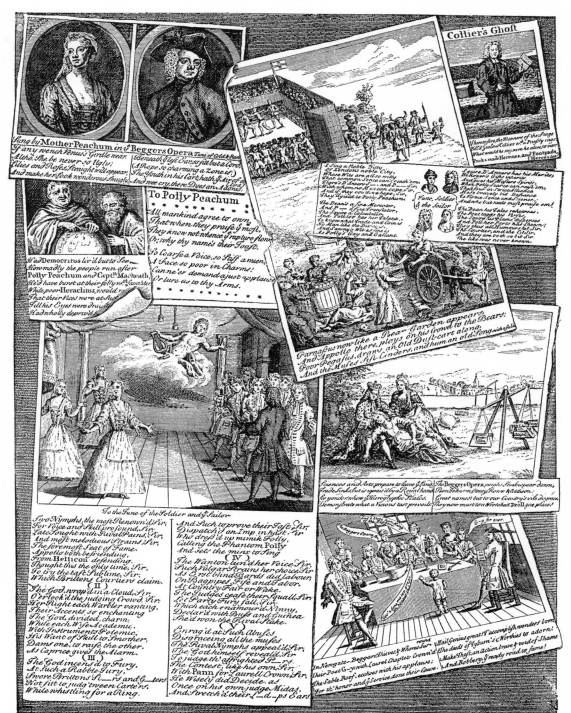

[Ap. 1728]

THE STAGE MEDLEY

REPRESENTING THE POLITE TASTE OF THE TOWN AND THE MATCHLESS MERITS OF POET
G—— POLLY PEACHUM AND CAPT^N. MACHEATH

Wm. Hogarth

THE BEGGARS' OPERA

contrasted with the misery of some beggars who are waiting outside a church, from which issue the figures of Britannia, Wisdom, and Piety. A Mercury flies through the air holding a scroll, on which are the words " Mascarades Destroyt."

On January 6th, 1724, the Bishop of London had preached so eloquent a sermon against masquerades that the Government had issued orders for this form of entertainment to be suppressed. The order must have been chiefly directed against Heidegger, a Swiss by birth, who had come to England in 1708 on a business mission from Zurich, and afterwards enlisted in the Guards, where he was known as the Swiss Count. Being patronised by the Prince of Wales (George II.), he got up subscription performances of opera in English, and introduced masquerades. He was appointed Master of the Revels by the King, and for many years directed the entertainments of the nobility. Allusions to Heidegger, to his physical uncomeliness and social pretensions, appear in the *Dunciad*, the *Tatler*, the farces of Fielding, and many other contemporary works.

After the censures levelled by critics and satirists against the "degraded taste" of the town, which was supposed to revel in the performances of jugglers, rope-walkers, and dancing dogs, it is refreshing to come across a high encomium upon the merits of the British theatre in Macky's *Journey through England* (*circa* 1724). "There are," he observes, "three very noble Theatres in London, the Haymarket for Opera, Drury Lane for History, Tragedy and Comedy, and Lincoln's Inn Fields for more miscellaneous entertainments. The English affect more the Italian than the French musick ; and their own compositions are between the gravity of the first and the Levity of the other. . . . No nation represents History so naturally, so much to the Life, and so close to Truth, as the English ; they have most of the occurrences of their own History, and all those of the Roman Empire, nobly acted. One Shakespeare, who lived in the last century, laid down a masterly foundation for this in his excellent plays ; and the late Mr. Addison has improved that taste by his admirable Cato. Their Comedies are designed to lash the growing Follies in every age ; and scarce a Fool or a Coxcomb appears in Town but his Folly is represented."

On January 29th, 1728, was produced at Lincoln's Inn Fields the piece that was said to have made Gay rich and Rich gay. This was, of course, the "Beggar's Opera," which temporarily drove even Italian opera out of the field, and enjoyed the unprecedented run of sixty-three nights in one season. The whole town went mad over Captain Macheath and Polly Peachum, scenes from the opera were painted on fans and screens, and the piece was played in nearly every town in the kingdom. Gay was consoled by this prodigious success for a long series of disappointments in his hopes of Court advancement, and compensated to some extent for his losses in the South Sea Bubble.

But the work was not without its detractors. The more puritanical cried it down as "immoral," declaring that it had the worst effect on the minds of the lower orders, and even going so far as to maintain that each time it was played it sent a man to the gallows. Like Italian opera and pantomime, it also became the subject of attack by the more conservative admirers of the legitimate drama. In April, 1728, a print was published called *The Stage Medley, Representing the Polite Tast of the Town and the matchless merits of Poet G——, Polly Peachum and Captain Macheath* (Pl. LVII.). In this a number of designs appear to be thrown carelessly together, including portraits of the principal performers, the Muses drinking together, a boxing match, the ghost of Collier rising from his grave, a party of Newgate prisoners carousing, with Gay at their head, and a pair of scales, in which the "Beggar's Opera" outweighs the works of Shakespeare, Jonson, and other giants of the past.

Hogarth also entered the field with an etching of no great merit, which represents a stage with a scene from the Italian opera on one side and from the "Beggar's Opera" on the other (Pl. LVIII.). The performers in Gay's work are drawn with the heads of animals—a bull, an ass, a pig, a cat, and an owl. Harmony is flying away, and Apollo sleeps beneath the stage. The idea of representing the characters with animals' heads is borrowed from the Dutch school, both Coypel and E. van Heemsherck[1] having produced caricatures in this style. Among a series of satirical designs by the latter (engraved by Toms) representing scenes from English life (*c.* 1730), there is one which deals with the subject of British admiration for foreign musicians (Pl. LIX.). This shows the interior of a large room, in which a band of animal-headed musicians play on mock instruments, such as tongs and shovel, tobacco-pipes, and a cow's horn; while in the background the rest of the company dance to the grotesque strains.

Rich Lun,[2] the harlequin proprietor of the theatre in Lincoln's Inn Fields, was a favourite target for the shafts of the satirists. In April, 1731, appeared *The Stage's Glory*, a large emblematical cartoon, which contains some smart satire upon Rich, and exposes the debased taste of the theatrical public (Pl. LX.). There is a mock-heroic dedication to Rich as "L'illustre, magnanime et heroique Arlequin, Génie Supreme et Ornement du Theatre, Sujet agréable des Pièces Dramatiques," etc. etc., and a numbered explanation, which is further elucidated by an article in *The Grub Street Journal*, April 15th, 1731. The design shows a triumphal arch, with a shield containing the Hero's arms—a mask, a harlequin's cap, and crossed batons—supported by a fox and a monkey. The crest is a Satyr's head, and the motto, "Craft is my lot." Within the arch sits Folly and her sister Fortune, towards whom the Hero (Rich) is ascending a rugged

---

[1] This was probably the son of the Egbert van Heemsherck (1645–1704) who settled in England in the reign of William III. He designed some humorous subjects, and Walpole tells us that he left a son who was also an engraver.

[2] "Immortal Rich! how calm he sits at ease
Mid snows of paper, and fierce hail of peas;
And proud his mistress' orders to perform,
Rides in the whirlwind and directs the storm."—*Dunciad.*

E. Heemskirck Inv.t et Sculp.t   *Toms Sculp.t*

IF MUSICK'S CHARMS CAN HEARTS ENTHRAL
THIS CONSORT'S SURE ABOVE 'EM ALL
HOW SWEET THE SOUND WHERE CATS AND BEARS
WITH BRUTISH NOISE OFFEND OUR EARS

JUST SO THE FOREIGN SINGERS MOVE
RATHER CONTEMPT THAN GAIN OUR LOVE:
WERE SUCH DISCOURAGED WE SHOULD FIND
MUSICK AT HOME TO CHARM THE MIND

[C. 1730]

THE STAGE'S GLORY

(W. Hogarth, inv et sculp) Price 6d

[Dec 18, 1732]

RICH'S GLORY
OR HIS TRIUMPHANT ENTRY INTO COVENT GARDEN

[1736]

THE JUDGMENT OF THE QUEEN'S COMMON SENSE
ADDRESS'D TO HENRY FIELDING ESQR.

path. Fortune holds a wreath for his head, and a purse turned upside down, from which coins fall into his hat. "For thy sake," she explains to Folly, "I'll continually heap my favours upon him." The Hero is supported on his upward path by the stock pantomime characters, Pierrot and the Doctor. Beneath is a cave inhabited by noxious creatures who attack the Hero with tongue and pen. Among them is a grand Critick, who declares, "I satirise on what is most sublime"; a thorough-paced Footman and ringleader of the upper gallery, who admits, "I'm very noisy"; a Female Wit, probably intended for Eliza Heywood, who says, "Nothing shames me"; and a formal, rigid Tragedy-writer, who complains, "I am uneasy to the world and myself." The design also includes scenes from the "Beggar's Opera" and the Italian opera, and shows the Hero preferring Momus to Apollo, the Hero diverting the town, the Hero and a singing lady burning the works of Shakespeare, Dryden, etc., and the landing of a party of French fiddlers and dancers in England.

On December 18th, 1732, Rich removed his company from Lincoln's Inn Fields to a fine new house which he had built in Covent Garden. The opening of the new theatre is the subject of a print ascribed to Hogarth (and said to have been suppressed) called *Rich's Glory, or his Triumphal Entry into Covent Garden* (Pl. LXI.). Here we see the exterior of the building, with its long colonnade, which a crowd is attempting to enter. A carriage approaches, drawn by six satyrs, and preceded by Gay, carried on a porter's back. On the box is a man in harlequin's dress, and inside are columbine and Rich in the character of a performing dog, a part which he played with success in one of the pantomimes. Among the crowds that follow are Theophilus Cibber,[1] Quin,[2] Ryan,[3] Walker[4] (the original Captain Macheath), and Hall (the original Lockit), all dressed in character. A cart brings up the theatrical properties, among which is a "Box of Thunder and Lightning." Addison, it may be remembered, had commented upon the excellent effect of the "new thunder"[5] some time before, and had complimented the operatic management upon the fact that "Their lightnings are made to flash more briskly than heretofore ; their clouds are also better furbelowed and more voluminous, not to mention a violent storm locked up in a big chest that is designed for the Tempest."

Projects for building new theatres attracted a good deal of attention at this time, and in April, 1735, Sir John Barnard[6] moved in the House of Commons for leave to bring in a Bill to limit the number of playhouses, and to restrain

[1] Theophilus Cibber, actor (1703–58), son of Colley Cibber. He made his début in 1721, and acted with varying success. He was the husband of the more famous Susannah Cibber (*née* Arne).

[2] James Quin (1693–1766), Garrick's chief rival. He acted either at Drury Lane or Covent Garden between 1714 and 1751.

[3] Lacy Ryan (1694–1760). He acted chiefly in Shakespearean characters, appearing at each of the London theatres in turn.

[4] Thomas Walker (1698–1744). He wrote a few plays and adaptations. His chief acting success was in Captain Macheath.

[5] Formerly thunder was produced by the aid of a mustard-bowl.—*Vide Dunciad.*

[6] Sir John Barnard (1685–1764). M.P. for City of London 1722–61. Lord Mayor 1737.

the licentiousness of actors. Barnard's supporters, among whom were Walpole and Pulteney, declared that the English nation was now so extravagantly addicted to idle diversions that the number of theatres in London was double that in Paris. They also complained that the Italian singers drew salaries equal to those of the Lord Treasurer and the Judges of England. The immediate cause of dispute seems to have been Giffard's unlicensed theatre in Goodman's Fields, Whitechapel, which had been temporarily suppressed in 1730. The Press took the matter up, and in April, 1735, the *Universal Spectator* published an article on " The Proposed Regulation of the Theatres," in which it is stated, " With reference to Mr. Giffard, what will ensue from new playhouses being erected may be seen from that in Goodman's Fields. The street (Leman Street) when it was built was inhabited by Silk-throwsters, Ribband-weavers, etc., who employed the *Industrious Poor;* immediately on setting up this Playhouse, the rents were raised, and now there is a bunch of grapes hanging at almost every door, besides an adjacent Bagnio or two ; an undoubted Proof that *Innocence* and *Morality* are not the certain Consequences of a Playhouse." The Bill was temporarily dropped on account of a clause which in the opinion of the House placed too arbitrary a power in the hands of the Lord Chamberlain.

A print suggested by the agitation for the better regulation of theatres, and entitled *The Player's Last Refuge; or, The Strollers in Distress*, was published on March 5th, 1735. The design, of no great merit, represents a ruined booth, in front of which sits Theophilus Cibber in profound dejection, with Despair and Poverty by his side, while Rich tries to console him with the offer of a mask and pistols. A young actress, Miss Lee, is drowning her sorrows in the gin-bottle, the corpse of Pistol, a favourite character of T. Cibber's, is carried in on a bier by Hamlet, Falstaff, Harlequin, etc., and Sir John Barnard is riding down Punch with drawn sword, and pointing in triumph to a black cloud which hangs over Goodman's Fields.

In April, 1736, Fielding's skit *Pasquin—A Dramatick Satire on the Times: Being the Rehearsal of Two Plays, viz. A Comedy called The Election; and a Tragedy called The Life and Death of Common Sense*, was produced at the little theatre in the Haymarket. This little piece, which contributed, it is said, to the passing of the Bill for licensing the theatres (finally carried the following year), inspired some unknown artist with a design called *The Judgment of the Queen o' Common Sense, Addressed to Henry Fielding*, Esq. (Pl. LXII.). The scene represents a stage with an alcove in the background, on which stands the Queen of Common Sense with a purse in one hand and a halter in the other. She gives the contents of the purse to Fielding, and hands the halter to Harlequin ; a pierrot, a tumbler, and representatives of the three learned professions are variously occupied, while in the foreground sits Shakespeare studying the scroll of *Hamlet*. Coming from behind, as though to remonstrate with the Queen, are a fashionably dressed lady and gentleman, who are supposed to represent the taste of the town. Another

THE ENRAGED MUSICIAN

Design'd, Engrav'd & Published by Wm Hogarth Nov^{br} the 30th 1741
Price 3 Shillings

design on the same subject is an etched benefit ticket for the author of *Pasquin*, ascribed to Hogarth, which introduces the Queen of Common Sense, her rival the Queen of Ignorance, and some of the allies of the latter potentate, among whom were (to quote from the play) " Two dogs that walk on their hind legs only, and personate human creatures so well they might be mistaken for them, a human creature that personates a dog so well that he might almost be taken for one, two Human Cats, and a most curious Set of Puppies."

Passing over the slight sketch of *Heidegger in a Rage*, somewhat doubtfully attributed to Hogarth, we come to the famous plate of *The Enraged Musician*, a subject which appeals no less to modern Londoners than to the contemporaries of Hogarth. This work, which was designed, engraved, and published by the artist on November 30th, 1741, and sold at three shillings, represents the exterior of a house in a London street, occupied by a professional musician, who, disturbed in his studies by the pandemonium outside, has rushed to the window, violin-bow in hand, to remonstrate. Among the noise-producers below are a milk-woman, a ballad singer, a hautboy player, a French drummer, a knife-grinder, a fish-seller, a dustman, and a paviour, to say nothing of romping children, barking dogs, and quarrelling cats (Pl. LXIII.).

The musician himself is said by Dr. Burney to have been intended for Signor Castrucci,[1] who was brought to England by Lord Burlington, and who led the Opera orchestra for some years. The violinist, Dr. Burney affirms, who was more than half-mad, is represented in one of Hogarth's prints as the *enraged musician*, "the painter having sufficient *polissonnerie*, previous to making the drawing, to have his house beset by all the noisy street instruments he could collect together, whose clamorous performances brought him to the window in all the agonies of auricular torture." According to Nichols and Stevens, however, the hero was John Festing,[2] the first hautboy and German flute player of his time, who on one occasion was infuriated by seeing a street hautboy player performing to a costermonger and being paid in onions. " Zounds, sir!" he cried. " This fellow is ridiculing my profession; he is playing on the hautboy for onions!" Being intimate with Hogarth, Festing mentioned the circumstance to him, and this, he declared, was the origin of *The Enraged Musician*.

On December 19th, 1741, David Garrick made his (nominal) first appearance at the unfashionable little theatre in Goodman's Fields, which only existed by stratagem. The new Licensing Bill had made it penal to represent plays outside the limits of the city of Westminster for gain or reward. This should have had the effect of closing the house in Goodman's Fields, but it was suggested to Giffard, the proprietor, that he might give a dramatic entertain-

---

[1] Pietro Castrucci (1689–1769), a pupil of Corelli, who came to London in 1715 as leader of Handel's orchestra. He invented an instrument called the violetta marina. In 1737 he was superseded by Michael Festing.

[2] John Festing was the son of a flautist who was engaged in the orchestra of the King's Theatre about 1727, and brother of the more celebrated Michael Christian, the violinist.

ment gratis, at the same time that he gave a concert for money. The hint was taken, and it was announced that on December 19th, 1741, would be performed "A Concert of vocal and instrumental music. Between the acts the audience will be entertained gratis with the tragedy of King Richard III. The part of Richard by a young gentleman, being his first appearance on any stage." The young gentleman was David Garrick, then in his twenty-fifth year, a well-known amateur performer, and with some experience gained on the boards of provincial theatres. His success was immediate and assured. The more accessible theatres were deserted, and the fashionable world flocked to Goodman's Fields to hear the new star. Early in 1742 the witty Miss Robinson, afterwards Mrs. Montagu, Queen of the Blue Stockings, writes to a friend: "On Saturday night I intend to go to Goodman's Fields to see Garrick as Richard III., that I may get one cold from a regard to sense. I have sacrificed enough to folly by catching cold at the great puppet-shows in town; if I have a rational constitution I shall not be the worse for my entertainment."

In 1743 Garrick was engaged at Drury Lane, where in this year a fierce dispute took place between the patentee, Fleetwood, and his company. The gentlemen of the Inns of Court had insisted the previous season that the prices of the pit and the gallery should be lowered, but the proprietors had then pleaded that, having engaged foreign dancers at high rates, they could not reduce the prices until the following year, when they undertook to do so. In order to fulfil their pledge, they were obliged to dismiss the dancers and dock the salaries of the actors. About a dozen of the leading members of Fleetwood's company, including Peg Woffington, Mrs. Clive, Mrs. Pritchard, Garrick, and Macklin, entered into an association, and presented a petition to the Duke of Grafton,[1] then Lord Chamberlain, for a licence to act at the Haymarket, or elsewhere. The Duke received them coldly, and expressed his surprise that a man could make five hundred a year by acting, adding that a cousin of his, a naval officer, risked his life for half that sum. The desired licence being refused, the actors were obliged to make terms with Fleetwood, who had signed a cartel with Rich, of Covent Garden, so that the two managers were able to play into each other's hands. Garrick and the leading members of the company obtained their former salaries, while the inferior performers were obliged to be content with half what they had previously received.

This dramatic rebellion excited a good deal of notice both from the press and the public, and among other satires, an engraving was published in October, 1743, called *The Theatrical Contest*, which deals with the hard fate of the discontented artists. The design shows the open space in front of Covent Garden. This is partly filled with a pool of water, across which the actors are endeavouring to swim on bladders (marked with the characters with which each was identified) to a group of gentlemen on the

[1] This was Charles, the second Duke, who succeeded his father in 1690, and died in 1757.

MR. WOODWARD IN THE CHARACTER OF MERCUTIO

Published by W. Herbert at the Globe on London Bridge 1753 *March* 1. *Price* 6⁰·

Patrick O Brian Sculp.

THE THEATRICAL STEEL-YARDS OF 1750

Publsh'a 27ᵗʰ April 1751

other side, among whom is the Duke of Grafton, who says, "I'll hear both sides," and Highmore, the patentee of Drury Lane (whose interest Fleetwood had acquired), who pronounces on his knees his favourite speech, "My Lord, I am a gentleman." In the doorway of the theatre a Harlequin (Rich) exclaims, "I've nicked 'em both." An actor declares, "I'll not play under £800 a year," and an actress (Mrs. Clive) observes, "I can do without 'em." Crowds are attempting to enter the theatre for an approaching performance, while a coster-woman and other bystanders look on the scene in amusement.

In 1747 the chronic rivalry between Covent Garden and Drury Lane entered upon an acuter phase. Garrick, who for a time had enlisted under the banner of Rich, where he had for colleagues Quin, Mrs. Cibber, and Mrs. Pritchard, was tempted by Lacy (who had superseded Fleetwood at Drury Lane) to accept a half-share in that theatre and the post of stage manager. On September 20th, 1747, a brilliant season opened at Drury Lane, several Shakespearean plays being revived with great success. In the autumn of 1749 both houses opened on the same night with *Romeo and Juliet*, Garrick presenting a new Juliet in the person of the afterwards notorious George Anne Bellamy.[1] Woodward[2] made an excellent Mercutio, and a portrait of him as he appeared when reciting the Queen Mab speech is interesting as showing how the part was dressed (Pl. LXIV.). It was generally considered that Garrick made the best Romeo, but Mrs. Cibber (at Covent Garden) the best Juliet.

The rivalry was not lessened when, at the beginning of the new year, Garrick brought out a pantomime, *Queen Mab*, in opposition to Rich, who for the past thirty years had made a *spécialité* of this form of entertainment. The rival pantomimes suggested the subject of a clever satirical design called *The Theatrical Steelyards, 1750*, engraved by Patrick O'Brian (Pl. LXV.). This is a representation of a huge steelyard suspended from the mask of a satyr. Rising high in the air on one side are the company at Covent Garden, including Mrs. Woffington, Mrs. Cibber, Quin, and Barry, while Rich in his harlequin's dress lies on the ground on the point of expiring from vexation. On the other side Garrick is weighing down the rival company unaided, though his harlequin, Woodward, is about to add Queen Mab to the scale.

In 1755 Garrick fell into disgrace with his hitherto adoring public in consequence of his having engaged a number of foreign dancers for a great spectacular piece, *The Chinese Festival*. The outbreak of war between England and France increased the British prejudice against foreign artists, and though the fashionable world took Garrick's part, the mob determined to stop the

---

[1] Bellamy, George Anne (*d.* 1788). She was an illegitimate daughter of Lord Tyrawley. She made her first appearance at Covent Garden in 1742. After a stormy career she published an Apology for her Life in 1785.

[2] Henry Woodward (1714–77). He made his début at Lincoln's Inn Fields in 1729, and later played at Covent Garden and Drury Lane, making his chief successes in comedy parts. During the latter part of his career he managed the Crow Street Theatre, Dublin, in conjunction with Spranger Barry. He was one of the few actors of the period who were praised by John Churchill in *The Rosciad*.

performances, and for some nights a free fight went on between the pit and the boxes. On November 18th, 1755, Mrs. Montagu writes to her sister: "There is a great bustle at Mr. Garrick's playhouse about some dancers, though they are chiefly German and Swiss the mob considers them as French, and I imagine they will be driven off the stage, though the dancers and scenery have cost Mr. Garrick an immense sum; this evening is to decide their fate, and I imagine at this time there may be a very bloody engagement." Mrs. Montagu was right; the theatre was wrecked, and the mob triumphed. The affair proved inspiring to a number of caricaturists, who treated it, however, from a political rather than a theatrical point of view. Among their productions may be mentioned a plate entitled *Britannia Disturbed*, which represents the invasion of a party of French vagrants who are forced on Britannia by members of the aristocracy.

DRAMATIC AND MUSICAL

PART II

TURNING to musical affairs, we find that Italian opera still held its place in the affections of the upper classes, who lavished money and attentions upon the performers as they had done in the days of Addison and Steele. Lord Chesterfield, in a satirical article contributed to the *World* in November, 1754, professes to believe that Italian singers came to England merely to oblige the English nobility. "They are exceedingly good and condescending," he writes, "to such of the nobility, or even gentry, as are desirous to contract an intimacy with them. They will, for a word's speaking, dine, sup, or pass the day with people of a certain condition, and perhaps sing or play if civilly requested. Nay, I have known many of them so good as to pass the two or three months of the summer at the country seats of some of their noble friends, and thereby mitigate the terrors of the country to my lady and her daughters. I have been assured by many of their chief patrons and patronesses that they are all *the best creatures in the world;* and from the time of Signor Cavaliero Nicolini down to this day, I have constantly heard the several great performers much more praised for their affability, the gentleness of their manners, and all the good qualities of their head and heart than for either their musical skill or execution."

The favourite of the hour was Regina Mingotti,[1] whose impertinences towards the public and quarrels with Vaneschi, the manager, brought her much unpopularity with the public. Writing to Mr. Bentley in October, 1755, Horace Walpole says, "I believe I scarce ever mentioned to you last winter the follies of the Opera : the impertinences of a great singer were too old and too common a topic. I must mention them now when they rise to any improvement in the character of national folly. The Mingotti, a noble figure, a great mistress of music, and a most incomparable actress, surpassed anything I ever saw for the extravagance of her humours. She never sang above one night in three, from a fever upon her temper ; and would never

---

[1] Regina Mingotti (1728–1807). She was born at Naples, and when little more than a child married Mingotti, the impresario of the Dresden Opera. She appeared in London during the season of 1755, and sang from time to time till 1763, when she finally retired to the Continent. Dr. Burney, who met her at Munich in 1772, says that she was a fine linguist, and knew as much about music as a Kapellmeister.

act at all when Ricciarelli, the first man, was to be in dialogue with her. Her fevers grew so high that the audience caught them, and hissed her more than once ; she herself once turned and hissed again." [1]

A little print called *The Idol* shows the prima-donna standing on a book inscribed £2,000 per annum, the amount of her salary. A group of admirers are standing or kneeling before her, among them Lord Holdernesse, one of the aristocratic syndicate which then "ran" the Opera, Henry Fox, afterwards Lord Holland, Lord Lyttelton, and a dignitary of the Church. A gentleman in the robes of a peer says to his wife, "We shall have but twelve songs for all this money" ; to which she replies, "Well, and enough too for the paltry trifle." Mingotti addresses her adorers with the lines :—

> "Ra Ru Ra Rot ye
> My name is Mingotti,
> If you worship me notti
> You shall all go to potti."

In an explanation to the design it is stated that "The great Distress of our Country at the time this print was published, was of more importance than the squalling of an Italian singer. However, she took some great people by the Ears, whose Likenesses in the print are very obvious."

In 1754 a caricature of Handel as *The Charming Brute* was produced by Goupy (Pl. LXVI.). The composer with the face of a pig, is seated on a beer-barrel, and playing an organ. He is surrounded by provisions —a ham, a goose, oysters, venison, etc.—to show his appreciation of the pleasures of the table ; while in allusion to his delight in a full orchestra and chorus, a number of sonorous instruments, such as kettledrums, trumpets, and bassoons, are included in the design. In a second plate, probably an adaptation of the first, a bill of fare hangs from the composer's pocket, proving that for dinner, besides oysters, he had consumed "A Codd 1/6, Quarter of Lamb and Asparagus 9/-, a Capon 2/6, Sausages 6ᵈ, two Quails 10/-, Tart 1/-, Wine 7/-, a Quartern Loaf, Sauce 1/6."

In her memoirs Letitia Hawkins, daughter of Sir John Hawkins, the historian of music, relates the incident that gave rise to this design. "At a time when Handel's circumstances were less prosperous than they had been, he invited Goupy to dine with him. The meal was plain and frugal, as he had warned his guest it must be, adding that he would give him as hearty a welcome as when he could treat him with claret and French dishes. Goupy returned a cordial reply, and they dined. Soon after dinner Handel left the room, and his absence was so long that Goupy at last, for want of other employ, strolled into the adjoining room, and walking up to a window which looked diagonally on that of a small third room, he saw his host sitting at a table covered with such delicacies as he had lamented his inability to afford his friend. Goupy was so enraged that he quitted the house abruptly, and

---

[1] Mingotti told Dr. Burney in 1772 that she was frequently hissed by the English for having a cold, a tooth-ache, or a fever, to which the good people of England would readily allow every human being to be liable except an actor or a singer.

Pub. March 21st 1754

THE CHARMING BRUTE

[A SATIRE ON HANDEL]

Drawn & Engrav'd by Gabⁱ· Smith

THE BUCK METAMORPHOSED

OR MR. FOOTE

IN THE CHARACTER OF THE ENGLISHMAN RETURN'D FROM PARIS

published the engraving in which Handel appears as a hog in the midst of dainties." [1]

In 1752 Samuel Foote, who had spent a year or two on the Continent, returned to town with a new comedy, *The Englishman in Paris*, which was successfully produced at Covent Garden. In October, 1753, Foote transferred it to Drury Lane, where he played the character of the Buck, which had previously been performed by Macklin. A caricature engraved by Gabriel Smith appeared about this time, under the title of *The Buck Metamorphosed; or, Foote in the character of the Englishman returned from Paris* (Pl. LXVII.). This shows a young man dressed in the height of the fashion, carrying a huge muff and wearing a peculiarly shaped wig with ears. He is standing in a complacent attitude in a street, and several of the passers-by are pointing at him in derision.

The complaints of the degradation of the stage and the frivolity of the public taste were quite as bitter at this epoch as they had been any time during the last fifty years. Goldsmith, through the mouth of his " Citizen of the World," observes that when the dramatic author is " well acquainted with the value of thunder and lightning, when versed in all the mystery of scene-shifting and trap-doors, when skilled in the proper periods to introduce a wire-walker or a waterfall, when instructed in every actor's peculiar talent, and capable of adapting his speeches to this supposed excellence, he knows all that can give a modern audience pleasure." This gloomy view of the requirements of the modern stage is partly corroborated by the fame attained by Mr. Maddox, Posture-master, and by Mrs. Midnight's Animal Comedians. A contemporary print shows Mr. Maddox as he appeared at Sadler's Wells in 1752, and it is remarkable that he is performing balancing tricks with chairs, cartwheels, straws, and glasses of water, which are quite as " advanced " as any that may be seen to-day at the modern music-hall. Mrs. Midnight's Animal Comedians were a troupe of highly trained dogs and monkeys, which in 1753 delighted the town with their performance as an amateur fire-brigade.

In 1761 " Thady " Fitzpatrick, an Irish journalist, attacked Garrick's acting in *The Craftsman*, and afterwards republished his criticisms. Garrick retaliated with a poem called *The Fribbleriad*, in which Fitzpatrick figures as " Fitzgigg." The title was taken from the character of Fribble in Garrick's farce of *Miss in her Teens*. Churchill also attacked Fitzpatrick in his *Rosciad*, describing him as

" A motley figure of the fribble tribe,
Which heart can scarce conceive or pen describe,
A six-foot suckling, mincing in its gait,
Affected, peevish, prim and delicate."

Fitzpatrick seems to have nursed his wrath till 1763, when it burst forth on the occasion of the famous half-price riots. At the beginning of this year

[1] Joseph Goupy was born at Nevers early in the eighteenth century. He came to England when quite a youth, and, in 1725, he was employed to paint scenes for the Italian Opera. He was drawing-master to Frederick, Prince of Wales, and also to Prince George (George III.). He died in 1763.

the managers of Drury Lane and Covent Garden had decided to abolish the custom of admitting persons for half-price at the end of the third act, at least in the case of new plays. Fitzpatrick and Francis (the supposed author of *Junius*) stirred up the indignation of the populace by means of handbills, and incited the audiences to riot. At Drury Lane the performances were stopped, the lustres broken, and the benches torn up. Garrick was not even permitted to argue the point, but was compelled to give an unqualified promise that he would revert to the old system. At Covent Garden the management made the same promise, but on February 24th, 1763, Dr. Arne's opera of *Artaxerxes* was given at full prices, whereupon the interior was wrecked by the rioters, even the pillars that supported the boxes being cut through. A caricature on this subject was engraved by L. P. Boitard, called *Fitz-giggo ; or, The New English Uproar, as it was performed at Covent Garden on Thursday last* (Pl. LXVIII.). This gives a representation of the interior of the theatre with the riots in full swing. Several members of the audience are clambering on the stage over the heads of the musicians, while the ladies in the boxes are gesticulating in terror. On the stage, which is lighted by five chandeliers (footlights not being introduced until 1765), are the principal singers and actors, Miss Brent,[1] Tenducci,[2] Beard,[3] Smith, and Woodward. Beard, the manager, had several of the ringleaders arrested, including Fitzpatrick, and these were taken before Lord Mansfield, who, however, discharged them with a severe reprimand.

In September, 1769, the Shakespeare Jubilee, held at Stratford-on-Avon, gave rise to some prints of a satirical character, which appeared in some of the contemporary magazines. Garrick stage-managed the Festival, which should have included a procession in costume, but this had to be abandoned on account of the weather. The remaining items, however, constituted a heavy programme, considering that it had to be worked through in three days. To begin with, at six a.m. on September 6th the performers from Drury Lane Theatre marched through the streets singing serenades to the ladies, in order, it may be supposed, that the latter should not oversleep themselves, and thus be late for the public breakfast that took place at nine. At eleven the oratorio of *Judith* was performed in the parish church, and Boswell, who wrote an account of the affair for the *London Magazine*, regrets that it was given without a service and a sermon ! At three there was a public dinner for ladies and gentlemen in the Amphitheatre, which lasted, with glees and catches, till six. The day concluded with a ball in the Assembly Room.

---

[1] Charlotte Brent (*d.* 1802). A favourite singer, who made her début in 1758, and sang chiefly at Covent Garden between 1759 and 1770. She married Thomas Pinto, the violinist.

[2] Tenducci, Giusto Ferdinandi, soprano, born at Sienna in 1736. Came to London in 1758, and succeeded Guadagni at the Opera. Later he toured with Dr. Arne, and made large sums, but was always in debt. He sang at the Handel Festivals as late as 1791. The date of his death is uncertain.

[3] John Beard, tenor (1717–91). A chorister of the Chapel Royal, he first appeared at Covent Garden under Handel in 1736, and migrated to Drury Lane in 1737. Two years later he married the widow of Lord Edward Herbert. He performed at one or other of the leading theatres till 1759, when, his first wife being dead, he married a daughter of John Rich, the patentee of Covent Garden. On Rich's death in 1761 Beard succeeded to his interest in that theatre. He retired in 1767. Handel composed for him the tenor parts in the *Messiah, Israel in Egypt, Judas Maccabeus,* and other oratorios.

L. Boitard

Feb 24 1763

FITZ-GIGGO,
A NEW ENGLISH UPROAR

Sold by E. Sumpter, Print and Bookseller, at the Bible and Crown, Three Doors from Shoe Lane, Fleet Street; and all the Print and Book-sellers in London and Westminster

J. Wale del

J. Miller sc.

JAMES BOSWELL ESQ

IN THE DRESS OF AN ARMED CORSICAN CHIEF, AS HE APPEARED
AT SHAKESPEARE'S JUBILEE, AT STRATFORD UPON AVON,
SEPTEMBER 1769

ΤΟΝ ΜΕΝΤΟΙ ΚΙΝΗΟΝ ΟΤΙ
ΕΣΤΙΝ ΩΣΤΙΣ ΟΥ

Paul Sandby   1781

SATIRE ON VESTRIS

JASON ET MEDEE   BALLET TRAGIQUE.

1781

BALLET TRAGIQUE

DRAMATIC AND MUSICAL

The next day Garrick delivered the Shakespearean ode that he had written for the occasion, and afterwards challenged the poet's enemies to advance in opposition. Tom King,[1] the comedian, thereupon delivered a smart ironic attack upon Shakespeare, speaking in the character of a modern modish man of the world. His speech, which is not reported in the magazines, surprised and annoyed those of the audience who were not in the secret of the joke. The evening wound up with a masquerade, at which Lady Crewe, Lady Pembroke, and Mrs. Bonner appeared as the witches in *Macbeth*, and Mr. Boswell was much admired in the character of a Corsican chief, of which a representation was published in the *London Magazine* for October (Pl. LXIX.). The great procession which, but for the rain, would have taken place next day, was first seen on the boards of Drury Lane.

A certain section of the public regarded the whole festival as a gigantic advertisement for Garrick, and Walpole, then in Paris, declares that he blushed when the papers came over from England " crammed with Garrick's insufferable nonsense about Shakespeare." A dissatisfied " Jubilite " (as he signs himself) wrote an indignant letter to the *Town and Country Magazine*, in which he asserts that the Jubilee must be classed among the humbugs of the age. His expenses for the week amounted to £49 2s., and he sums up the " value received " in the following fashion: "A scarcity of provisions, a want of conveyances, a rotunda that was not waterproof, and masquerade dresses at five guineas a-piece form a pretty collection of omissions and impositions." The " Jubilite " encloses a satirical design representing a man's head emerging from the neck of a bottle, which stands upon a tripod. The legs of the tripod are labelled respectively " Stratford Jubilee," "Al Fresco," and " Bal Paré," while the motto is "Audita Utraque Parte, Judicia."

The theatrical satires of the latter part of the century are taken up in great measure with the relations of certain actresses with the royal princes— Perdita with the Prince of Wales, Mrs. Jordan with the Duke of Clarence, and Mrs. Billington with the Duke of Sussex. Certain of these will be dealt with in the chapter devoted to royalty. The chief theatrical events of this period were the appearance of Mrs. Siddons at Drury Lane in 1782, and that of her brother, John Kemble, a year later. The caricaturists were more occupied, however, with the sensational success of Vestris the dancer about the same date. This was " le grand Vestris," of whom it was said that the House of Commons on one occasion adjourned on purpose to attend his performance, though Burke was about to introduce an important Bill. His wife was the first *danseuse* of the day in the grand style, and by another celebrated dancer, Marie Allard, he had a son, Auguste, who inherited the gifts of both parents. A clever caricature by Paul Sandby shows the famous dancer stand-

---

[1] Thomas King, actor-dramatist (1730–1805). An excellent comedian, who was engaged by Garrick for Drury Lane in 1748. He was afterwards connected with the management of Drury Lane and Sadler's Wells. King was the original Sir Peter Teazle and the original Puff in the *Critic*.

ing on one leg, with the other raised high in the air (Pl. LXX.). At the two lower corners of the design are representations of geese, to which Vestris is supposed to be setting an example. The picture is intended to illustrate Plutarch's anecdote of the stranger at Sparta, who, after standing long upon one leg, said to a Lacedemonian, " I do not believe you can do as much." " True," replied the Lacedemonian, " but any goose can." Other caricatures on the same subject show Vestris as a fox dancing before English geese, as *A Modern Mercury with his Two Wings*, and as taking part in a *Ballet Tragique*—that of Jason and Médée (Pl. LXXI.).

After a glance at a caricature portrait by Bartolozzi of *Dr. Arne playing Rule Britannia* (Pl. LXXII.), we pass on to an early Gillray representing Mrs. Siddons as *Melpomene* (1784), her pockets full of banknotes and gold, grasping a purse which is held out to her at the end of a pitchfork (Pl. LXIII.). Mrs. Siddons' economical methods, so unlike the prodigality of the typical artist, had led to accusations of avarice being made against her, and it was also said that she required to be handsomely paid for acting at the benefits of distressed colleagues. This statement, which was quite unfounded, afflicted her so deeply that she had serious thoughts of retiring from the stage.

In 1789 Vanbrugh's Opera-house in the Haymarket was burned down, and while it was rebuilding there was some difficulty in finding another asylum for the singers and dancers. At one time an appeal to charity was contemplated as a possible solution of the difficulty; at least, if we may judge from Rowlandson's etching, *The Prospect before us, No. 1, Humanely inscribed to all those Professors of Music and Dancing whom the Cap may fit.* In this the opera company is represented perambulating the streets clothed in rags, some of the members playing and dancing, while others solicit the alms of the charitable. They carry with them a big model of the new house, on which is inscribed, " Pray remember the poor dancers."

The difficulty was arranged by the transformation of the Pantheon Theatre into an Opera-house, which was opened to the public on February 17th, 1791, with a performance of *Armida*. We have a representation of this fine theatre, which was burned to the ground only a year later, in Rowlandson's plate, *The Prospect before us, No. 2, Respectfully dedicated to those Singers, Dancers and Musical Professors who are fortunately engaged with the Proprietor of the King's Theatre, Pantheon* (Pl. LXXIV.). Here we see two of the leading dancers, M. Didelot and Madame Théodore, performing in the ballet of *Amphion and Thalia* before a brilliant audience, which included the King and Queen and most of the leaders of fashion.

This seems to have been an unfortunate period for London theatres, for not only had Covent Garden to be practically rebuilt, but in 1791 Drury Lane was condemned as unsafe, and had to be pulled down, a new theatre being built upon the site in the course of the next three years. It is evident that Drury Lane was known to be in a dangerous state prior to its condemnation, since for February 4th, 1791, we have another design by Rowlandson

Publd. Dec 6th, 1784, by

MELPOMENE

J. Ridgeway, No 196, Piccadilly, London

DR. ARNE

DONE FROM AN ORIGINAL SKETCH BY F. BARTOLOZZI

Pub. May 10th 1782 by Wm Humphrey, No 227, Strand

[*Rowlandson*]

THE PROSPECT BEFORE US

(2)

RESPECTFULLY DEDICATED TO THOSE SINGERS, DANCERS AND MUSICAL PROFESSORS WHO ARE FORTUNATELY ENGAGED WITH THE PROPRIETOR OF THE KING'S THEATRE
AT THE PANTHEON

Pub.ᵈ Jan 13, 1791, by S. W. Fores, Piccadilly

Qui Capit invent

Ille Habet fec.

CHAOS IS COME AGAIN

MUSIC HATH CHARMS TO SOOTHE THE SAVAGE BREAST
TO SOFTEN BRICKS AND BEND THE KNOTTED OAK

Pub by S. W. Fores, Piccadilly
Feb 4th 1791

T Rowlandson del

ACTOR RECITING TO A MANAGER

THE CASTLE SPECTRE AND HER ERNEST ADMIRER

London. Published by Willm Holland, No 50 Oxford Street, March 14 1793

entitled *Chaos is come again.* *Qui capet inven. ille habet fec* with the motto:—

> "Music hath charms to soothe the savage breast,
> To soften bricks and bend the knotted oak."

This is an imaginary sketch of the collapse of the old theatre in the course of a performance. The roof is falling in and the supports of the gallery giving way, while the panic-stricken audience rushes out over the débris (Pl. LXXV.). Before quitting the subject of Rowlandson's dramatic caricatures, mention must be made of his water-colour drawing, *An Actor Reciting to a Manager* (Pl. LXXVI.). The manager and the importunate mime were probably sketched from life, though neither can now be identified.

During the last decade of the century the theatrical topics which attracted most attention from the caricaturists were the marriage of Miss Farren[1] to Lord Derby, the episcopal crusade against the costumes of the ballet-dancers, and the success of certain melodramatic productions at Drury Lane. Miss Farren had long maintained a friendship, generally believed to be platonic, with Lord Derby. Lady Derby died in March, 1797, and Miss Farren, who continued to appear on the stage down to the middle of April, was married to Lord Derby on May 1st, 1797. Her promotion aroused some jealousy among her colleagues, while the incongruity between her tall, thin figure and the squat proportions of Lord Derby fired the malicious imagination of James Gillray, who produced at least three designs on the loves of the earl and the actress. The earliest of these is called *A Peep at Christie's; or, Tally-ho and his Nimeney-Pimeney taking their Morning Lounge.* This shows Miss Farren, who created the part of Nimeney-Pimeney in General Burgoyne's play *The Heiress*, in company with her dumpy lover examining the pictures in Christie's auction-rooms. Lord Derby is looking with evident appreciation at a picture of the *Death of Reynard*, while Miss Farren gazes over his head at a work representing *Zenocrates and Phryne*. A little later, on March 20th, 1797, Gillray produced another caricature on the same lady, called *Reflections on a Coronet* (Pl. LXXIX.). Lady Derby had died only six days before, and the actress, seated at her toilette-table, is ecstatically regarding a coronet placed on a wig-block, which bears a strong resemblance to Lord Derby's curiously shaped head. Cosmetiques and a genealogical chart of British nobility are on the dressing-table, and half-concealed beneath its drapery is a bottle of gin. The actress is soliloquising: "A coronet! Ah! it must be mine; now there's nobody left to hinder! And then for my Lady Nimi
ney-Piminey! O Gemmini! No more straw-beds in barns, no more scowling managers, and curtseying to a dirty public, but a coronet on my coach! Dashing at the opera; shining at the Court! O dear, dear; what I shall come to!"

---

[1] Elizabeth Farren (*c.* 1759–1829). She made her début at the Haymarket in 1777, and later appeared at Drury Lane, where she made her chief successes in high comedy parts—Lady Teazle, Lydia Languish, Lady Towneley, etc.

By far the best pictorial joke on this subject, however, and one of the cleverest that Gillray produced, was a parody of Payne Knight's Marlborough gem, *The Union of Cupid and Psyche* (Pl. LXXVIII.). In this Miss Farren as Psyche towers above her corpulent little Cupid, who carries a dove and is led by a little Love, while another holds the coronet above his head. Robert Dighton also produced a print on the subject of the ill-assorted lovers called *Darby and Joan*, which shows the pair seated in a box at the theatre, the ex-actress eagerly following the performance of her former colleagues.

In 1796 an English opera-dancer, Miss Rose, a plain woman with a beautiful figure, created a sensation, and started, or rather developed, the fashion for wearing very scanty clothing. Gillray caricatured her in a plate entitled *No Flower that Blows is like this Rose*, published on April 12th, 1796; and in *Modern Grace; or the Operatical Finale to the Ballet of Alonzo e Caro*, in which three dancers are depicted, the two females being quite insufficiently clad. Two years later, in March, 1798, in the course of a debate upon a Divorce Bill in the House of Lords, the Bishop of Durham remarked upon the frequency of such Bills, for which he blamed the French, who, finding that they were not able to subdue us by arms, sent over persons to this country who gave indecent performances in our theatres. He proceeded to state that it was his intention to move an address to be presented to His Majesty, beseeching him to order all such dancers out of the kingdom as persons who were likely to destroy our morals and our religion. For once a debate in the House of Lords had some result. The theatrical authorities took fright, and the ballet of *Bacchus and Ariadne*, which was to have been produced the next night, was postponed, while new costumes were prepared with more drapery, and white stockings instead of flesh-colour.

This agitation provided Gillray with a good deal of effective material. On March 14th, 1798, he published his well-known etching, *Operatical Reform; or, la Danse à l'Evêque*. In this three *danseuses* are portrayed, wearing episcopal aprons and very little else, and engaged in performing a *pas de trois*. On March 19th appeared from the same hand *Ecclesiastical Scrutiny; or, The Durham Inquest on Duty*, a design which shows the bishops superintending the dressing of the opera-dancers and busily engaged in measuring the skirts and bodices of the performers, and arranging that the garments shall be worn in the most unbecoming fashion.

The popular successes at Drury Lane of *The Castle Spectre*, *The Stranger*, and *Pizarro* were regarded with some disapproval by those who had no taste for melodramatic " tragedy," and who considered that the genius of the Kembles was sacrificed to unworthy objects. An unsigned caricature for the year 1797 shows Mrs. Siddons as *The Castle Spectre, with her Ernest Admirer*, an allusion presumably to the appreciation of the Duke of Cumberland (Pl. LXXVII.). Another print in the Burney collection, by R. Dighton, represents the same lady as Elvira, the heroine of Sheridan's adaptation of Kotzebue's *Pizarro* produced with amazing success in 1799 (Pl. LXXX.). Into Rolla's address

THE MARRIAGE OF CUPID & PSYCHE

J. G. fec. from ye antique

Pub^d May 3, 1797, by H. Humphrey, 27 St James' Street

Pub. March 20th 1797 by H. Humphrey, Bond S^t & St James Street

J^s G^y inv. & f^t

CONTEMPLATIONS UPON A CORONET

to his soldiers Sheridan is said to have put some choice extracts from his own speeches, which Pitt recognised with amusement when he attended the theatre. The King and Queen, though they regarded Sheridan with no favour, were present at one performance with the young Princesses, and duly appear in a caricature called *A New Play; or, The Drury Lane Masquerade*. Sheridan's many enemies attributed the success of the play entirely to Kemble's acting, and a plate, designed by Gillray, appeared in the *Anti-Jacobin Review*, which shows Sheridan borne triumphantly aloft on John Kemble's head. This is accompanied by an allusion to the playwright's assumption of the character of a patriotic statesman, the following lines being put into his mouth :—

> " This season, true, my principle I've sold,
> To fool the world I pocket George's gold ;
> Prolific mine, Anglo-Peruvian food
> Provoked my taste, and candidate I stood ;
> While Kemble, my support, with loyal face,
> Declares the people's choice with stage-struck grace."

HOLD !—PIZARRO—HEAR ME !—IF NOT ALWAYS *JUSTLY*, AT LEAST ACT ALWAYS *GREATLY*.

Drawn, Etch'd & Publish'd by Dighton, Char⁹ Cross, Dec 14ᵗʰ 1799

LITERARY AND ARTISTIC

PART I

THE eccentricities of artists and authors have always received less attention from the caricaturist than the eccentricities of actors and opera-singers. This neglect may be partly explained by the fact that the great majority of the caricaturist's patrons belong to the class that frequents the playhouse, and is well acquainted with the scandals and squabbles that are associated with the personalities of popular actors, but takes little or no interest in the private affairs of the professors of art and literature. Again, writers and painters are sometimes dangerous persons to attack, because they possess weapons wherewith they may not only defend themselves, but even carry the war into the enemy's country.

One of the earliest artistic caricatures is Hogarth's satire on Kent's altar-piece in St. Clement's Danes Church. The original picture gave offence to the congregation, " being a musical representation variously explained, some finding in it St. Cecilia and her Harp, and some Princess Sobieski and her Son, but the generality agreeing it was not a thing proper to be placed there ; upon complaints to the Bishop of London at his last visitation of the said Church, we hear his Lordship, in order to secure the solemnity of the place of worship, hath lately very prudently ordered the churchwardens to take it down " (*Postman* for August 25th, 1725). Hogarth's parody (1725) is a deliberately ill-drawn and mawkishly sentimental composition. It includes an angel playing on an organ, above which a dove hovers, a second angel playing the harp, and a third holding a lute, while two cherubs are in attendance (Pl. LXXI.). According to the appended explanation, this print was " exactly Engraved after the Celebrated Altar-Peice in St. Clement's Church which has been taken down by order of the Lord Bishop of London (as 'tis thought) to prevent Disputes and Laying of Wagers among yᵉ Parrishioners about the Artist's meaning in it. For publick satisfaction here is a particular Explanation of it, humbly offered to be writ under the Original that it may be put up again, by which means the Parish'es 60 pounds which they wisely gave for it, may not be entirely lost.

" 1st. 'Tis not the Pretender's Wife and Children as our weak brethren imagine.

[By Hogarth]   *[1725]*

A SATIRE ON THE ALTAR-PIECE BY KENT

IN St CLEMENT DANES CHURCH, WESTMINSTER

[By Hogarth]   Price 6ᵈ

[1731]

TASTE

THE GATE OF BURLINGTON HOUSE

THE DUNCIAD
with NOTES
VARIORUM.

His
HOLINESS
and his
PRIME MINISTER.

A
Letter
to the
Publisher
Art of
Politiks

THE PHIZ AND CHARACTER OF AN ALEXANDRINE HYPER-CRITICH & COMENTATOR

[1728]

Nosce te Ipsum, price 6ᵈ

" 2ly. Nor St. Cecilia, as the Connoisseurs think, but a Choir of Angells playing in Consort.

" A an Organ. B an Angel playing on it. C the shortest joint of the Arm. D the longest joint. E an Angel tuning a Harp. F the inside of his Leg, but whether right or left is yet undiscovered. G a hand playing on a Lute. H the other leg judiciously omitted to make room for the Harp. I and K smaller Angels, as appears by their Wings."

In the early part of the century there are but few literary caricatures of importance, with the exception of those levelled at Pope, who, by his own hard hitting, provoked many counter-attacks from his victims. The publication of *The Bathos; or, the Art of Sinking*, and of the *Dunciad*[1] was followed by an avalanche of retorts and return-strokes, pictorial as well as printed. One of the most effective designs is called *Fronti Fides, Martini Scribleri vera Effigies*. In this Pope is represented in the form of an ape, crouching on a pedestal, his head on his hand, and his elbow resting on a pile of his own books, while an ass stands at his side. Another print of almost exactly similar design is called *His Holiness and his Prime Minister. The Phiz and Character of an Alexandrian Hypercritick and Commentator. Nosce te Ipsum* (Pl. LXXXIII.). Below are inscribed the lines from Pope's own character of Thersites :—

> " Aw'd by no shame, by no Respect controul'd,
> In Scandal busy, in Reproaches bold.
> Spleen to Mankind his envious Heart possest,
> And much he hated all, but most the Best."

This print was sold separately for sixpence, and also published as the frontispiece to a feeble counterblast against the *Dunciad* by John Dennis[2] and George Duckett,[3] *Pope Alexander's Supremacy and Infallibility Examined.* It is interesting at the present day to read the strictures of forgotten Grub Street upon " this insipid Poem, the outcome of this Pigmy Animal's malice, which, if it should endure to be read by posterity, would endure only as a monument of Infamy." The reception accorded to the *Dunciad* by the town proved, we are assured, that " the Performance was thought as mean as the Design, the lines being prosaick, the Transitions unnatural, the whole Tale loose and unconnected, and the too-frequent parodies on the most admired passages of the Ancients poorly worked up."

Many of the pictorial satires in which Pope figures are not detached cartoons, but small woodcuts prepared as frontispieces to the various printed attacks upon himself and his works. There is a print of the " Medley " *genre*, however, entitled *Mr. Alexander Pope*, which deserves a word of

---

[1] The first edition of the *Dunciad* was published anonymously in 1712, but an enlarged edition appeared in 1729. The authorship was an open secret, though the poem was not acknowledged till 1735.

[2] John Dennis (1657–1734). Dramatic writer and critic. Having been attacked by Pope, he replied in *Reflections Critical and Satirical.* He wrote some forgotten tragedies and comedies, and *The Advancement and Reformation of Modern Poetry.*

[3] George Duckett (*d.* in 1732). He was a Commissioner of Excise and M.P. for Calne. He published *Homerides*, an attack on Pope's *Iliad.*

notice, if only because it seems to have been designed by a partisan of the poet's. In this, as in other Medleys, we have the effect of a little heap of engravings thrown loosely together. One of these contains a portrait of Pope, another of the Fop, from the *Rape of the Lock*, a third illustrates some lines in the poem of *Windsor Forest*, and a fourth represents some rustics dancing round a maypole. Beneath the design, which is signed " G. A. Delin. Sculp. 1731," is engraved " An Encomium on Mr. Pope and his Poems, by his Grace yᵉ late Duke of Buckingham."

Both art and literature come under the lash in Hogarth's famous engraving, *Taste; The Gate of Burlington House* (Pl. LXXXII.). Here we see Pope on a platform, in the guise of a plasterer, whitewashing the obnoxious gate, and splashing the coach of the Duke of Chandos, which is passing below. On a ladder, in the dress of a bricklayer's labourer, stands Lord Burlington, the " architect earl," to whom Pope had addressed his Essay on Taste. In this the poet had criticised the house and grounds of Timon, who was supposed to be intended for the Duke of Chandos, though Pope had received much kindness from the Duke. Hogarth bore a grudge against Lord Burlington on account of his patronage of Kent, the artist, who was the chief rival of Mrs. Hogarth's father, Sir William Thornhill. On the top of the gate a statue of Kent stands between the recumbent figures of Michael Angelo and Raphael. Pope was, it is said, greatly annoyed at this satire, but he never ventured to retaliate upon Hogarth, preferring to use his weapons against his less dangerous foes.

Among the series of animal-headed caricatures produced by Van Heemskerck (*circa* 1730), is one of an auction-room during a sale of pictures (Pl. LXXXV.). The auctioneer, who offers a picture of *Boors Drinking*, has the head of a fox; the porter who holds it represents an ass; and the various bidders appear in the likenesses of bulls, goats, monkeys, or cats. Apparently the artist did not approve of an auction as a method of disposing of pictures, for beneath the design are engraved some rather acrimonious lines beginning :—

> " An auction is a public sale
> That injures those who fairly deal,
> While South Seas, Indies, Companies
> Are nought but meer Monopolies."

From jeremiads many and bitter we know that the lot of the literary man in the first half of the century was not an enviable one. Drudge of the bookseller, parasite of the patron, he passed his days compiling, editing, translating—

> " For ever reading, never to be read."

This phase in the history of English literature is illustrated by *The Distrest Poet*, " invented, painted, engraved, and published by William Hogarth " in 1736. The plate, a companion subject to *The Enraged Musician*, is too

THE DISTREST POET

Invented Painted Engraved & Published by Wm Hogarth December the 15, 1740   according to Act of Parliament.   Price 3 shillings

E. Heemskirck invᵗ et Pinxᵗ   *Toms sculp*

SATIRE ON A PICTURE AUCTION

[C 1730]

[*By Thomas Patch*]   [1750]

UNI SE HUMILIAT EXALTABITUT
CHI SI UMILIA SALTA SALTA

No 13, Se ipsum pinx et sculp.   [SIR HORACE MANN]

well known to require detailed description, even if it did not tell its own story (Pl. LXXXIV.). The young poet, who has been identified with Theobald, the hero of one version of the *Dunciad*, sits at a table in his squalid attic, engaged on a poem on " Riches," while his pretty wife mends his breeches, the baby squalls, a milk-woman clamours for the payment of her bill, and a dog steals the meagre piece of meat that was to serve for supper. In one state of the engraving the following lines from the *Dunciad* supplement the design :—

> " Studious he sat with all his books around,
> Sinking from thought to thought, a vast profound.
> Plunged for his sense, but found no bottom there :
> Then writ and floundered on in sheer despair."

Another Hogarthian plate, which can hardly be overlooked in this connection, is the *Characters and Caricaturas*, published in 1743. The artist gives the following explanation of the not too enlightening design : " Being perpetually plagued from the mistakes made among the illiterate by the similitude in the sound of the words *character* and *caricatura*, I ten years ago endeavoured to explain the distinction by the above print ; and as I was then publishing *Marriage à la Mode*, wherein were characters of high life, I introduced the great number of faces there delineated (none of which are exaggerated), varied at random, to prevent if possible personal application when the prints should come out." In the sub-title of this engraving, which formed the subscription-ticket for the series of *Marriage à la Mode*, it is explained that the design contains three " characters " and four " caricaturas," and the public are referred for a further elucidation of the difference between the two terms to the passage in the Preface to *Joseph Andrews*, which has already been quoted. The profiles, upwards of a hundred in number, contained in this design, are arranged in the most admired disorder, except the seven which occupy the lower compartment. Of these the three characters are taken from Raphael's cartoons, and the four caricaturas from " Annibal Charraci " (*sic*), " Cavl. Chezzo," and Leonardo da Vinci (Pl. I.).

In the early fifties Thomas Patch,[1] an English artist living at Florence, began a series of caricatures of English tourists, which attracted some attention when specimens found their way to England. Patch arrived in Rome about 1750, where he associated with Reynolds, and was patronised by Lord Charlemont and other distinguished travellers. Having got into some trouble with the ecclesiastical authorities he moved to Florence, where he was made welcome by Sir Horace Mann. Writing of him some years later, Sir Horace said, " He really is a genius, and all his productions have merit. . . . I took much to him, and though he does not live in my house, he is never out of it a whole day. He has an excellent turn for caricature, in which the young English often employ him to make conversation-pieces of any member, for which they draw lots ; but Patch is so prudent as never to caricature anybody

---

[1] Patch published some volumes of engravings from Florentine frescoes. He died in 1782.

without his consent, and a full liberty to exercise his talents." Patch, whose work was much admired by Horace Walpole, produced a caricature of Sir Horace Mann as a bull lying down in a field, with the city of Florence in the background (Pl. LXXXVI.). Beneath is engraved the verse :—

"Qui se humiliat exaltabitur
Chi se Umilia salta salta."

During the latter part of Hogarth's career the state of art in England, and what he considered the too subservient attitude of both public and professors towards the works of the old masters, occupied his thoughts more and more. He does not appear to have been in favour of an Academy of Painting, or of annual exhibitions of pictures, but he fully believed in his own power to instruct students in the theory and technique of his art. In 1752 it was announced that Mr. Hogarth would shortly publish by subscription a tract called *The Analysis of Beauty*, together with two explanatory prints, *A Statuary's Yard* and *A Country Dance ;* and that these would be accompanied by a great variety of figures, tending to illustrate the new system contained therein. The author, it is further explained, had endeavoured to render the book " useful and interesting to the Curious and Polite of both Sexes, by laying down the Principles of personal Beauty and Deportment, as also of Taste in general, in the plainest, most familiar, and most entertaining manner."

It is unnecessary here to discuss the theories stated in the Analysis, even that relating to the famous " Line of Beauty," but a brief account of its reception may serve to introduce the pictorial war that was afterwards waged against the author. Horace Walpole, in common with most of the dilettanti, declared that Hogarth's book was " very silly," but Warburton admired it, and Benjamin West, writing many years later, maintained that it was a work of the highest value to everyone studying the art. Hogarth, added West, was " a strutting, consequential little man, and made himself many enemies by that book, but now that most of them are dead, it will be examined by disinterested readers, unbiassed by personal animosities." The vanity and arrogance of the artist made him more enemies, probably, than his book, but the book gave an opportunity to his enemies, and Hogarth exaggerated but little when he said, " I have been assailed by every profligate scribbler in town, and told that though words are man's province, they are not my province. . . . By those of my own profession I am treated with yet more severity. Pestered with caricature drawings, and hung up in effigy in prints, accused of vanity, ignorance and envy ; called a mean and contemptible dauber ; represented in the strangest employments and pictured in the strangest shapes ; sometimes under the hieroglyphical semblance of a satyr, and at others in the still more ingenious one of an ass." The satirist, it will be observed, winced as sensitively under attacks of his colleagues as though he himself had never inflicted chastisement with the graving tool.

Wm. Hogarth   Feb 28th 1745

THE BATTLE OF THE PICTURES

THE BEARER HEREOF IS ENTITLED (IF HE THINKS PROPER) TO BE A BIDDER FOR
MR. HOGARTH'S PICTURES, WHICH ARE TO BE SOLD ON THE LAST DAY OF THIS MONTH

G. Bickham   1753

AN APE PAINTING AN ASS

W. Hogarth inv et delin.

L. Sullivan sculp.
[1753

FALSE PERSPECTIVE

LITERARY AND ARTISTIC

The leader of the campaign against Hogarth and his theories was Paul Sandby (1725–1799), who has been termed the father of English water-colour. In 1752 Paul was living at Windsor, where he, in conjunction with his brother Thomas, executed numerous drawings of the castle and of the neighbourhood. He took an active interest in the academy in St. Martin's Lane, and, regretting the meagre opportunities enjoyed by the art-student in England, earnestly desired to establish a permanent and effective system of art-teaching. The project was ridiculed by Hogarth, who regarded academical methods, more especially those based upon a study of the old masters, with something nearly approaching contempt. In the auction ticket which he had etched in 1745, under the title of *The Battle of the Pictures*, he had shown a number of conventional Italian paintings, the *Rape of Europa*, *St. Andrew and his Cross*, *Apollo flaying Marsyas*, etc., jostling and being jostled by some of his own best productions, including *Marriage à la Mode* (Pl. LXXXVII.).

That Hogarth regarded himself as being better qualified than any of his colleagues to impart such instruction as might be needed by the student, seems proved by the rather aggressive fashion in which he gave his *Analysis of Beauty* to the world, and also by the private testimony of a feminine admirer, Mrs. Pendarves, who writes to her sister the joyful news that " Mr. Hogarth has promised to give me some rules about drawing that will be of great use—some rules of his own that he says will improve me more in a day than a year's learning in the common way." It cannot be said that Hogarth's illustrations of his artistic ideas are among the most successful of his productions, though there are both humour and ingenuity in the design which he made for the frontispiece to Kirby's[1] edition of *Dr. Brook-Taylor's Method of Perspective made Easy, both in Theory and Practice*. In this elaborate artistic joke, which is said to have been suggested by the mistakes made by Sir Edward Walpole, who was learning drawing without a knowledge of perspective, we have a landscape in which the farther the various objects are from the spectator the larger they appear. A bridge springs from the middle of a river, in which a man is fishing with a rod about fifty yards long. Another sportsman aims (in the wrong direction) at a bird which is out of all proportion to the tree in which it sits, while a traveller lights his pipe from a candle held out of an upper window in an inn on the opposite side of the river (Pl. LXXXIX.).

But it was the *Analysis of Beauty*, with its glorification of the serpentine line, which chiefly roused the antagonism of Hogarth's antagonists, the supporters of convention and classic tradition. On December 1st, 1753, Paul Sandby opened fire with a caricature called *Burlesque sur le Burlesque*, " ou le grand progres du Dogme dans l'art de Peinture, avec ses inventions pour

---

[1] John Joshua Kirby (1716–74). Clerk of the Works at Kew, and teacher of perspective to the Prince of Wales (George III.). He published Brook Taylor's *Method of Perspective* in 1754. In 1768 he was elected President of the Incorporated Society of Artists. He was the father of Mrs. Trimmer, of pious memory.

produire les Effets de tous les grand Peintres depuis Raphael, et sa production pour montrer combien il a inveintéz et excellez dans la composition, dans l'effet et dans le coloris" (Pl. XC.). Here we have an artist's studio, with Hogarth, represented as half man half dog, painting a picture of *The Sacrifice of Isaac* in the style of the Dutch school. A large window is hung with shutters which change the lights, and are labelled, " Pour Raphael, pour Rubens, pour Vandyke,"[1] and so forth. Included in the design are various uncomplimentary methods of disposing of the *Analysis of Beauty*, copies of the work being sketched on their way to a cookshop in a wheelbarrow, sold by the hundredweight to a trunkmaker, carried round by a hawker on a pole, and exposed at a bookstall among volumes ticketed " Choisir à 4 Sous."

Pugg's Graces, etched from his Original Drawing, is the title of another engraving by Sandby, which shows Hogarth, still with a dog's hindquarters, painting his picture of *Pharaoh's Daughter*, while a friendly connoisseur points admiringly to three ungraceful Graces, one fat, one thin, and one deformed. Scattered about the studio are various articles suggested by the *Analysis of Beauty*, mostly in mockery of the famous serpentine line, together with an open book inscribed " Reasons against a Publick Academy." Below are engraved some doggerel lines, concluding with the couplet :—

> "Dunce connoisseurs extol the Author Pugg,
> The senseless, tasteless, impudent Hum Bugg."

On the back is printed a burlesque address to the public, beginning, " I propose to publish by subscription an Analysis of the Sun, in which I will show the constituent Parts of which it is composed, and how it ought to have been composed. I will compute exactly its Magnitude and Quantity of Matter, both as it is, and as it ought to have been constructed," etc. etc. Among the other satires levelled against Hogarth by his chief enemy, three may be specially mentioned : *The Author Run Mad*, an etching representing the artist in a lunatic asylum, painting with his left hand upon the wall ; *The Painter's March from Finchley*, dedicated to the King of the Gypsies as an Encourager of Arts, etc., a parody of Hogarth's *March to Finchley*, which was dedicated to the King of Prussia in revenge for the neglect of George III.; and *The Burning of the Temple at Ephesus*, perhaps the most effective of the three. This last represents a night scene, illuminated by the flames that are consuming the Temple of Diana (Pl. XCI.). At the foot of a column, elaborately ornamented with portraits in relief of famous painters and sculptors, Hogarth, attended by an admirer and his dog, is grubbing under the pedestal with a palette-knife. A satyr is descending to scourge him, and a flock of geese are devouring all that he can pick up with his " impious quill and pallate knife." According to the printed explanation, this is the presentment of " A Self-conceited Arrogant Dauber, grovelling in

---

[1] It must be remembered that Hogarth openly boasted of his ability to paint in the style of the great masters, whose alleged superiority to the moderns he regarded as chiefly due to the kindly offices of Time.

The Progress of the *mpdag* en *ŷ* Art of Painting with his Invention by a Variety of Lights A.B.C.D.E.F to produce *ŷ* Effect of all *ŷ* great Painter, Shewing how *far* in his Opinion he has *excell'd* them, in Design Colouring and Taste.
1. an Infant learning *ŷ* Painter with variety
2. a History piece suitable to *ŷ* Painter's Capacity, from a Dutch Manu
3. Old prints from whence he steals Figures for his Design
4. his Brains taken out & his Soul serving for a Magic lanthorn, Paul before Felix is reflected from it on *ŷ* Wall
5. his Layman
6. Roast Beef
7. his Disciples
8. Lives of All the best Painters torn in pieces for his window blind
9. *postil* bringing him a bone to pick as *ŷ* Line of beauty

[By Paul Sandby]

BURLESQUE SUR LE BURLESQUE
AVEC PRIVILEGE DU ROI DECEM^R I, 1753

[*By Paul Sandby*]   [1753]

THE BURNING OF THE TEMPLE AT EPHESUS

vain to undermine the ever Sacred Monument of all the best Painters, Sculptors, Architects, etc., in Imitation of the Impious Herostratus, who with Sacrilegious Flames destroyed the Temple of Diana, to perpetuate his Name to Posterity."

The *Portrait of an Artist*—an ape painting an ass—is also supposed to be an attack on Hogarth by a humble colleague, George Bickham the younger, son of a famous writing-master, who published *The Universal Penman*, with illustrations engraved by himself (Pl. LXXXVIII.). The younger Bickham, who died in 1758, was one of the caricaturists who worked, for the most part anonymously, for the Bowles' firm in St. Paul's Churchyard. He also engraved a few serious subjects, as well as a number of graceful illustrations to a song-book, *The Musical Entertainer*, which appeared in 1737. It is probable that he practised as a drawing-master, since in 1747 he published a technical work under the title of *An Introductive Essay on Drawing, with the Nature and Beauty of Light and Shadows.*

LITERARY AND ARTISTIC

PART II

THE curious personality of Sterne and his not altogether reputable methods of self-advertisement brought him under the lash of the satirists. A little print, which may be ascribed to the early sixties, shows *Sterne at Ranelagh* soliciting subscriptions for the sermons which he published under his pseudonym of Yorick, much to the scandal of the orthodox (Pl. XCII.). The *Monthly Review* commented in the strongest terms upon the lack of taste evinced by the appearance of the name of Yorick upon the title-page of such a work, observing that this was "the greatest outrage upon sense and decency that has been offered since the first establishment of Christianity—an outrage which would have scarce been tolerated even in the days of Paganism!" Another design for about the same period, called *The Scheming Triumvirate*, shows Sterne, Whitefield, and Foote, each engaged in hawking his special wares: Sterne his *Tristram Shandy*, Whitefield his tracts and hymns, and Foote his play, *The Minor*.

Sterne's death on March 18th, 1768, inspired Thomas Patch, who had probably met the author during his Italian travels in 1765, with the idea for an etching called *Sterne and Death* (Pl. XCIV.). The scene is laid in Yorick's study, and the dying man is portrayed in the act of rising from his chair to welcome Death, who enters in the guise of a skeleton, holding out an hourglass. Among the accessories are a statuette of the Ephesian Diana, the works of Aristotle and Ovid, and a machine for tearing books to pieces, in allusion to the plagiarisms of Sterne. Below is an emblem of the soul as a butterfly hovering over a torch, and a quotation from *Tristram Shandy:* "And when Death himself knocked at my door, ye bade him come again; and in so gay a tone of careless indifference did ye do it, that he doubted of his commission. 'There must certainly be some mistake in this matter,' quoth he."

Returning to 1761, we find that in this year Hogarth etched a frontispiece and tail-piece for the catalogue of pictures exhibited by the Society of Artists in Spring Gardens. The first shows Britannia watering three small trees, inscribed "Painting," "Sculpture," "Architecture." In a niche over a fountain is a bust of George III., presumably as a patron of Art, with the motto, " Et

[c 1760]

STERNE IN RANELAGH GARDENS

SOLICITING SUBSCRIPTIONS FOR YORICK'S SERMONS

W. Hogarth inv^t et del

C. Grignion sculp

FRONTISPIECE TO THE ARTISTS CATALOGUE

Published according to Act of Parliament May 7, 1761

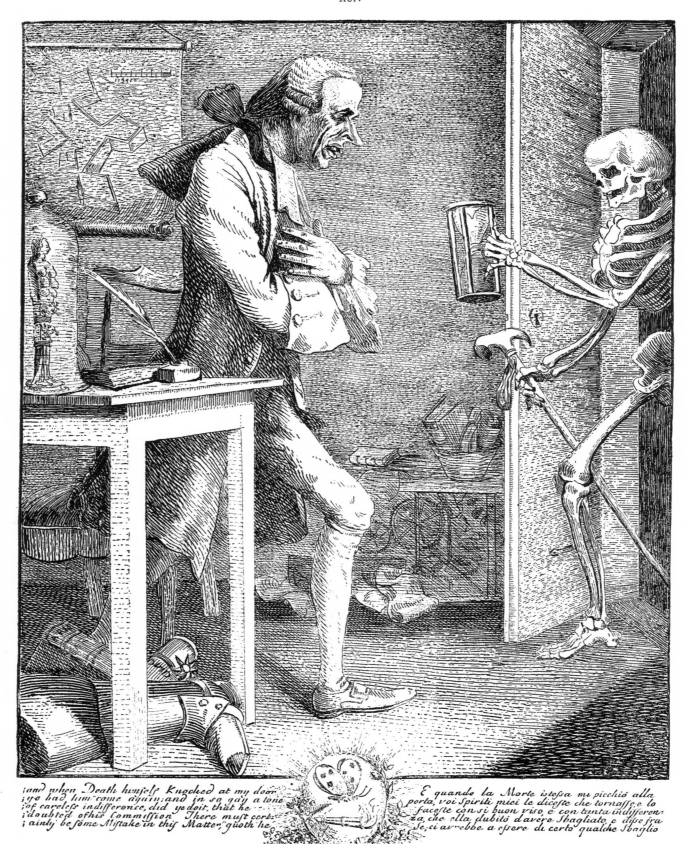

;and when Death himself Knocked at my door
;ye bad him come again; and in so gay a tone
;of careless indifference, did ye do it, that he
;doubted of his Commission" There must cert-
; ainly be some Mistake in this Matter" quoth he

E quando la Morte istessa mi picchiò alla
porta, voi Spiriti miei le diceste che tornasse, e lo
faceste con si buon riso, è con tanta indifferen-
za, che ella dubitò d'avere Sbagliato, e disse fra
Se; ci avrebbe a essere di certo qualche Sbaglio

STERNE AND DEATH

Price half crown

Patch pinx et sculp.
[1768]

spes et Studiorum in Cesare tantum " (Pl. XCIII.). In the tail-piece we see a connoisseur in the guise of a monkey tending some dead shrubs in flower-pots. These are described as " Exoticks," the first being labelled " Obit 1502," the second " Obit 1600," the third " Obit 1606." The monkey has a large magnifying glass with which to view the beauties that are hidden from ordinary eyes. Ireland explains that Hogarth introduced these " dwarfish importations of decayed nature " to indicate the state of " those old and damaged pictures which are venerated for their antiquity, and exalted above all productions, from the name of a great master, rather than from any intrinsic merit."

The same idea is illustrated by the subscription ticket etched by Hogarth, in 1761, for the proposed engraving from his historical picture *Sigismunda with the Heart of Guiscard.* This picture, it will be remembered, was painted with the object of proving that ancient pictures are not intrinsically superior to the works of modern masters, but owe much of their supposed excellence to the mellowing processes of time. Sir Richard Grosvenor, who had given the artist a commission for an historical painting, was dissatisfied with the *Sigismunda*, and refused to buy it, and the engraving from the picture was not proceeded with, owing probably to the unsatisfactory nature of the subscription. In the ticket, *Time Smoking a Picture*, which has for motto Whitehead's line, " While statues moulder into worth," Time as an aged man is seated before an easel on which is a landscape (Pl. XCV.). He has a pot of varnish beside him, and is engaged in " mellowing " the canvas, which his scythe has pierced, with the smoke that he produces from a long pipe. Below are engraved the lines :—

> " To Nature and yourself appeal,
> Nor learn of others what to feel.—*Anon*."

For the year 1762 we have records, pictorial and other, of an elaborate artistic joke organised by Bonnel Thornton,[1] George Colman the elder, Robert Lloyd,[2] and Joseph Hill, all members of the Nonsense Club. This was suggested by the annual picture exhibition established by the Society of Arts. In March, 1762, it was announced in the *St. James' Chronicle* that " The Society of Sign-painters are preparing a most magnificent collection of portraits, landscapes, fancy-pieces, etc., etc., designed by the ablest masters, and executed by the best hands in these Kingdoms." The exhibition was held at the house of Bonnel Thornton, who drew up a comic Catalogue, on which was a notice to the effect that " the Society of Sign-painters take this opportunity of refuting a most malicious suggestion that their Exhibition is intended as a ridicule on the Society of Arts. They intend theirs only as an appendix or companion to the other."

According to a contemporary account, the spectator on entering the

---

[1] Born in 1724, died in 1768. He was a schoolfellow of William Cowper's and a friend of Dr. Johnson's, who much admired his Burlesque Ode on St. Cecilia's Day, which was performed at Ranelagh. Thornton contributed to the *Adventurer* and the *Connoisseur*, and at one time edited the *St. James' Chronicle*.

[2] Robert Lloyd (1733-64). He edited the *St. James' Chronicle*, and published a collection of poems in 1762. He was a friend of Garrick's, and wrote a comic opera called *The Capricious Lovers*.

room found himself in a commodious apartment, round the walls of which was hung a curious collection of wooden signs, together with the poles, balls and sugar-loaves that had once dangled from the pent-houses of shops. Among the items set forth in the catalogue are *The Vicar of Bray*, represented by an ass in full canonicals, *The Irish Arms*, a pair of thick legs, and *A Man*, nine tailors at work. Hogarth is supposed to have taken part in the joke, and it is even alleged that by means of a few touches with a piece of chalk he heightened the humorous effect of certain exhibits. In revenge, probably, for this assistance, a poor and coarsely-executed etching was published by "Justitia Brushwell" under the title of *A Brush for the Sign-Painters*. The design contains a caricature portrait of Hogarth at work upon a signboard rendering of his *Sigismunda*, with Envy guiding his brush. The poster of the exhibition hangs near, bearing the inscription, "Here we expose our Heads and Hearts, price 1/-." Folly is seen in the clouds above, holding a label on which is the text : "It is an Honour for a Man to cease from Strife ; but every Fool will be meddling."

Passing over the Hogarth, Wilkes, and Churchill squabble[1] in 1763, the origin of which was mainly political, we come to an etching by De Louther-bourg[2] called *The Reviewers' Cave*, which is interesting from a literary point of view, though its artistic merit is of the slightest (Pl. XCVI.). The design seems to have been prepared as a frontispiece to *The Powers of the Pen*, a satirical poem published by Evan Lloyd (1734–76), a Welsh parson, in 1765. This, his first production, brought Lloyd some literary reputation, but another poem in the same style, *The Curate and the Methodist*, was rewarded by a term of imprisonment for libel in the King's Bench. Later, in an *Epistle to David Garrick*, he defended the actor against the attacks of Kenrick, who replied with *A Whipping-post for a Welsh Parson*. Garrick, in gratitude for this championship, presented Lloyd with a drinking-cup made out of the wood of Shakespeare's mulberry tree.

In *The Powers of the Pen* Lloyd describes a sort of reviewers' dungeon, the walls being papered with title-pages, and the doors guarded by printers' devils. With the audacity of a provincial Churchill he attacks Johnson's "Scholastic Pedantry" and "Testy Prefaces," describing the sage as a "Catacomb of Words," while Warburton is "Learning turned to Curds." The reviewers in general are branded as

> " Mechanic Judges of the Brain
> As weather-glasses are of Rain."

---

[1] Hogarth's political print, *The Times*, brought upon him attacks by Wilkes and Churchill. He retaliated with a caricature of the squinting Wilkes with his cap of Liberty and of Churchill as *The Bruiser*. But the quarrel embittered his last years, and the depression of his sturdy spirit is shown in the tail-piece which he etched for his works, *The Bathos ; or, the Art of Sinking in Sublime Painting* (1764). Hogarth died at his house in Leicester Fields on October 25th, 1764.

[2] Philippe Jacques de Loutherbourg was born at Strassburg in 1740. Although he attained some success in Paris, where he was appointed Court Painter to the King, he migrated to London in 1771, where he was employed by Garrick to design scenery and decorations for Drury Lane. He executed several works dealing with naval and military episodes, and was elected a Royal Academician in 1781.

W. Hogarth   1761

TIME SMOKING A PICTURE

[De Loutherbourg]

Etched by Mortimer
[1765]

THE REVIEWERS CAVE

LITERARY AND ARTISTIC

The etching portrays the cave or dungeon, with the goddess of Dulness asleep overhead. The reviewers sit round in solemn conclave, while a porter carries towards an altar a basket of books, including the *Sentimental Journey*, Churchill's *Poems*, and the *Powers of the Pen*. For the rest we are shown the accessories described in the poem, the scalps of authors, the torn title-pages, the sleepy owl, and the ass that brays at the approach of Sense.

The middle of the century saw a great increase in the number of print-shops in London, while the art of caricature was rapidly gaining in popularity. In June, 1765, a letter appeared in the *Public Advertiser*, which condemns in ironical fashion the growth of these pictorial libels. After expressing his satisfaction that all the terrors of the law had lately been let loose on those authors and publishers who had abused the liberty of the Press, the writer desires to draw the attention of ministers to the licence of the rolling-press. "The Rolling-press, Mr. Printer, as you very well know," he continues, "is the machine from which the Impression of Plates and Cuts is taken, as that of the sheets of Books, Pamphlets and Newspapers is taken from the Common Press. The first of these, it is easy to conceive, is more liable to abuse, and the abuse of it is of more consequence than the latter. Books are confined to one language, and the knowledge of that language to the inhabitants of one nation, but Prints are an universal Language, understood by Persons of all Nations and Degrees. . . . Every window of every Printshop is in a manner glazed with libels. One Arch-libeller in particular has rendered himself more than a hundred times liable to Prosecution for Scandalatum Magnatum. There is scarce a distinguished person in the Kingdom whom he hath not exhibited in caricature. He has dealt his grotesque cards from house to house, and circulated his defamatory Pictures from Town's end to Town's end. . . . Twenty Columns of your paper would not create an insurrection among the Weavers so soon as one pack of the Cards above-mentioned. I could draw this Arch-libeller's character in the most lively colours ; but however faintly he is crayoned out in this letter, I dare say that most people will know and abominate him."

The letter is signed George Bout-de-Ville, otherwise George Townshend (afterwards first Marquis Townshend), who produced a large number of political cards and prints, by which he made himself many enemies. Horace Walpole considered that Townshend's genius for likeness in caricature was astonishing, but observes, "As his parts lie entirely in his pencil, his pen has no share in them ; the labels are very dull." Townshend, who had served under the Duke of Cumberland at Culloden, and under Wolfe in the expedition against Quebec, was appointed Lord Lieutenant of Ireland in 1767, but the unpopularity which he had earned by his caricatures seems to have followed him in this new capacity.

Among the famous firms of print-sellers, that of Carington Bowles[1]

---

[1] Many of Carington Bowles' prints were issued in conjunction with John Bowles, of 13, Cornhill.

(afterwards Bowles and Carver), of St. Paul's Churchyard, holds a foremost place, its *spécialité* being the hand-coloured mezzotints which were aimed at the professional foibles and middle-class follies of the day. Among other well-known print-sellers were Robert Sayer (himself an engraver), in Fleet Street, whose wares were mainly political; Matthew Darly, at the Golden Acre, Strand, who turned the Maccaronies to good account; John Smith, at Hogarth's Head, Cheapside; George Bickham, in May's Buildings, Covent Garden; William Holland, of Oxford Street; and, in later days, S. W. Fores, at the corner of Sackville Street, Piccadilly, where the name may still be seen over the door; William Dickinson, of Bond Street; Humphrey, whose name was so closely associated with that of Gillray, more especially during the years that Mistress Humphrey reigned over the shop in St. James' Street; and Rudolf Ackermann, of the Repository of Arts in the Strand, who was one of Rowlandson's chief employers.

The exterior of a print-shop was a favourite subject with the caricaturist, Darly's premises in the Strand being sketched by Topham in 1772 under the title of *The Maccaroni Print-shop* (Pl. CV.). This shows the outside of the shop-window, the panes of which are filled with caricatures of Maccaronies, miniature representations of the prints that were then in actual circulation. Among the spectators are an elderly man, an officer, and a country squire, who gaze in at the window with amused appreciation, but a gentleman of the Maccaroni type regards the counterfeit presentments of his kind with evident disgust and annoyance. A hand-coloured mezzotint belonging to the same period gives a view of Carington Bowles' print-shop in St. Paul's Churchyard, the windows of which contain portraits of popular preachers as well as a large number of caricatures. Bowles, like Fores and other leading print-sellers, issued portfolios of caricatures, which were hired for the evening by persons who were giving a party, and desired to entertain their guests with a fashionable amusement; while exhibitions of satirical prints were frequently organised, to which the public were admitted on payment of a small fee. In spite of the large demand for their wares, the majority of caricaturists were wretchedly paid, the market being cheapened by the amateurs, whose designs were touched up and " executed gratis " by enterprising tradesmen.[1]

The caricaturists of the " seventies " were, as we have seen, chiefly taken up with the vagaries of the Maccaronies, male and female, and even the artistic profession was not wholly free from these fashionable vanities. Thus, in *The Maccaroni Painter; or, Billy Dimple sitting for his Portrait*, a hand-coloured mezzotint drawn by Dighton[2] and engraved by Earlom,[3] we have a caricature sketch of Richard Cosway, R.A., in the act of painting a typical

---

[1] The important Act known as " Hogarth's Act," which protected designers from piracy, came into operation in 1735.

[2] Robert Dighton (*c.* 1752–1814). Etched a number of satirical portraits of professional types in *A Book of Heads*. Exhibited occasionally with the Royal Academy and the Free Society of Artists. In 1806 he abstracted some valuable prints from the print-room of the British Museum and sold them, but the majority were recovered.

[3] Richard Earlom (1743–1822), who obtained a great reputation as a mezzotint engraver during the latter half of the eighteenth century.

[*R. Dighton*]   [C. 1770]

THE MACARONI PAINTER, OR BILLY DIMPLE SITTING FOR HIS PICTURE

Printed for Bowles & Carver, Map & Printsellers, No 69, in St Paul's Churchyard, London.

[R. Dighton]

[C. 1770]

THE PAINTRESS OF MACCARONI'S

Printed for Carington Bowles, Map & Printseller, No 69, in St Paul's Churchyard, London

Chas. Brandoin Inv^t el delin^t

R. Sayer Excudit

Richd Earlom fecit

THE EXHIBITION OF THE ROYAL ACADEMY OF PAINTING OF THE YEAR 1771
FROM AN ORIGINAL DRAWING IN THE POSSESSION OF ROB^T SAYER

Printed for Robt Sayer, No 53 in Fleet Street

Pub^d 20th May, 1772

C

U⟨ª⟩.G⟨ᵛ⟩]

OLD WISDOM

BLINKING AT THE STARS

Pub March 10ᵗʰ 1782 by W. Rennie

Cl

DR. JOHNSON IN HIS TRAVELLING DRESS
AS DESCRIBED IN BOSWELL'S TOUR

Publish'd Jan 18, 1786 by Geo. Kearsley
No 46, Fleet Street

Price 1ˢ 6ᵈ

Drawn from the Life
and Engrav'd by T. Trotter

Maccaroni, resplendent in red coat, green waistcoat, brown breeches, white stockings, and voluminous wig (Pl. XCVII.). The artist himself, who is scarcely less elaborately costumed, was described by a contemporary as an exceptionally dirty boy, who grew up into one of the smartest men of his time. "Indeed, so ridiculously foppish did he become that Mat. Darly introduced an etching of him in his window, as the *Maccaroni Miniature-painter*. . . . I have often seen Mr. Cosway at the elder Christie's picture-sales, full-dressed in his sword and bag, with a small three-cornered hat on the top of his powdered toupet, and a mulberry silk coat, profusely embroidered with scarlet strawberries." A companion print to the above is called *The Paintress of Maccaronies*, and represents a comely young woman in a huge frilled cap, sitting before an easel on which is the portrait of a young man wearing a maccaroni wig (Pl. XCVIII.). The Paintress may have been intended for Mrs. Cosway, or possibly for Angelica Kauffmann.

The Royal Academy held its first exhibition in 1768, and in 1771 Charles Brandoin[1] executed a clever drawing of the *coup-d'œil* of the exhibition for that year, which was engraved in mezzotint by Earlom (Pl. XCIX.). Among the spectators are connoisseurs, dandies, clergymen, fashionable ladies, and children, who, armed with spy-glasses and catalogues, examine the pictures on the walls (which seem to be mostly in the sacred or classic genre), quiz each other, or rest on the hard wooden benches in the middle of the room.

Dr. Johnson and his faithful Boswell enjoyed a larger share of attention from the caricaturists than any other literary men of the period. The most celebrated of the pictorial attacks upon Johnson is the etching by Gillray, which appeared in 1782 under the title of *Old Wisdom Blinking at the Stars* (Pl. C.). The sage, who is here represented with the body of an owl, stands on his own *Lives of the Poets* and blinks with a sour and supercilious expression, eminently suggestive of his "testy Prefaces," at the busts of Milton, Pope, and other great poets, which are surrounded by the stars of immortality. A couple of years earlier Rowlandson had produced a little sketch called *A Scene at Streatham*, in which Mrs. Thrale and Boswell are depicted at high words over their proposed biographies of Dr. Johnson. A stout man with a violoncello, who has been variously identified as Sir John Hawkins and Signor Piozzi, is vainly trying to pacify the combatants. On a bookshelf in the background is a copy of Sir John Hawkins' *History of Music*, over which a spider has spun its web.

The publication of Boswell's *Tour in the Hebrides*, however, was the signal for a sudden outbreak of caricature and parody. In 1785 appeared a portrait of *Dr. Johnson in his Travelling Dress*, done from the life and engraved by T. Trotter (Pl. CI.). The Doctor, who stands in the midst of a treeless landscape, is giving utterance to his famous speech about the loss

---

[1] Charles Brandoin, a German artist, known as L'Anglais, came to England about 1771. He produced some water-colour views as well as caricatures, and died in Germany *circa* 1790.

of his walking-stick in the Hebrides: "No, no, my Friend, it is not to be supposed that any man in Mull who has got it will part with it. Consider, Sir, the value of such a piece of timber here."

A year later was published that witty satire, *The Picturesque Beauties of Boswell*, which contains twenty plates, designed by Samuel Collings and etched by Rowlandson, illustrative of Boswell's tour to the Hebrides. The frontispiece to the first part shows Boswell in a go-cart, being dragged along by Johnson and Paoli, the Corsican hero, the while he indulges in his famous imitation of the mooing of a cow. Beneath is inscribed the legend, "All Hail Dalblair! Hail to thee, Laird of Auchinleck!" Each of the etchings is based upon a passage in the famous Journal; for example, in No. 2, a portrait of *The Journalist, with a view of Auchinleck; or, the Land of Stones*, Boswell is depicted in Highland costume and an heroic attitude, with his Journal for a claymore and his manuscript materials for the Life of Johnson for a shield, is accompanied by the following quotation :—

"I am, I flatter myself, completely a 'Citizen of the World.' In my travels through Holland, Germany, Switzerland, Italy, Corsica, France, I have never felt myself from home; and I sincerely love every kindred and tongue and people and nation. . . . My great-grandfather, the husband of the Countess Veronica, was Alexander, Earl of Kincardine. From him the blood of Bruce flows in my veins; of such ancestry who would not be proud, and glad to seize a fair opportunity to let it be known?" (Pl. CII.).

The other illustrations include *The Embrace at Boyd's Inn*, Edinburgh, where the fellow-travellers met on August 14th, 1773; *Tea at the Journalist's House in St. James' Court*, where Johnson's conversation temporarily charmed his hostess into forgetfulness of his uncouth appearance (Pl. CIII.); *Veronica, a Breakfast Conversation*, at which Boswell's baby daughter, Veronica, showed so marked an approval of the strange guest that her father declared she should have "five hundred pounds of additional fortune"; and *Setting out from Edinburgh* for the Tour. In the frontispiece to the second part, we see the journalist engaged in *Revising for the Second Edition, under the Inspection of a Learned Friend*. The revision consisted chiefly of cutting out certain libellous passages relating to Lord M'Donald, who had threatened reprisals. Among the other incidents chosen for illustration in this part, we find *Sailing among the Hebrides—the Journalist holding a Rope's end*, which, he confesses, had been given him to keep him quiet; *Scottifying the Palate*, which shows Boswell forcing dried fish down Johnson's throat; *The Recovery*, after a drinking-bout on the part of Boswell at Corrichnatachin; and *Contest at Auchinleck*, when Johnson and the Laird of Auchinleck came to loggerheads over the dangerous topics of Whiggism and Presbyterianism, Toryism and Episcopacy. Boswell, we are assured by a contemporary, was far from being mortified by these and other pictorial satires, but rather gloried in such tokens of notoriety. "He had a large collection of these caricatures upon 'self and company,' as he used facetiously to inscribe them, and boasted at

THE JOURNALIST, WITH A VIEW OF AUCHINLECK

OR THE LAND OF STONES

Pub. May 1786 by E. Jackson, 14 Marylebone Street, Golden Square

[1786]

TEA AT THE JOURNALIST'S HOUSE

STARVING POET AND PUBLISHER

[FROM A WATER-COLOUR DRAWING BY ROWLANDSON]

THE MACARONI PRINT SHOP

Pub. by M. Darly, Strand, July 14ᵗʰ 1772

[T. Rowlanason]

THE HISTORIAN ANIMATING THE MIND OF A YOUNG PAINTER

[1784]

James Gillray design et fecit

Pub. June 20th 1789, by H. Humphrey
No 18, Old Bond Street

SHAKESPEARE SACRIFICED; OR THE OFFERING TO AVARICE

[c. 1786]

GEORGE MORLAND

[FROM A WATER-COLOUR DRAWING
BY ROWLANDSON]

the Judge's table that his History would be more copiously illustrated than the Lord Chancellor Clarendon's."

That a Society for the Prevention of Cruelty to Authors was badly needed at this period is implied by Rowlandson in a couple of etchings, *Bookseller and Author* and *Starving Poet and Publisher* (Pl. CIV.). The first, which was executed from a design of Henry Wigstead's in 1784, shows a shabby half-starved author in the book-lined sanctum of a prosperous and apparently purse-proud publisher, who looks contemptuously upon the manuscript that is proffered by his visitor. The second, a water-colour drawing, is here reproduced. A more attractive subject, treated by the same artist in the same year, is entitled *An Historian Animating the Mind of a Young Painter* (Pl. CVI.). In a sparsely furnished studio a young artist sits with a crayon in his hand, and a large volume for drawing-board, while he listens to the sublime ideas declaimed by the historian. The painter's wife is playing with her little son, who has evidently just been posing to his father in the character of a cupid or cherub. It was probably in or about 1787 that Rowlandson sketched the portrait of his friend, George Morland,[1] then a dashing young man about town, who always expected, according to Angelo, to be "king of his company," preferring to reign over the Bohemian society of Soho taverns, rather than find his level among men of education and repute (Pl. CVII.).

In June, 1789, Gillray published his famous cartoon *Shakespeare Sacrificed, or the offering to Avarice*, which, by its wealth of imagination and skill in grouping, shows his talent at the highest level (Pl. CVIII.). The victim of this ferocious satire was Alderman Boydell (1719–1804), who had made a large fortune out of the publication of engravings from the works of English artists. In 1786 Boydell conceived the idea of establishing a Shakespeare Gallery, to which the leading painters of the day were invited to contribute. Reynolds, Romney, Northcote, Opie, Fuseli, and West lent their support to the scheme, and in 1789 the Gallery was opened with thirty-four pictures, the number being afterwards increased to a hundred and sixty-two. By the majority of his contemporaries Boydell's enterprise seems to have been regarded with approval, while those artists who had hitherto been compelled to paint portraits for lack of encouragement to undertake historical work, were quite pathetically grateful for the opportunity thus afforded them. The exhibition prospered for a time, but the export trade in engravings being temporarily ruined by the war with France, Boydell fell into difficulties, and in 1802 was obliged to dispose of the Gallery and its contents by means of a public lottery.

[1] George Morland (1773–1804). As soon as he could free himself from his artistic apprenticeship to a harsh father, he took up his quarters at a picture-dealer's shop, swaggered about with potboys, ostlers, and jockeys, and usually appeared in a green coat, with large yellow buttons, and top boots, "the very extreme of foppish puppyism." It is difficult, however, to reconcile the quality and quantity of his work with this character for incessant dissipation.

Although Northcote declared that Boydell had done more for English art and artists than all the patrons put together, he seems to have laid himself open to charges of sharp practice, or at least illiberality, in his dealings with young painters who were not in a position to make their own terms. In Gillray's design we see the Alderman in his civic robes (which he wore when attending at the Gallery) preparing an oblation to the Demon of Avarice, who, hugging his money-bags to his breast, is seated on a volume of Subscribers to the Sacrifice, *i.e.* the collection of engravings from the Shakespearean pictures. On the Demon's shoulder is the figure of Puck blowing bubbles of immortality. The fuel for the burnt-offering is supplied by the Plays of Shakespeare, and in the smoke that arises are seen parodies of the scenes and personages that were treated by Boydell's artists. Thus we have Northcote's Richard III., Reynolds' Macbeth, Romney's Infant Shakespeare, and Fuseli's Caliban, each with the original defects of conception or execution cleverly exaggerated, while Death, as the grave-digger in *Hamlet*, is employed in digging the Alderman's grave.

The Ireland forgery of Shakespearean documents, which was exposed in 1796, was a fruitful topic of satire and caricature. It will be sufficient to remind the reader that in 1794 William Henry Ireland (1777–1835), then a boy of seventeen, just articled to a solicitor, professed to have discovered some Shakespearean relics in an oaken chest belonging to a gentleman who did not wish his name to be divulged. Emboldened by the readiness with which his statements found belief, more especially from his father, an engraver with antiquarian tastes, the boy, who had access to some old parchments, forged a deed purporting to be signed by Shakespeare, a transcript of *Lear*, a Shakespearean Confession of Faith, and finally composed a tragedy called *Vortigern and Rowena*, which he put forward as an unpublished play by Shakespeare. Parr, Warton, Pye, and several other men of letters who examined the relics, formally attested their belief in the authenticity of these "discoveries," and a facsimile of the documents was published by the elder Ireland at four guineas a copy. The tragedy was accepted by Kemble, and produced at Drury Lane on April 2nd, 1796, when the bubble, which had already been pricked by George Steevens, Malone, and Porson, finally burst. The elder Ireland protested his good faith to the last, but the boy quitted his home after confessing his guilt, and, a few months later, published a history of the forgeries in *An Authentic Account of the Shakespearean MSS.*, in which he denied his father's complicity in the fraud.

In 1796 *The Oaken Chest; or, the Gold-mines of Ireland* was produced by W. Nixon, who is described as "of the Bank," in contradistinction to his more famous namesake, "the facetious Nixon" (Pl. CX.). In this design we see the whole Ireland family, including two daughters, busily engaged upon the forgeries which were to be discovered later in the famous oaken chest. Another cartoon on the same subject, *The Ghost of Shakespeare appearing*

Designed & Engraved by W. Hogarth & found in an old chest   [1796]

THE SPIRIT OF SHAKESPEARE APPEARING TO HIS DETRACTERS

CX

[W. Nixon]   [1796]

THE OAKEN CHEST
OR THE GOLD MINES OF IRELAND. A FARCE
"The Earth has Bubbles as the Water has and these are of them."—*Shakespeare*

Sold at No 32, Lombard Street, & to be had of all the Printsellers in London & Westminster

[*Gillray*]

SATAN IN ALL HIS GLORY;—OR—PETER PINDAR CROUCHING TO THE DEVIL

SKETCH'D FROM THE PEEP-HOLE AT SCALEGILL

TO THE WORTHY INHABITANTS OF CUMBERLAND THIS IMPARTIAL REPRESENTATION OF THE VIRTUES OF HIS INFERNAL MAJESTY IS RESPECTFULLY DEDICATED

Pub. May 8th 1792 (for the proprietor) by H. Humphrey, No 18, Old Bond St

to his Detractors, " Designed and engraved by William Hogarth, and found in an old Chest," shows Ireland and his children shrinking in terror from the apparition of the injured poet (Pl. CIX.). In 1797 Gillray published a satirical portrait of Samuel Ireland as the first of his series of *Notorious Characters*. The following lines by the poet Mason are appended to the design :—

> " Four forgers, born in one prolific age,
> Much critical acumen did engage :
> The first[1] was soon by doughty Douglas scared,
> Tho' Johnson would have screened him had he dared.
> The next[2] had all the cunning of a Scot ;
> The third[3] invention, genius—nay, what not ?
> Fraud now exhausted, only could dispense
> To her fourth son,[4] their threefold impudence."

Ireland seems to have been more enraged by this portrait than by any of the other pictorial attacks of which he was the subject, for he contemplated bringing an action for libel against the artist, and is said to have smashed the windows of the shop in which the print was exposed for sale.

In 1792 Gillray's caricature of Peter Pindar was published by H. Humphrey " for the proprietor," under the title of *Satan in all his Glory ; or, Peter Pindar crouching to the Devil—sketched from the Peep-hole at Scalegill*. " To the worthy inhabitants of Cumberland this impartial representation of the Virtues of his Infernal Majesty is respectfully Dedicated." This shows Dr. Wolcot[5] pleading for mercy to Satan,[6] who has one of his claws upon a sack of coals for the infernal pit, consisting of Cruelty, Avarice, Malice, etc. Pindar's many and various misdeeds radiate in flames from Satan's person, and a recording Demon marks them down in his book (Pl. CXI.). In response to Pindar's prayers the Devil exclaims :—

> " No, Peter, no, in vain you sue,
> 'Tis my turn now ; the Devil must have his due."

It would be impossible, even in the most summary notice of the artistic caricatures of this period, to pass over Gillray's elaborate satire upon the reputed discovery by a Miss Provis of the secret of Venetian colouring. This etching, published in 1797, is entitled *Titian Redivivus ; or, the Seven Wise Men consulting the Venetian Oracle—a Scene in the Academic Grove*. The art dictionaries are discreetly silent upon the subject of Miss Provis, but it is reported that she imposed upon a large number of the Royal Academicians, who bought her secret at an exorbitant price. The following is a slightly summarised version of the description of this plate in the *Works of James Gillray*, by Mr. Grego.

---

[1] Lauder.   [2] Macpherson.   [3] Chatterton.   [4] Ireland.

[5] John Wolcot (1738–1819). He studied medicine and also took Orders with the hope of preferment. After spending some years in Jamaica, he settled at Truro as a medical practitioner. In 1781 he came to London with literary aims, and after gaining notoriety with his Odes to the Royal Academicians, began a series of attacks upon the King with the *Lousiad* (1785) and the *Ode upon Odes* (1787).

[6] Satan is intended for Lord Lonsdale, whom Wolcot had attacked, and who had threatened an action for libel.

"Mounted on a rainbow stands the ragged impostor, boldly dashing off a head in positive light and shade. Above the canvas rises a phœnix, bursting forth from flames and lightenings, with the famous Venetian Manuscript. Fame cries through his trumpet, 'You little stars, hide your diminished heads,' whereon the stars (Michael Angelo, Raphael, etc.) drop out of the firmament. Pegasus, as a scrubby Jackass, is kneeling down to drink from the magic paint-pot. The tattered figure of the impostor ends in a train of peacock's feathers, which the three Graces submissively support. The lower compartment exhibits the interior of the Royal Academy. The foremost seats are occupied by the Academicians, Opie, Westall, Farringdon, Hoppner, Stothard, Smirke, and Rigaud, the chief dupes of the secret, who are immersed in the discovery. Behind the Seven Wise Men are crowds of artists, all changing into monkeys, and clambering up the rainbow after the deluding Miss Provis. The names of Northcote, Lawrence, Downman, etc., are distinguishable amidst their palettes. The figure of Sir Joshua Reynolds, rising from the grave, expresses astonishment at the infatuated Academicians. Three figures in the immediate foreground are stealing away in evident mistrust : Benjamin West, the President, who was not a convert to the 'Venetian Humbug'; Alderman Boydell, in alarm for the prospects of his Gallery ; and Macklin, bearing a sack of tickets, marked 'Lottery. Five guineas a dip,' with his Bible in his pocket, indicating his anxiety respecting the success of his lottery for these grand illustrations."[1]

[1] Presumably Thomas Macklin, an engraver who executed the plates for Bunbury's Shakespeare.

SPORT AND GAMES

AN examination of the sporting prints of the eighteenth century leads the student to the melancholy conclusion that the English of that period were not, in our modern sense of the phrase, a nation of sportsmen—certainly they were not as yet given over to the cult of athleticism. The cock-pit and the prize-ring had their patrons, it is true, both numerous and enthusiastic, while Newmarket was already a racing centre; but in days when men made long journeys perforce in the saddle, hunting was scarcely regarded with the same keenness as to-day (George III.'s equerries used to complain bitterly of their master's devotion to the sport), and shooting was simply a cheap method of supplying the larder. Football and cricket were not yet become highly organised national sports, but were played on village greens by schoolboys and yokels, without a thought of gate-money or paragraphs in the daily papers.

The coarser forms of sport were regarded with disfavour by men of intellect and breeding, who considered that fencing, riding (according to the rules of the *manège*), and dancing were the only kinds of exercise worthy the attention of a gentleman. Lord Chesterfield was particularly strong in his denunciation of field-sports. " Eat as much game as you please," he writes to his godson, " but I hope you will never kill any yourself; and indeed I think you are above any of those rustick illiberal sports of guns, dogs, and horses, which characterise our English Bumpkin Country Gentlemen. . . . For my part I never in my life killed my own meat, but left it to the poulterer and butcher to do it for me. All those country sports, as they are called, are the effects of the idleness and ignorance of country esquires, who do not know what to do with their time, but people of sense and knowledge never give in to those illiberal amusements." Again, writing from Bath in 1769, he complains of the strange mixture of company, including Bucks, Bloods, and Bumpkins. " The two first are offensive by their ill-manners, the latter sort are only ridiculously awkward. They hunt all the morning, and appear, often in the Publick Rooms, in their boots and spurrs, their leathern caps and deerskin waittescoats, which are commonly the Opima Spolia of their morning's atchievements. How glad am I to be convinced that you will never appear anywhere in any of these ridiculous and offensive characters, and to know that you have already a just contempt for them all."

The general neglect of physical exercise, together with the contempt for fresh air and the tendency to over-indulgence in the pleasures of the table, were not conducive to stability of health, slimness of figure, or length of days in the men, more especially the townsmen of the period. It is better, from the point of view of physical fitness, to play the part of a "flannelled fool" or a "muddied oaf" than to assist at a cock-fight or attend a professional sparring match in the character of a noble patron.

The majority of the sporting caricatures belong to the latter half of the century, being the work of Collet, Bunbury, Gillray, and Rowlandson, but two or three may be mentioned that appeared at an earlier date. A print by E. van Heemsherck, called *The Bruising Match*, is undated, but probably belongs to the decade 1730-40. In his portrayal of character and attitude van Heemsherck was superior to many of his fellows, and this representation of the flooring of one champion by his opponent, and the intervention of an umpire or second, is by no means ineffective, while the curious costume of both bruisers and onlookers may be studied with interest by the modern patrons of the noble art of self-defence[1] (Pl. CXII.).

For illustrations of the social games most in vogue at this period, we must turn to a series of paintings executed by Francis Hayman[2] for the ballroom at Vauxhall in 1743. These pictures are not, strictly speaking, caricatures, but being conceived in a spirit of comedy, they may be admitted in this connection. From Hayman's designs we may pick out three which deal with the indoor amusements of the upper classes, viz. *Battledore and Shittlecock* (engraved by N. Parr[3]), played by a man and a girl, with another girl looking on (Pl. CXIII.); *Quadrille*, a party of two men and two ladies seated at an old card-table, with the corners hollowed to hold money or counters (Hayman's furniture is always worth noting), while a maid and a negro boy are about to serve tea (Pl. CXIV.); and *Building a House with Cards*, engraved by L. Truchy,[4] in which we see a gentleman building a house of card, while a group of spectators follow his progress with interest. One man is trying to blow down the erection, while another raises his hand in protest. Two little girls are playing the same game at a low table or stool (Pl. CXV.).

Among the amusements in low life we have *Leap-frog* (L. Truchy *sc.*), *Sliding on the Ice* (R. Parr *sc.*), *Blindman's Buff*, and *Cricket*, the last being

---

[1] Although this design was published with an English title, it was obviously "made in Holland," since the models were evidently Dutch boors.

[2] Hayman (1708–56) had a distinguished career as an historical painter, and was one of the forty original Royal Academicians.

[3] Nathaniel Parr (fl. 1730–60), together with his brother Remigius, engraved several of the Vauxhall paintings. Both brothers worked for the firm of Bowles in St. Paul's Churchyard.

[4] L. Truchy (1731–64). A French engraver, who executed some of J. Highmore's designs for *Pamela*, and engraved after Teniers and Boydell.

C. 1730

THE BRUISING MATCH

[VAN HEEMSKERCK]

F. Hayman Pinx.   Publish'd according to Act of Parliament 1743

N. Parr sculp. from the original Painting
in Vauxhall Gardens

BATTLEDORE AND SHITTLECOCK

Printed for Thos Bowles in St Paul's Chuchyard & John Bowles at the Black Horse in Cornhill

F. Hayman pinx.   *London.   Printed for Rob.t Sayer Map and Printseller, at No 53 in Fleet Street*   *Truchy sculp.t*
[C 1743]

QUADRILLE   LE QUADRILLE

F. Hayman pinx^t

S. Truchy sculp.
C 1743

BUILDING HOUSES WITH CARDS
ENGRAVED AFTER THE ORIGINAL PAINTING IN VAUXHALL GARDENS
Printed for John Bowles at the Black Horse in Cornhill and Carington Bowles in St Paul's Churchyard, London

played with a narrow curved bat, not unlike a golf stick, and primitive wickets, composed of two pieces of stick for stumps, and a third laid across them for bail. Below are printed a couple of verses eulogising the activity of the players, of which the second may be quoted :—

"Britons, whom Nature has for War designed,
In the soft Charms of Ease no joy can find.
Averse to waste in Rest th' inviting Day,
Toil forms their Game, and Labour is their Play."

While professional horse-racing was a much less national affair than it is at the present day, there were probably a larger number of amateur events, friendly matches in which one country gentleman backed his chestnut mare to run against his friend's grey gelding, and invited a few neighbours to witness the race.

The young bucks and bloods, so abhorrent to Lord Chesterfield, sometimes added to the gaiety of the sporting world by inventing new sporting "events," which were carried out with the utmost solemnity, and seldom failed to justify their *raison d'être*—the winning or losing of large sums of money. A wager of this kind attracted a good deal of public attention in the autumn of 1756. According to a paragraph in the *Gentleman's Magazine*, "A match has been made at Newmarket between a nobleman and a gentleman in the army, to be walked from Norwich to Mile-end Turnpike between five geese and five turkeys, that person to win who brings in most *Cattle* alive to the turnpike. Both parties have begun to train for the expedition, which is to be performed on the 10th day of December and the following days. This article was at first imagined to be a burlesque upon our military men, but it is now certainly to be fact." Horace Walpole alludes to this or a similar event in a letter to Mann, dated October 17th, 1756. "My Lord Rockingham and my nephew, Lord Orford," he writes, "have made a match for five hundred pounds between five turkies and five geese to run from Norwich to London. Don't you believe in the transmigration of souls? And are you not convinced that this race is between Marquis Sardanapalus and Earl Heliogabalus?"

The result of the race does not appear, but it was supposed beforehand that the chances would be fairly even, since though the turkeys could move faster than the geese, they would roost in the trees at night, and some time would be lost in starting them again in the morning, whereas the geese would rest on the ground, and move on again without delay. Some thirty years later Colonel Hanger is said to have won large sums of the Prince of Wales over a similar wager—thanks to his knowledge of the roosting habits of turkeys. The original match seems to have taken hold of the popular imagination, and the caricaturists turned it to good account, not only by imaginary representations of the actual race, but by symbolical designs showing the Duke of Newcastle and Mr. Fox urging along their respective flocks. One of the non-political prints is called *The Pleasures of the Turf*, and portrays two gentlemen, one wearing a fool's cap and carrying a bauble, and the other armed with a halberd, driving their respective teams of geese and turkeys.   Below are engraved the lines :—

> " Birds of a Feather will flock together.
> Like to like, as the Devil said to the Collier."

On November 5th, 1759, was published Hogarth's engraving of the *Cock-pit*, the subject of which is said to have been suggested to the artist by some lines which appeared in the *Gentleman's Magazine* for 1747.   In a bare room a large round table with a raised rim constitutes the field of battle, upon which two cocks are engaged in the conflict.   Round the table is a bench with a high back on which are seated the spectators, each so carefully individualised as to give the effect of a portrait from the life (Pl. CXVI.).   Several, indeed, have been identified as contemporary sportsmen, notably the central figure, a blind man, said to be Lord Albemarle Bertie, second son of the Duke of Ancaster ; the man holding a cock in a bag, supposed to be Jackson, a well-known jockey ; the public hangman (!) ; and a dandy chimney-sweep, who was a notorious contemporary character.   According to the laws of the cock-pit, the man who does not pay his debts of honour is liable to exaltation in a basket, and in this plate the shadow of a man hung from the ceiling in a basket is cast upon the table. He is holding out his watch and seals as his stake upon the fight in progress.

The popular sports of bear-baiting, bull-baiting, and dog-fighting were usually held at Hockley-in-the-Hole, Clerkenwell, where too was the prize-ring, visited by Steele, the scene of many an encounter, not only with fists, but also with swords or daggers.   Women frequently challenged each other to single combat, fighting with half a crown in each clenched fist, the one who dropped her money first to lose the battle.   Sometimes they took part in the matches arranged by men, as in an event mentioned by Malcolm, when " Sutton, the champion of Kent, and a courageous female heroine of that country fought Stokes at Tigg's [in the Oxford Road] and his much-admired consort of London.   Forty pounds was to be given to the male and female who gave most cuts with the swords, and twenty pounds for most blows at quarter-staff, besides the collection in the box."   Mrs. Stokes is elsewhere alluded to as the City Championess.   A rather popular subject with the mid-century caricaturist is a scene in which one of these Amazons—generally a Billingsgate fishwife—administers a thrashing to a Frenchman or a Maccaroni.

Even the women of the upper classes, now held up to their descendants as models of all that was gentle and feminine, were not exempt from these sporting tastes, as may be proved by a glance at the works of John Collet.[1]

---

[1] John Collet (born *c*. 1725, died 1780) is said to have been a pupil of Hogarth, and it is certain that he studied in the art school in St. Martin's Lane, in which Hogarth was interested.   He exhibited some serious work with the Free Society of Artists in 1761 and the following season, but after 1762 he produced, for the most part, humorous studies of contemporary life.   His pictures are more valuable for the light they throw upon the middle-class society of his time than for their artistic merits.   According to an Academician (quoted by Angelo), Collet's works were " less satirical than narrative, more ludicrous than witty, and oftentimes displeasing without conveying any moral instruction."   Late in life Collet, who is described as a modest, retiring man, inherited a small fortune, and went to live in Cheyne Row, where he remained until his death on August 6th, 1780.

Pit   Royal Sport   Ticket

Design'd and Engrav'd by Wm Hogarth

THE COCK-PIT

Publish'd according to Act of Parliament
Nov. 5th 1759

THE SPORTING LADY

London.   Printed for R. Sayer & J. Bennett, No 53, Fleet Street, 1 Octr 1776

[C 1770]

MISS WICKET AND MISS TRIGGER

MISS TRIGGER YOU SEE IS AN EXCELLENT SHOT, AND FORTY-FIVE NOTCHES MISS WICKET'S JUST GOT

FROM THE ORIGINAL PICTURE BY JOHN COLLET, IN THE POSSESSION OF CARINGTON BOWLES

Printed for Carington Bowles at his Map & Print Warehouse in St Paul's Churchyard. London

THE ISIS MACARONI

Pub. by M. Darly, accord. to Act, May 27ᵗʰ 1772 (39) Strand

Stayner sculp

A TAYLOR RIDING TO BRENTFORD

ENGRAV'D FROM AN ORIGINAL PICTURE PAINTED BY MR. JOHN COLLETT

Printed for R. Sayer No 53, Fleet Street & Jno. Smith No 35, Cheapside, June 20, 1768

SPORT AND GAMES

For example, in *The Female Fox-hunter*, a hand-coloured mezzotint after Collet (*c.* 1770), we see a girl mounted on a grey pony in the act of leaping a gate. A man has just parted company with his steed, but another lady gallops triumphantly ahead. The women, it may be noted, are generally allowed to outshine the men, at least by the gallant caricaturist, and even in the minor art of skating, a lady is represented sailing gracefully over the ice, with a contemptuous glance for a couple of men who, having lost their balance at the same moment, lie prone at her feet. *The Sporting Lady* (after Collet, *c.* 1770) shows a young woman tramping across country, with a fowling-piece over her shoulder (Pl. CXVII.). In another mezzotint after the same artist, *Miss Wicket and Miss Trigger* (1773), we have a couple of girls standing in a field, the one holding a cricket-bat, the other carrying a gun and several head of game (Pl. CXVIII.). Miss Trigger is followed by a brace of pointers, and is trampling on a paper marked " Effeminacy." Below is engraved the couplet :—

> " Miss Trigger you see is an excellent shot,
> And forty-five notches Miss Wicket's just got."

Several prints published about this period throw ridicule upon the troubles and embarrassments of inexperienced horsemen. An engraving by J. Stayner after Collet, *The Taylor riding to Brentford*, represents a snip much worried by the behaviour of his horse, which is taking fright at an ass eating cabbage by the wayside. The tailor has *Rules for Bad Horsemen* sticking out of his pocket, while on a wall near by is a poster announcing " Various Feats of Horsemanship performed this Evening by the famous Samson" (Pl. CXX.).

The vagaries of the Maccaroni sportsmen have not been left unchronicled by contemporary satirists. An engraving by Caldwall[1] after a picture by Collet portrays *A Maccarony taking his Morning Ride in Rotten Row*. A number of persons are represented, but most prominent among them is an awkward person, with very short stirrups, round shoulders, and an obviously precarious seat. He is arrayed in all the paraphernalia of his tribe—cane, bouquet, and club of plaited hair. Even more extraordinary, however, is the costume of the *Isis Maccaroni* (1772), in an etching, possibly by Bunbury (Pl. CXIX.). This gentleman stands upright in a canoe which he is paddling along a river. He wears a tight-fitting garment trimmed with frogs of braid, a flat hat ornamented with bows of ribbon, and the usual artificial coiffure.

The Maccaronies were the chief patrons of the cabriolet, a form of vehicle which had been invented prior to 1755. In June of that year Horace Walpole wrote to Mann : " All we hear from France is that a new madness reigns there, as strong as that of Pantins was. This is *la fureur de cabriolets;* Anglice, one-horse chairs, a mode introduced by Mr. Child [brother of Earl Tilney]; they not only universally go in them, but wear them ; that is, every-

---

[1] James Caldwall (born 1739). A pupil of Sherwin who engraved portraits and a few subject pieces.

thing is to be *en cabriolet;* the men paint them on their waistcoats, and have them embroidered for clocks on their stockings ; and the women, who have gone all the winter without anything on their heads, are now muffled up in great caps, with round sides, in the form of, and scarce less than, the wheels of chaises." In an etching attributed to Bunbury called *The Cabriolet* (1770), we see one of these new-fashioned carriages drawn by two bobtailed horses and guided by a postillion. The occupant, a gentleman in maccaroni dress and wig, is bowing to a friend on foot, who carries one of the newly introduced umbrellas. A footman, with his hair worn long, clings to the back of the carriage. Beneath is engraved the following quatrain in French, which contains a boast to be sadly falsified twenty years later :—

> " Barbares Anglois ! qui du même couteau
> Coupent la tête au Roi et les queues aux Chevaux,
> Mais les Francais polis laissent aux Rois leur Têtes
> Et encore comme vous les queues à leur Bêtes."

In 1776 the fashionable high headdress seems to have been accompanied by a passion for lofty vehicles in the female breast. Thus in *Phaetona ; or, Modern Female Taste*, we have a presentment of a lady driving a phaeton, which is built with a small body, hung on very high wheels, and with abnormal length from back to front, a vehicle which must have embarrassed the two undersized wooden-looking horses that are supposed to draw it (Pl. CXXII.). A curious mezzotint for the same year is called *The New-fashioned Phaeton —Sic Itur ad Astra*. In this design the phaeton, raised upon towering springs, is drawn up close to the front of a house, and a lady, assisted by a gentleman, is stepping into it out of a first-floor window, while the neighbours look on in astonishment (Pl. CXXIV.).

By the year 1781 another novel vehicle had come into fashion, and in a caricature for this year we have *The New Gig*, which is something like a cabriolet in shape, but hung on two high wheels instead of four, and drawn by a pair of horses harnessed tandem, the leader being ridden by a postillion (Pl. CXXI.). A dashing design by Bunbury, called *Sir Gregory Gigg*, depicts a beau of the period (1782) driving one of these new-fangled conveyances, but this specimen resembles a curricle rather than a cabriolet (Pl. CXXIII.). It may be remembered that that braggart sportsman John Thorpe in *Northanger Abbey* describes his gig and its purchase to Catherine in the following terms : "Curricle-hung, you see, seat, trunk, sword-case, splashing-board, lamps, silver moulding, all, you see, complete ; the iron-work as good as new, or better. He [the first owner] asked fifty guineas ; I closed with him directly, threw down the money, and the carriage was mine."

Ladies continued to distinguish themselves as whips, and the passion for driving seems to have spread to the lower classes, if we may judge from a mezzotint called *A Lesson Westward*, in which a young woman is being taught to handle the ribbons by Tom Longtrot, who advertises that he " teaches young ladies to drive in a fortnight, gig, whiskey, or phaeton—

Colley fecit
[1781]

THE NEW GIG

PHAETONA, OR MODERN FEMALE TASTE

Pub. by M. Darly, 59 Strand. Nov 6 1776

Design'd by H. W. Bunbury Esq.

SIR GREGORY GIGG

Published July 23ᵈ 1732, by J. R. Smith, No 83, Oxford Street, London

THE NEW FASHIONED PHAETON

SIC ITUR AD ASTRA

London.   Printed for R. Sayer & J. Bennett No 53, Fleet Street 22ᵈ Febʸ **1776**

H. Bunbury Esq. Delin.   *W. Dickinson Excudit*

RICHMOND HILL

London: Publish'd March 1st 1782, by Wm. Dickinson, Printseller & Engraver, No 158, New Bond Street

single lessons half a crown." In this case the pupil is evidently a beginner, for she is driving over a pig, and terrifying an old gentleman, who clings to a post for safety. Other lady whips are shown in Bunbury's drawing, *Richmond Hill*,[1] engraved by Dickinson[2] in 1782 (Pl. CXXV.). The central group in this design is a party of pleasure, whose overladen horses have jibbed half-way up the ascent. A laughing lady dashes past them driving a young buck in his own curricle, while another lady is driving a chariot with an old gentleman inside and a servant on the roof.

In these days aeronauts are regarded as sportsmen of the most pronounced type, therefore it will not be out of place here to glance at Lunardi, who astonished the Londoners with his balloon in 1784. Vincenzo Lunardi (1759–1806) was a native of Lucca, and Secretary to the Neapolitan Ambassador to St. James'. He boasted that he was the first to make an aerial voyage from English ground, and he certainly has good claims to be regarded as a pioneer of aerostatics, since his first ascent from the grounds of the Hon. Artillery Company on September 15th, 1784, took place only a year later than the first flight of Pilâtre de Rozier, and a few days after that of John Tytler at Edinburgh. His balloon measured thirty feet in diameter, and was provided with a car, a parachute (to break the force of the fall in case of an explosion), and four wings or paddles with which he professed to be able to navigate it. It was filled with "rarefied air composed of zinc, oil of vitriol, and steel shavings," under the direction of Dr. Fordyce, the famous chemist. Lunardi made the ascent in the presence of nearly two hundred thousand spectators, including the Prince of Wales, Pitt, Fox, Sheridan, and Burke, while the King watched the balloon as it sailed over London through a telescope from a window in St. James'. The aeronaut, who took no companion with him except a cat, a dog, and some pigeons, remained in the air over three hours, reached at one time an alleged altitude of three miles (?), and safely alighted near Ware. He had intended, after circling the town, to work his way back to the Artillery grounds by means of his wings, but unfortunately one of these broke off early in the journey.

Lunardi afterwards wrote an account of his impressions in a series of letters to his guardian, and a couple of years later published a volume upon *Five Aerial Ascents* which he made in Scotland. For a few months he was the rage in London, where no one could think or speak of any topic but the " Flying Man," and his gaudily decorated balloon was exhibited at the Pantheon. A caricature, dated September 23rd, 1784 (Pl. CXXVI.), shows the first ascent of the aeronaut from the Artillery grounds, while in another (drawn by L. Byron and engraved by Valentine Green)[3] we see the airship as it appeared in the large room at the Pantheon.

---

[1] Presented by him to Horace Walpole.

[2] William Dickinson (1746–1823). Mezzotint engraver and print-seller. Engraved chiefly after Sir Joshua Reynolds.

[3] Valentine Green, F.R.S., F.S.A. (1739–1813). Mezzotint engraver. Keeper of the British Institution 1805–13. Published a large number of plates, and a *Review of the Polite Arts of France.*

The fickle public soon tired of this new toy, which, in its then state of development, could not be put to purposes either of use or pleasure, and by the autumn of 1786 the aeronaut seems to have fallen into neglect. His misfortunes are recorded by Rowlandson in *Aerostation out at Elbows; or, the Itinerant Aeronaut*, which shows poor Lunardi in rags, carrying the framework of his balloon over his shoulder (Pl. CXXVII.). The design is explained in the following lines :—

> "Behold a hero, comely, tall and fair !
> His only food is philogistic air.
> Now on the wings of mighty winds he rides,
> Now torn through hedges, dashed in ocean tides.
> Now drooping roams about from town to town,
> Collecting pence to inflate his poor Balloon.
> Pity the wight, and something to him give
> To purchase gas to keep his frame alive."[1]

In 1781 Bunbury produced a series of plates called *Hints to Bad Horsemen*, which seven years later were incorporated in his famous book, *The Academy for Grown Horsemen*, containing the Compleatest Instructions for Walking, Trotting, Cantering, Galloping, Stumbling, and Tumbling. Also the Annals of Horsemanship, Containing Accounts of Accidental Experiments and Experimental Accidents, Communicated by various Correspondents to the Author, Geoffrey Gambado, Esq., Riding Master, Master of the Horse, and Grand Equerry to the Doge of Venice. The designs to this edition, which is in quarto, are engraved by W. Dickinson,[2] but an octavo edition was published in 1798, and again in 1808, with coloured plates etched by Rowlandson.

"When," says the author in his preface, "I have told the Reader how to chase a horse, how to tackle him properly, in what sort of dress to ride him, how to mount and manage him, and, above all, how to ride him home again ; if he is not a complete horseman in the course of ten or twelve summers, I will be bold to foretell that neither the skill of Mr. Astley, nor the experience of Mr. John Gilpin will ever make him one."

The humour of the letterpress is somewhat too primitive for modern taste, the following specimen from " Directions for the Road " being rather above than below the general level of the work : " Take care never to throw your horse down, it is an unlucky trick, and fit only for boys. Many gentlemen of my acquaintance, and I too, have been thrown down by our horses ; yet I scarce know an instance on record of a gentleman throwing his horse down, but many have complained to me of their servants doing it for them." Fortunately the spirit has not evaporated from the designs in the course of a hundred years or so, and many of them may be found appropriate to the troubles of amateur horsemen in the present day. For example, in *How to make the most of a Horse*, we see a spirited animal being shown off by a

---

[1] Lunardi died in a convent at Lisbon in 1806.

[2] The plates reproduced are from Dickinson's engravings in the edition of 1788, which differ in some of the details from Rowlandson's etchings.

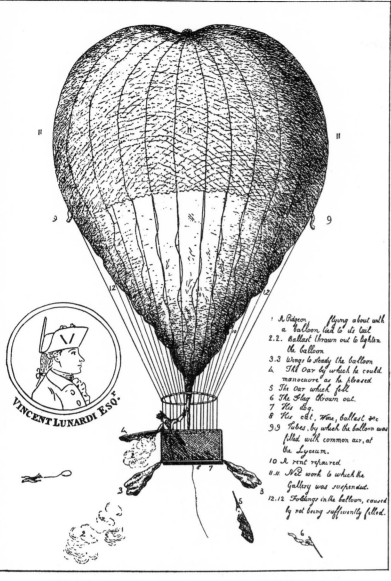

1. A Pidgeon flying about with a balloon tied to its tail
2.2. Ballast thrown out to lighten the balloon
3.3. Wings to steady the balloon
4. The Oar by which he could manœuvre as he pleased
5. The Oar which fell
6. The Flag thrown out.
7. His dog.
8. His cat, Wine, ballast &c
9.9. Tubes, by which the balloon was filled with common air, at the Lyceum.
10. A rent repaired
11.11. Net work to which the Gallery was suspended.
12.12. Foldings in the balloon, caused by not being sufficiently filled.

THE ENTERPRIZING LUNARDI'S GRAND AIR BALLON

WHICH TOOK ITS FLIGHT FROM THE ARTILLERY GROUND SEPT 15, 1784; AMIDST THE ACCLAMATIONS OF 300,000 SPECTATORS. THIS WONDERFUL MACHINE RAISED TO THE AMAZING HEIGHT OF NEAR THREE MILES, CONTINUED FLOATING ON THE AIR FOR NEAR THREE HOURS, AND THEN ALIGHTED ABOUT 5 MILES BEYOND WARE IN HERTFORDSHIRE, 26 MILES FROM LONDON

Pub by S. W. Fores, No 3 Piccadilly, Sept 23, 1784

[*Rowlandson*]

[1786]

AEROSTATION OUT AT ELBOWS
OR THE ITINERANT AERONANT

H. *Bunbury Esqr Delin*

HOW TO MAKE THE MOST OF A HORSE

London. Publish'd March 25, 1791 by W Dickinson, No 24, Old Bond Street

H. Bunbury Esqr Delin

HOW TO MAKE THE LEAST OF HIM

QUANTUM MUTATUS AB ILLO HECTORE

London, Publish'd March 25, 1791, by W. Dickinson, No 24, Old Bond Street

CXXXI

H. Bunbury Esq.r Delin

W. Dickinson Excudit

THE MISTAKEN NOTION

London, Publish'd June 25th 1787, by W. Dickinson Bond Street

CXXX

H. Bunbury Esq.r Delin

W. Dickinson Excudit

A BIT OF BLOOD

London, Publish'd Aug. 1st 1787, by W. Dickinson, Engraver & Printseller, No 158 Bond Street

dealer's man to an admiring customer (Pl. CXXVIII.); while *How to make the least of Him* is a representation of the same steed being feebly urged along by his inexperienced purchaser (Pl. CXXIX.). *A Bit of Blood, with no Flesh or Bone* (Pl. CXXX.) is the portrait of an Irishman on a weedy screw, and *The Mistaken Notion* is a study of a dandy who evidently has a " mistaken notion" of his own appearance on horseback (Pl. CXXXI.). Among the other plates, *How to be Run Away With, How to Lose your Way, How to Ride up Hyde Park, How to do Things by Halves,* and *How to Travel Upon Two Legs in a Frost,* are among the most effective, and sufficiently explain themselves without the aid of Mr. Gambado's letterpress, some portions of which are said to have been contributed by Captain Grose.

Before quitting the subject of Henry Bunbury's most popular production it will be desirable to give a brief account of the artist. The second son of the Rev. Sir Charles Bunbury, of Mildenhall, Suffolk, Henry was born in 1750. While still at the University he began to produce comic drawings and etchings of Cambridge scenes and personages, several of which were published, and during the grand tour which followed his college career he made many clever studies of the peasants and postillions whom he observed *en route.* In 1771 he was married to Catherine Horneck, Goldsmith's " Little Comedy." He was a great favourite in society, and though he never took his art very seriously, he exhibited occasionally at the Academy between 1780 and 1808. Among his best-known productions are *The Coffee-house Patriots, A Barber's Shop in Assize-time, A Windy Day in Hyde Park, Richmond Hill, A Country Club, A Long Story,* and *The Long Minuet.* Bunbury was appointed Equerry to the Duke of York, with whom he was a great favourite, in 1787, but upon the death of his wife in 1798 he retired to Keswick, where he died in 1811.

Genuine and spontaneous as was his talent, it is obvious that he was somewhat overrated by his contemporaries, a fact that was probably due to his personal charm. Walpole described him as a second Hogarth, and in 1781 acknowledges the gift of the drawing of *Richmond Hill* in a style of the most high-flown compliment. Again, we learn from a letter to Lady Ossory (1787) that he has lost no time in buying a print of *The Long Minuet,* and that he gets everything he can of Mr. Bunbury's. Garrick, who was another intimate friend, composed some lines called *The Old Painter's Soliloquy upon seeing Mr. Bunbury's Drawings,* from which the following stanzas may be quoted :—

> " Shall I so long, old Hayman said, and swore,
>   Of Painting till the barren soil ?
> While this young Bunbury, not twenty-four,
>   Gets fame for which in vain I toil.
> With Reynolds' grace and Hogarth's power
>   (Again he swore a dreadful oath)
> This boy had rather trot ten miles an hour
>   And risk his neck, than paint like both."

According to Malcolm, Bunbury was one of the few caricaturists who might look over a collection of his own works without experiencing a sensation of remorse, and his obituary notice in the *Gentleman's Magazine* describes a being almost too bright and good for this sinful world. Apart from his talent for humorous design, he is said to have been a good classical scholar and an excellent judge of poetry, while " his social and moral qualities, as long as any remain who shared his friendship, will continue the objects of fond admiration and regret. No ribaldry, no profaneness, no ill-natured censure, ever flowed from his lips, but his conversation abounded in humour and pleasantry : no one was ever in his company without being pleased with him ; none ever knew him without loving him. His feelings were the most benevolent, his affections the most delicate, his heart the most sincere," etc. etc. (Pl. CXXXII.).

A portrait with more shading has been drawn by Fanny Burney, to whom Bunbury was introduced at the Equerries' table at Windsor in 1787. There was nothing striking, she says, in his conversation, nothing bespeaking character or genius, and she continues, with evident misgiving : " So now we may all be caricatured at our leisure ! He is made another of the Equerries to the Duke. A man with such a turn, and with talents so inimitable in displaying it, was a rather dangerous character to be brought within a Court." Later she gives a long and interesting analysis of the character of Mr. Bunbury, who, she explains, " did not open upon me with that mildness and urbanity that might lead me to forget the strokes of his pencil and power of his caricature ; he early avowed a disposition to laugh at censure, or despise all around him. . . . Notwithstanding the general reverence I pay to extraordinary talents, Mr. Bunbury did not win my good will. His serious manner is superficial and haughty, and his easy conversation wants rectitude in its principles. For the rest, he is entertaining, gay, full of talk, sociable, willing to enjoy what is going forward, and ready to speak his opinion with perfect unreserve. Plays and players seem his darling theme ; he can rave about them from morning till night, and yet be ready to rave again when morning returns. . . . This, however, is not his only subject, love and romance are equally dear to his discourse, though they cannot be introduced with equal frequency. Upon these topics he loses himself wholly—he runs into rhapsodies that discredit him as a father, a husband, and a moral man. He asserts that love is the first principle of life, and should take place of every other ; holds all bonds and obligations as nugatory that would claim a preference ; and advances such doctrines of exalted sensations in the tender passion as made me tremble when I heard them. He adores Werter,[1] and would scarce believe I had not read it, still less that I had begun it, and left it off, from distaste at its evident tendency. I saw myself sink instantly in his estimation, though till this little avowal I had appeared to stand in it very honourably."

---

[1] The publication of *The Sorrows of Werter* in English had made a literary sensation a couple of years previously, and in 1786 Bunbury's friend Rowlandson had etched some satirical illustrations to the story from the designs of Collings.

Laurence pinx^t   Ryder sculp^t

HENRY BUNBURY ESQ^R

MLLE LA CHEVALIÈRE D'EON DE BEAUMONT

FENCING AT CARLTON HOUSE, 9TH APRIL, 1787

PARODY OF L'ECOLE DES ARMES

May 1, 1773

J. Gillray del et fec.

*Pub. April 24th by J. Lewis & Sold by
J. Aitken, Castle Street, Leicester Field
Price 3|*

MENDOZA

[1788]

SPORT AND GAMES

Both Rowlandson and Gillray, owing to their friendship with the famous fencing-masters, Domenico Angelo[1] and his son Harry, executed a number of subjects connected with the science of tierce and quarte. Rowlandson made several drawings, and also engraved a series of plates for the younger Angelo, but most of these were destroyed when the Opera House was burnt down in 1789, Angelo having stored them in a room which he rented over the pit entrance. To go back a little in point of date, a clever caricature was published anonymously in 1772, ostensibly intended as a parody of the illustrations to Angelo's famous work, *L'École des Armes* (Pl. CXXXIV.). A coloured man is represented in the act of fencing with a tall masculine-looking woman, whose features are concealed by a mask. The story of this design is told at length in Harry Angelo's *Reminiscences*.

The Duchess of Queensberry (Prior's Kitty) having adopted a little negro boy, educated and made a pet of him instead of keeping him in his proper place as a page. Soubise, as he was called, was allowed to attend Angelo's *manège* in Soho, and being quick and clever, he soon became an accomplished rider as well as a brilliant fencer. Nor did his talents end here, for he sang and danced well, composed sonnets, and earned the reputation of a gay Lothario. To humble his pride the Duchess articled him to the elder Angelo, but without the desired effect. Soubise continued to play the part of a young man of fashion, ran up long bills with tailors and liverymen, which the Duchess paid, and drove down to Eton, where he gave lessons at the College, in a chaise and four, with a *chère amie* at his side. Gainsborough and Zoffany painted his portrait, while the elder Sheridan taught him elocution, and declared that he was the best-behaved minion of the great he had ever known. At length, however, his excesses lost him his situation, and by Angelo's advice the dusky Cherubino was sent out to India. He established a successful *manège* at Bengal; but his career was brought to a premature conclusion by a vicious Arab steed. The caricature, above described, represents Soubise fencing with his eccentric patroness, the Duchess of Queensberry.

Fencing matches were frequently held at Carlton House, and in 1787 Gillray produced a sketch of one of these encounters, in which the combatants are the Chevalier D'Eon (after he had adopted feminine costume) and that famous swordsman the Chevalier St. George, among the spectators being the Prince of Wales and Mrs. Fitzherbert (Pl. CXXXIII.).[2] A year later Rowlandson issued a plate called *A Fencing Match*, which represents a scene at Angelo's saloon. But it is by no means an attractive example of the artist's work, the persons portrayed being nearly all of advanced age and repulsive appearance. The prize-ring also came in for a share of attention, especially during the period that it was patronised by the Prince of

[1] Domenico Angelo (1716–1802). Italian fencing-master. He came to London about 1755, and opened a school of arms and *manège* in Soho Square, which soon became fashionable. In 1763 he published his splendidly illustrated *Ecole des Armes*. His son Henry (1760–*c.* 1839) succeeded to his business, and published his *Reminiscences* about 1830. The two Angelos were intimate with most of the artistic celebrities of their period.

[2] In the engraving reproduced the Chevalier St. George does not appear. It was probably one of several similar subjects etched by Gillray.

Wales.[1] Gillray etched a large portrait of the champion bruiser Mendoza[2] (1788) standing on a platform in a fighting attitude (Pl. CXXXV.), and also a plate called *Foul; or, Humphreys and Johnson a Match for Mendoza*, into which the portraits of several sporting celebrities are introduced.

About the same period a couple of etchings, *The Royal Academy* and the *Royal Society*, were published by Austin, a minor caricaturist, who by his devotion to Fox had earned the name of "Fox's Fool." The first is a representation of the Prince of Wales taking his first lesson in the noble art of self-defence at a boxing academy kept by an instructor named Martin (Pl. CXXXVI.). The second shows the Prince at a banquet, urging his guests to drink, the only idea, according to the satirist, of a Royal Society. In 1789 an anonymous caricature appeared under the title of *St. George and the Dragon, and Mademoiselle riposting* (Pl. CXXXVII.). Here we have the Prince again, bitterly complaining because Mademoiselle D'Eon has landed him "one in the eye," while his friend, Colonel Hanger, has been beaten in a fencing bout by the Chevalier St. George. A printed notice states that "Gentlemen and Ladies are taught the polite arts of boxing and dancing."

That Amazons were not wanting in contemporary society may be gathered from a paragraph in a daily paper, the writer of which expresses a hope that "the popular dramatist [Sheridan?] in his rage for hunting down the follies of the day, will not forget to be *in* at the *death* of our masculine women of fashion. Their hunting, shooting, drawing, driving, cricketing, faroing, and skating, present a monstrous chaos of absurdity."

Racing subjects are fairly well represented about this period. Rowlandson is to the fore with an etching called *Going to the Races* (Pl. CXXXIX.), and two series, the one called the *High-mettled Racer*, showing the gradual descent of a thoroughbred from being the pride of the training stable to his death between the shafts of a cart (Pl. CXXXVIII.), and the other consisting of four plates entitled respectively *The Start, The Betting-post, The Course*, and *The Mount*, wherein figure various well-known "horsy" characters, including Colonel O'Kelly, the fortunate owner of Eclipse. For November, 1791, we have a pair of racing satires, also by Rowlandson, called *How to Escape Winning* and *How to Escape Losing*, which deal with an old sporting scandal. At one of the Newmarket events this autumn, it was popularly supposed that the Prince of Wales' horse Escape was "pulled" by his jockey Chiffney,[3] and there were some who did not scruple to hint that Chiffney was only acting under orders. On November 6th the Prince wrote to Sir Charles Bunbury (brother of the caricaturist), one of the stewards of the Jockey Club, to protest against "the infamous and rascally lies fabricated relative to the affair that happened at

---

[1] The death of a prize-fighter in the ring disgusted the Prince with this form of sport, and he never afterwards attended a sparring match.

[2] Daniel Mendoza (1764–1836). A distinguished pugilist, who retired from the ring in 1820. He published *The Art of Boxing* in 1789.

[3] Samuel Chiffney the elder (*c.* 1753–1807). Well-known jockey and trainer. He won the Derby in 1789. It is doubtful whether he or his royal employer was to blame for what looked like dishonest riding in 1790. He published his *Autobiography* in 1795.

THE ROYAL ACADEMY

Published 13th April 1786, by S. W. Fores, at the Caricature Warehouse, No 3 Piccadilly

London. Pubd Oct 12, 1789, by S. Fores, No 3, Piccadilly

ST GEORGE & THE DRAGON & MADLLE RIPOSTING

[*Rowlandson*

[1789]

THE HIGH METTLED RACER

[*Rowlandson*]

GOING TO THE RACES

CXL

[*Rowlandson*]

[*Nov.* 22 1791]

HOW TO ESCAPE WINNING

By the la' Harry
This shall not go for Nothing

J. Kay

COCK OF THE GREEN

Engraved from an Original Drawing

by H. Bunbury Esq

PATIENCE IN A PUNT

London, Publish'd May 1st 1792, by W Dickinson, Engraver & Printseller, No 24, Old Bond Street

Publ.sh'd Apri. 8th 1800 by H. Humphrey, No. 27, S James's Street

B.

J.s Gy fect

HOUNDS THROWING OFF

Published April 8th 1800 by H. Humphrey, 27, St James's Street

B

J.s Gy fect

COMING IN AT THE DEATH

London. Publish'd November 12th 1800, by——
I. C. Esqr delt

H. Humphrey, 27, St James's Street
Js Gy fect

COCKNEY SPORTSMEN RECHARGING

Publish'd November 12th 1800
by H. Humphrey, 27, St James's Street
London

I. C. Esqr delt

Js Gy fecit

COCKNEY SPORTSMEN FINDING A HARE

Newmarket, by republican scribblers, and studiously circulated through the country." He judges it necessary that these calumnies should be contradicted, but leaves the method of contradiction to be arranged by Bunbury and Sheridan.

In the first of Rowlandson's plates Chiffney is portrayed in the act of pulling his mount, while Escape makes gallant efforts to struggle to the front (Pl. CXL). The horse's near fore-leg is fastened to his off hind-leg with the Prince's Order of the Garter, on which the motto "Honi soit qui mal y pense" is visible. In the foreground stands a sportsman, intended either for the owner or trainer, with his finger to his nose, and a self-congratulatory expression on his face. In the second plate the race still continues, and Escape is leading, the garter being broken, but heavy weights are slung over the jockey's shoulders and round the horse's neck, and the personage in the foreground maintains his attitude of complacency.

The royal and ancient game of golf, though it had scarcely yet become nationalised in England, was being played with all due diligence north of the Tweed. Among the etchings of John Kay, the Edinburgh caricaturist, of whom more hereafter, is a small sketch called *Cock o' the Green*, which represents Alex. McKellar, a famous player, preparing for a drive (Pl. CXLI.). "By the la' Harry," says the champion, "this shall not go for nothing," and the spectator feels assured that his is no vain boast.

After a passing glance at Bunbury's capital satire on amateur fishermen, *Patience in a Punt* (Pl. CXLII.), we may conclude this section with an examination of some sporting prints engraved by Gillray, from the designs of an anonymous amateur, in the year 1800. The first series consists of four plates, entitled respectively, *Hounds Finding*, i.e. "finding" some provisions in the pocket of a fallen rider; *Hounds in Full Cry*, a horseman being run away with through the midst of the pack, which is in "full cry" owing to the injuries received from the horse's hoofs; *Hounds Throwing Off* (Pl. CXLIII.), three horses, excited by the hounds, have "thrown off" their riders; and *Coming in at the Death*, two horsemen taking a blind leap, and landing in a deep pool (Pl. CXLIV.).

The second series, published on November 12th of this year, deals with the adventures of two City sportsmen, out for a day's sport in Hornsey Wood with their dogs, a poodle and a mongrel spaniel. The first plate is called *Cockney Sportsmen Marking Game*. One of the sportsmen has discovered a "covey" of crows hovering over a dead horse, and in his excitement nearly brings down his comrade by the accidental discharge of his gun. In *Shooting Flying*, the same impulsive youth is firing (without effect) at a flock of pigeons while jumping over a stile. In *Recharging*, the elder sportsman is recharging himself with a hearty lunch, while the younger, who has bagged a cock, has reloaded his piece in very amateurish fashion (Pl. CXLV.). In *Cockney Sportsmen Finding a Hare*, we see the two citizens stealing towards poor Puss, who is lying in some furze, with the obvious intention of catching her with their hats! (Pl. CXLVI.).

87

POPULAR DELUSIONS AND IMPOSTURES

PART I

AMONG the social crazes of the eighteenth century which have afforded material for the pencil and the graver of the satirist, the South Sea Bubble stands forth pre-eminent, but as a whole library of books and pamphlets has arisen round this fruitful subject, it will only now be necessary to consider the effect of this sudden outbreak of Stock Exchange mania upon contemporary art and contemporary society. France, it will be remembered, set the Bubble fashion, dazzled by the Aladdin-like abilities of that enterprising Scotchman, John Law,[1] of Lauriston. Law obtained the monopoly of the Mississippi trade for a company which volunteered to take over the national debt, and relieve the Government from the bankruptcy with which it was threatened. This was in 1717, and the company prospered until 1719, when its operations were largely extended, and the stock rapidly increased in value. The Government was rescued from its embarrassments, undreamed-of fortunes glittered before the eyes of speculators, and John Law, the creator of this new Tom Tiddler's Ground, was appointed Controller-General of the Finance of France.

Meanwhile England looked on with an envious eye at her neighbour's good fortune, and English speculators, with friends in Paris, contrived to pull a few plums out of this apparently inexhaustible pie. Mrs. Howard (afterwards Lady Suffolk), bed-chamber woman to the Princess of Wales and mistress of the Prince, received "tips" from Lord Islay (afterwards Duke of Argyll), who was then in Paris. Writing in September, 1719, when the Mississippi Company seemed to be at the height of its prosperity, he says, " I have laid out the money you bade me. It is very difficult in a letter to give you an idea of the funds of this country; but in fact everybody has made estates that has been concerned in them four or five months. As a little instance, Cousin Jack has got near £10,000, and has lost near the half of that sum by a timourous silly bargain he made."

The stocks were then at 950, and Lord Islay assured his correspondent

---

[1] John Law, of Lauriston (1671–1729). He killed a man in a duel in 1694, and being sentenced to death, escaped to France, where he founded the Banque Générale in 1716. On the failure of the Mississippi scheme he fled to Italy, and died at Venice.

that they were likely soon to reach 1,500, and that " her master " might in a few months make himself richer than "*his* master." This was probably intended to reach the ear of the Prince of Wales, who, if rumour may be believed, was not slow to act upon the advice. In January, 1720, Mrs. Howard's amateur stock-broker tells her that her money matters go very well, though the shares have fallen from 1,900 to 1,750. This he attributes to the fact that a number of speculators were selling in order to buy a new issue. However, the fall of Mississippi stock continued, and Law gradually lost his hold upon the credulous multitudes, though supported by the Regent to the last.

Towards the close of 1719 an imitation of the Mississippi scheme was started in England in connection with the South Sea Company, which had been in existence since 1711. The projectors of the new monopoly proposed to take over the government loans and public annuities, which were to be made part of the capital stock of the company, whereby, it was alleged, the national debt would be reduced and public credit restored. The scheme received the enthusiastic support of Aislabie, Chancellor of the Exchequer, Lord Sunderland, Sir John Barnard, and other members of the Tory party. Walpole, then out of office, opposed the measure, and issued a warning pamphlet against it, but to no effect. The South Sea Bill was carried, the bubble was blown, and in the eyes of the people it appeared in the likeness of a sphere of gold.

Some of the most curious illustrations of the social aspect of the South Sea Bubble are to be found in the correspondence of Pope and his friends. As early as 1716 the poet had bought South Sea stock for himself and Martha Blount,[1] and the pair had further speculated in lottery tickets, which then bore interest, payable in annuities. In March, 1720, he writes to Miss Blount that " he has borrowed money on their lottery orders in order to buy more stock at 180, and that the shares had since risen to 184." Later in the month he wrote to his friend, James Eckershall, who seems to have acted as his agent :—

" I daily hear such reports of advantages to be gained by one project or another in the Stocks that my spirit is up with double zeal in the desires of our trying to enrich ourselves. . . . To be serious, I hope you have sold the lottery orders, that the want of ready money may be no longer an impediment to our buying in the Stock which was very lucky at that time. I hear the South Sea fell since, and should be glad we were in. . . . Let but fortune favour us, and the world will be sure to admire our prudence. If we fail, let's e'en keep the mishap to ourselves. But 'tis ignominious (in this age of hope and golden mountains) not to venture."

Mrs. Howard was again in the movement, with a royal purse to back

---

[1] Martha Blount (1690–1762). Famous for her friendship with Pope, who dedicated to her his *Epistle on Women*, and left her part of his fortune.

her, and received many congratulations from her friends upon her splendid prospects. One correspondent, Mrs. Molesworth, probably expresses the emotions of a numerous class when she declares that she is " South-sea mad," and finds that the philosophic temper of mind which made her content with her circumstances, when there seemed no possibility of bettering them, forsakes her on this occasion, and she cannot help bitterly regretting that for want of a little money she is forced to let slip an opportunity which is never likely to occur again. Lady Mary Wortley Montagu dabbled in speculation as she dabbled in literature and gallantry, and as usual burnt her fingers. Pope, with whom she was still on friendly terms, was employed to buy stock for her, and in May he wrote to an inquiring friend :—

" The question you ask about the fair ladies' gains and my own is not easily answered. There is no gain till the stock is sold, which neither theirs nor mine is. So that, instead of wallowing in money, we never wanted more for the uses of life, which is a pretty general case with most of the adventurers. . . . One day we were worth two or three thousand, and the next day not above three parts of the sum. For my own particular, I have very little in ; the ladies are much richer than I, but how rich, as you see, there is no telling by any rule of arithmetic."

Meanwhile a multitude of parasite companies had sprung into being, in defiance of the proclamation against all such unlicensed schemes. Change Alley had become the centre of fashion, and speculation the absorbing occupation of all classes. By the month of June there were a hundred and four bubble companies in existence, and the shares of all were at a fancy premium. Some few of these schemes were founded on ideas of practical utility, such as the companies formed for making china in England (the earliest proposal for such a manufacture), for developing the national fisheries, for cleansing and paving the streets, and for supplying water to certain parts of the metropolis. The majority, however, were mere " wild cat " projects, such as those promoted for discovering the secret of perpetual motion, casting nativities and insuring against divorce, or for extracting butter from beech-nuts, silver from lead, and oil from poppies. The shares of all, good, bad, and indifferent, were eagerly snapped up by the public, whose appetite for speculation only grew by what it fed on.

The few voices that were raised in warning and protest against this madness which had overtaken an entire nation were drowned in the jingle of gold and the din of Change Alley. In May, Steele was pointing out the true nature of the gamble in his paper, *The Theatre*, while Swift, more keen-sighted than Pope, compared Change Alley to a gulf in the South Sea, since

"Subscribers here by thousands float,
And jostle one another down,
Each paddling in his leaky boat,
And here they fish for gold and drown."

[1720]

THE BUBBLERS BUBBL'D
OR
THE DEVIL TAKE THE HINDMOST

[1720]

THE BUBBLER'S MEDLEY. OR A SKETCH OF THE TIMES

In Paris, John Law had nearly reached the end of his tether, being mobbed by the populace in the month of June, when English statesmen were still congratulating themselves upon their successful adaptation of his financial methods. In France and Holland the caricaturists were hard at work upon satires which were to make Europe merry over the Bubblers' follies. The earliest caricature on this subject that appeared in England is said to have been *The Bubblers Bubbled; or, Devil take the Hindmost*, which was advertised in *The Post-boy* for June 21st, 1720 (Pl. CXLVII.). This was a copy of a Dutch print dealing with the Mississippi scheme, but the inscriptions are printed in English. It represents a building, evidently intended for a Stock Exchange, the keeper of which points to a long list of bubble companies, while various speculators comment on their good or evil fortune. "I have got £4,000 out of nothing," says one; "A gaol must be my portion," wails another; "I live in hopes," declares a third; while a fourth observes, "I have lost a thousand pounds this day." Beneath the design are printed some warning verses in the usual doggerel, of which the following is a fair specimen :—

> "Our Trade we shun, to South we run,
> We bubble and are Bubbles.
> In stock we're rich, by stock undone,
> O Britain ! mourn thy troubles."

But the public was suffering from too sharp an attack of speculation mania to heed either satire or warning. "The London language and conversation is, I find, quite changed since I left it, though it is not above three or four months ago," writes Mr. Robert Digby to Pope on July 9th; "I am pleased with the thoughts of seeing nothing but a general good-humour when I come to town; I rejoice in the universal riches I hear of, in the thought of their having this effect. They tell me you was soon content; and that you cared not for such an increase as others wished for you. By this account I judge you the richest man in the South Sea, and I congratulate you accordingly."

On August 7th the South Sea stock touched its highest point, 950, the rise being the result, it was said, of artificial engines and secret springs; but by the middle of the month the fall had begun, a mere accidental fluctuation as it was supposed. The company, however, had already taken the first step towards its own ruin by the issue of writs of *scire facias* against the numerous unauthorised enterprises. The pricking of these lesser bubbles seems to have opened the eyes of the public to the airy composition of the parent company, since by the end of September South Sea stock had fallen to 175, and ruin was widespread. Some great fortunes had been made, but the losers were innumerable, and drawn from nearly all classes of society.

Though it was commonly reported that Pope had lost the profits on his translation of Homer, he put a good face on the matter when writing to his friends, more especially to Atterbury, who appears to have foreseen disaster.

"I have some cause since I last waited on you at Bromley," he writes on September 23rd, "to look upon you as a prophet in that retreat, from whom oracles are to be had, were mankind wise enough to go thither to consult you. The fate of the South Sea scheme has, much sooner than I expected, verified what you told me. Most people thought the time would come, but no man prepared for it. . . . As for the few who have the good fortune to remain with half of what they imagined they had (among whom is your humble servant), I would have them sensible of their felicity. . . . Indeed, the universal poverty, which is the consequence of universal avarice, and which will fall hardest on the guiltless and industrious part of mankind, is truly lamentable. The universal deluge of the South Sea, contrary to the old deluge, has drowned all but a few *unrighteous* men ; but it is some comfort to me that I am not one of them, even though I were to survive and rule the world by it. I am much pleased with a thought of Dr. Arbuthnot's ; he says the Government and South Sea Company have only locked up the money of the people, upon conviction of their lunacy (as is usual in the case of lunatics), and intend to restore them as much as may be fit for such people, as fast as they shall see them return to their senses."

With the bursting of the Bubble came a whole flood of satires in every form, ballads, pamphlets, and caricatures. One of the most admired of the emblematical prints on this subject was an English adaptation of Picart's,[1] *A Monument of Folly*, dedicated to Posterity in commemoration of ye incredible Folly transacted in the year 1720. Here we see Folly in her triumphal chariot, drawn by six emblematical figures, bearing the titles respectively of South Sea, Mississippi, West (India Company) Bank, Assurance, and India (East India Company). On the wheels are inscribed some of the most popular and absurd of the bubble schemes. The chariot is being dragged through an open space intended for Change Alley in the English version, and for the Rue Quinquempoix (the scene of Law's operations) in the French and Dutch versions. The Devil riding on a cloud blows bubbles, while Fortune scatters the shares of companies on the speculators who are grouped outside the Stock Exchange. An explanation of the symbolical figures is appended to the design, though it is stated that "those who will give themselves the trouble of examining the print may discover many things which are not here explained, that the curious may have room to guess at."

A popular form of caricature at this period was the *Bubbler's Medley*, a representation of a number of prints which seem to be thrown one on the top of another. One of these, dated August 10th, 1720, shows a considerable variety of subjects, such as a view of Change Alley with groups of financiers, a party of stock-broking ladies, a speculator

[1] This was Bernard, son of Etienne Picart, called Le Romain. Bernard, who was born in Paris in 1673, settled at Amsterdam in 1710, where he died in 1733. He was a prolific engraver, producing portraits, book-illustrations, and a few more important original designs.

laughing at an ass eating thistles, a couple of beggars mounted on horseback, an unlucky investor in prison begging for alms through the bars, and a number of persons trying to climb up a tree, from which some of them fall off into the water, *i.e.* the South Sea. Among the sets of verses inscribed beneath the various prints is *A South Sea Ballad*, which is said to have been publicly hawked in Change Alley, much to the annoyance of the speculators whose folly it satirised (Pl. CXLVIII.).

The public consequences of the bursting of the Bubble are a matter of common knowledge—the flight of Robert Knight, the cashier of the South Sea Company, to the Continent, the disgrace of Aislabie,[1] the removal of the directors from all public offices, the appointment of a committee to inquire into the whole matter, and finally the break-up of the Government. After the catastrophe every wiseacre was ready to echo the opinion of Atterbury, that "had the project taken root and flourished, it would by degrees have overturned our constitution. Three or four hundred millions was such a weight that whichsoever way it had leaned, it must have borne down all before it."

It would scarcely have been surprising if such widespread disaster had led to serious public disturbances, even to revolution, but the fairy gold seems to have melted away with less confusion than might have been expected. Pope, as we have seen, declared that he was unhurt by "these times or fates," and his friends the Miss Blounts were gainers in a small way. Lady Mary Wortley Montagu, however, suffered serious losses, and was terribly worried by the demands of a French admirer, M. Rémond—a ridiculous little man, according to St. Simon—who had placed a considerable sum in her hands for investment. When the crash came he demanded the whole back, and threatened to send her rather indiscreet correspondence to her husband. Years afterwards Horace Walpole, commenting on the affair in his usual pleasant style, declared that Lady Mary had cheated her lover out of £5,000.

Poor Gay, who had invested £1,000, raised by a subscription volume of poems, in South Sea stock, at one time found himself master of £20,000—on paper. His friends begged him to sell out at least as much as would secure him a clean shirt and a shoulder of mutton a day for the rest of his life. But he held on to the last, and lost his whole fortune. For a time the calamity so preyed upon him that his life became in danger. He seems to have recovered his spirits, however, before he wrote the *Epistle to Mr. Snow*, in which he ridicules his folly and thus apostrophises his friend :—

> "Oh thou whose penetrative wisdom found
> The South Sea rocks and shelves where thousands drowned,
> When credit sunk, and commerce gasping lay,
> Thou stoodst, nor sent unpaid one bill away.

. . . . . .

---

[1] John Aislabie (1670–1742). He was Chancellor of the Exchequer from 1714 to 1718, but was expelled from the House in 1721.

Why did Change Alley waste thy precious hours
Among the fools who gaped for golden showers?
No wonder if we found some poets there,
Who live on fancy, and can feed on air ;
No wonder they were caught by South Sea schemes,
Who ne'er enjoyed a guinea but in dreams :
No wonder that their third subscriptions sold
For millions of imaginary gold."

We hear but little of those lucky or prudent investors who retired at the psychological moment, but there are occasional allusions to those who had held what Pope called "the true and important doctrine of selling out" in contemporary literature. Macky, writing c. 1724, observes that Caen Wood, formerly a seat of the Duke of Argyll's, "now belongs to one Dale, an upholster, who bought it out of the Bubbles." Again, speaking of the towns in the neighbourhood of London, he declares that these are prodigiously improved since the South Sea scheme. "Chelsea, by its new Buildings fronting the River, is more like a City than a Village." A mezzotint entitled *The Bubbler's Mirror; or, England's Folly (Joy)*, shows a lucky speculator holding up a full purse, the result of a fortunate investment realised in the nick of time (Pl. CXLIX.). A companion print with the same title, except that the word "Joy" is changed to "Grief," represents a gentleman with a lugubrious countenance, who is holding up an empty purse (Pl. CL.). Both figures are surrounded by emblematical designs and scrolls inscribed with the titles of the bubble companies, and the highest prices at which the shares of each were sold.

The Prince of Wales, the King's mistresses, and other distinguished persons being involved in the Bubble speculations, there were difficulties in the way of a full investigation, and it was found impossible to bring the South Sea directors or the absconding cashier to justice. Knight having fled to Antwerp, the Brabanters refused to deliver him up, and it was generally believed that the Duchess of Kendal and Countess Platen had been bribed to protect him, for though a reward of £2,000 had been offered for his apprehension, the British authorities did not seem particularly anxious to have him back. In the spring of 1721, when the public was still smarting from its losses, a number of prints were published dealing with the case of Knight, and the inquisition into the responsibilities of the directors. One of these, *The Brabant Skreen*, shows the interior of a large room, with a high screen extending about half-way across the floor. Behind the screen, but reflected in a mirror, are three gentlemen, probably intended for directors, one of whom is engaged in writing. On the left stands the absconding cashier, ready dressed for a journey, and evidently in a state of alarm and agitation. He is receiving a letter from a lady, who may be intended for Mrs. Howard, or for another royal favourite. On the screen hang a number of pictures, representing, among other subjects, Knight showing a list of sums paid for secret services ; Great Britain and Ireland swamped in the South Sea ; adventurers tearing the same countries to pieces, and a gallows

94

[1720]

Printed for Carington Bowles next
y^e Chapter House, St Paul's Churchyard. London.

THE BUBLERS MIRROUR, OR ENGLANDS FOLLEY

(GRIEF)

Printed for Carington Bowles, next y^e Chapter House
in St Paul's Churchyard. London

[1720]

THE BUBLERS MIRROUR, OR ENGLANDS FOLLEY

(JOY)

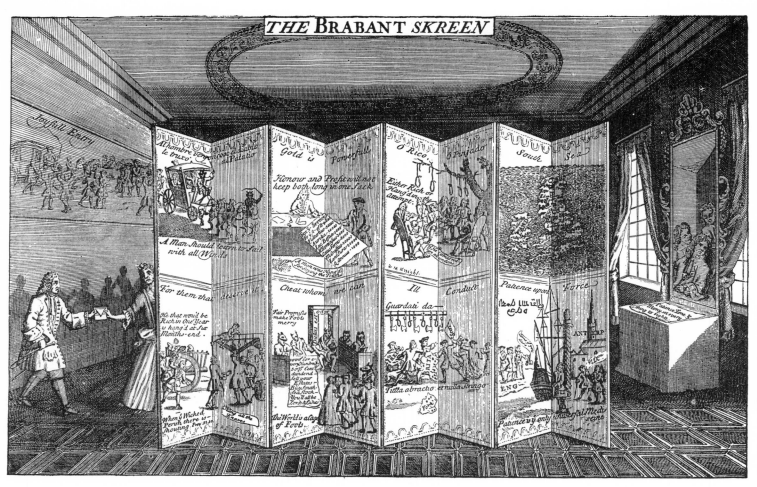

[Ap 29, 1721]

THE BRABANT SKREEN

[1721]

A SATIRE ON THE SOUTH SEA COMPANY

and cart with culprits (Pl. CLI.). In the verses engraved below the design, "Great George" is implored to assist in procuring justice, and to

"Let no cursed Traitor, tho' of high Degree,
Eclipse the Beams of Sacred Majesty !
Throughout ye Realm our loud Complaints are sent,
Oh King and Father ! All our griefs prevent !"

One of the most remarkable results of the whole Bubble agitation was the stimulus given by a subject so fertile and so general in its appeal to the art of pictorial satire. No longer content to imitate or adapt Dutch designs, the English artist-engraver was beginning to use his own imagination and to produce original designs, suggested by the events, social or political, of his day. William Hogarth, then (1721) just four and twenty, and at the end of his 'prentice years, was inspired by the South Sea troubles to put forth a rather ambitious emblematical engraving. This is not, it must be confessed, a very successful production, its chief interest lying in the fact that the great original artist of the future is to be seen still in leading-strings, still under the influence of that contemporary taste for confused symbolism which he was to do so much to reform.

This design, which was sold at a shilling, shows a roundabout worked by South Sea directors, whereon a number of typical personages are whirling round (Pl. CLII.). In the background is the London Monument, on the pedestal of which is inscribed, "This Monument was erected in Memory of the Destruction of this City by the South Sea in 1720." The Devil standing behind a counter cuts slices from a figure of Fortune and tosses them to the crowd. Self-interest is breaking Honesty upon the wheel, and a Villain is flogging Honour. Among the bystanders is a small, thin man, with his hand in the pocket of another, the thief being intended, it is said, for Pope, against whom Hogarth seems to have nourished some grudge, though the poet wisely refrained from satirising so dangerous an opponent. A number of women, among whom may be discovered the old maid afterwards introduced into the plate called *Morning*, are rushing into a building, over the door of which is written, "Raffling for Husbands with Lottery fortunes in here." It is probable that this idea was borrowed by Hogarth from a print which illustrated a skit entitled *A Good Husband for 5s. ; or, Esquire Bickerstaff's Lottery for London Ladies*, published in 1710. In this the author proposes that all ladies who have lost their husbands in the war on the Continent shall become candidates for fifty-five prizes, composed of highly respectable public characters, a selection of which are humorously described.

POPULAR DELUSIONS AND IMPOSTURES

PART II

APART from the Bubble mania there are some half-dozen examples of popular insanity which deserve a word of notice, if only because they afforded such excellent material to the industrious caricaturist. These are the hoax of the Bottle Conjurer, the Earthquake panics of 1750, the case of Elizabeth Canning, the Cock Lane Ghost, and—it must be added—the ever-recurring State Lotteries. Taking the last first, we find that the lotteries in the early part of the century were arranged somewhat on the same plan as the issue of government bonds at the present day. For example, in 1710 a loan of £500,000 was negotiated by means of a lottery. The tickets cost £10 apiece, holders of blanks being entitled to annuities of 14s. a year for a period of thirty-two years, holders of prizes to annuities varying from £5 to £1,000 for the same period.

Private lotteries were forbidden, but the Government when in straits, which happened on an average about two years out of three, resorted to this method of raising money, which was at least more amusing to its victims than the levy of income tax. This point of view is ironically considered by Steele, who in January, 1710, saw crowds on their way to the Bank, struggling who should first get their money into the newly erected lottery. " It gave me a great notion of the credit of our present government and administration," he writes, " to find people press as eagerly to pay money as they would to receive it ; and at the same time a due respect for that body of men who have found out so pleasing an expedient for carrying on the common cause, that they have turned a tax into a diversion. The cheerfulness of spirit and the hopes of success which this project has occasioned in the great city lighten the burden of the war."

In 1721 Hogarth published as a companion subject to his *South Sea Scheme*, a plate in the same style called *The Lottery* (Pl. CLIII.). Here we have no actual portrayal of a contemporary lottery being drawn by real men and women, but, which is far less interesting, a representation of Fortune drawing the blanks and prizes from one lottery wheel, while Wantonnesse draws the numbers from another, and various other symbolical figures are appropriately engaged. For example, National Credit is leaning on a pillar supported by

Justice, Suspense is turned to and fro by Hope and Fear, Misfortune is oppressed by Grief, Fraud is tempting Despair with money, and Good Luck is seized on the one hand by Pleasure and Folly, while on the other Fame persuades him to raise sinking Virtue and the Arts. The only realistic details are the lottery wheels, which are of the same pattern as those represented in engravings forty or fifty years later.

An interesting and important lottery, representations of which have come down to us, was that by which money was raised for the building of Westminster Bridge in 1739-40. A print engraved by B. Roberts, called the *State Lottery*, gives the interior of the hall in which the tickets are being drawn. On a raised platform is a table at which sit the Lottery Commissioners, and at each end is a lottery wheel from which the Bluecoat boys, who were always employed for this purpose, draw the numbers. To prevent cheating, each boy was obliged to have his coat closely buttoned and his pockets sewn up, and to hold one hand behind him, while he handed the tickets to a gentleman stationed by him. In spite of these precautions, a boy, bribed by speculators, sometimes contrived to draw two numbers at a time, and conceal one about his person. One case was made public in which a man had got possession of one of these numbers, and insured it no less than seventy-nine times in the course of one day.

Although the lotteries were not invariably a success, the Government on one occasion losing £7,000 by their venture, ministers resorted to them in time of financial stress throughout the greater part of the century. In 1763, Lord Bute's finance minister, Sir Francis Dashwood,[1] produced a budget which included a scheme for two lotteries to be drawn in May and December. On this occasion, in consequence of the frauds that had been practised in connection with former lotteries, the wheels were escorted from Whitehall to the Guildhall by a detachment of the Horseguards. The Bluecoat boys were still employed to draw the numbers, but this practice was denounced in the Press, and the scheme generally seems to have met with little approval from the better part of the public, a fact which may have been partly due to the unpopularity of Lord Bute's ministry. It was on this occasion that Horace Walpole was among the prize winners. "T'other day, coming from my Lady Townshend's," he writes to Lord Hertford on December 29th, "it came into my head to stop at one of the lottery offices to inquire after a single ticket I had had, expecting to find it was a blank, but it was £500. Thank you! I know you wish me joy. It will buy twenty pretty things when I come to Paris."

A contemporary etching shows the interior of the Guildhall while this lottery was being drawn, with the Lottery Commissioners and the Bluecoat boys on a platform, and the ticket-holders and spectators grouped on the floor of the hall eagerly awaiting each turn of the wheel. It was on this, or a similar occasion, that a lady, having bought a ticket, desired the

---

[1] Afterwards Baron Le Despencer (1708–81). He is best known as the founder of the Hell-fire Club at Medmenham Abbey, but he was Chancellor of the Exchequer 1762–3.

prayers of the congregation at her parish church " for the success of a person engaged in a new undertaking " !

In the year 1749 the public fell a victim to an absurd hoax played off upon it by a person calling himself the " Bottle Conjurer." Early in January advertisements appeared in the papers to the effect that on the evening of January 16th, a gentleman would appear at the Haymarket Theatre who would play on a common walking-stick the music of every instrument to surprising perfection ; that he would get into a tavern quart bottle, and while there sing several songs, and allow any spectator to handle the bottle ; lastly, that in a private room he would produce the representation of any dead person, with which the " party " requesting it should converse some minutes, as if alive. " These performances," it was added, " have been seen by most of the crowned heads of Asia, Africa, and Europe, and never appeared publick anywhere but once ; but will wait of any at their houses, and perform as above for five pounds."

The hoax is said to have been invented by the Duke of Montagu,[1] to test the credulity of the public, and the result must have more than equalled his expectation, for we read that "a great company came, waited till seven o'clock ; then growing impatient and noisy, a person came before the curtain, and declared that if the performer did not appear, the money should be returned. One in the pit then cried out, 'For double prices the conjuror will go into a pint bottle,' a tumult began, and a person in the boxes threw a lighted candle on the stage. The greatest part of the spectators hurried out, and the mob breaking in, they tore down the inside of the house, and burnt it in the street, making a flag of the curtain, which was placed on a pole in the middle of the bonfire. During this confusion the money, which was secured in a box, according to contract with the owner of the house, was carried off."

Naturally the satirists saw their opportunity in this amazing instance of popular gullibility. One of the earliest caricatures on the subject is dated January 24th, and entitled *The Bottle Conjuror from Head to Foot without Equivocation*. This shows the crowds rushing out of the theatre, the bonfire in the street, and at a window Lord Chesterfield holding up a bottle with a man inside it. Another appeared under the title of *The Magician ; or, the Bottle Cungerer (sic). English credulity ; or, ye're all Bottled* (Pl. CLIV.). In this we see the hero himself in the guise of a satyr, standing behind a table on which is a quart bottle. He holds a purse, and points to a mirror on which is inscribed, " Veluti in speculum." A number of persons, encircled by a cord, are led in by Folly, who exhorts them, " Doubt me not, for I've long led ye." Among the crowd are members of various ranks and professions, including the Butcher Duke of Cumberland, who says, " Show me Alexander, Cæsar, and Marlboro'," and a dignitary of the Church who exclaims, " Miracles will now be confirmed."

[1] John, second Duke of Montagu (*c.* 1688–1749). He held several important offices of state under George I. and George II.

[1721]
Price one Shilling

THE LOTTERY

THE MAGICIAN, OR BOTTLE CUNGERER

Publish'd according to Act of Parliament the 5th of March 1748/9

ENGLISH CREDULITY; OR YE'RE ALL BOTTLED

CLV

AN APOLOGY TO THE TOWN

POPULAR DELUSIONS AND IMPOSTURES

John Potter, the proprietor of the Haymarket, wrote to the papers to explain that he was not responsible for the imposition. The person who took the theatre, he stated, was a man of "genteel appearance," who said that his name was William Nicholls, and gave the Bedford Coffee-house as his address. Potter, suspecting a trick, insisted that he should be allowed to put one of his own officials in the box-office, in order that the money should be returned if no performance took place. But the audience, instead of accepting the offer, had stolen the money, wrecked the theatre, and obliged the officials to fly for their lives. This letter was made the subject of a print called *An Apology to the Town, for Himself and the Bottle, by J. Nick-all, Bedford Coffee House, Covent Garden* (Pl. CLV.). This represents the conjurer in the act of entering a quart bottle by means of a large funnel.

Just a year later the town was agitated, both mentally and physically, by a couple of earthquake shocks, the first of which occurred on February 8th, 1750, the second a month later. In the "new houses about Grosvenor Square" the chairs were shaken and the pewter rattled, and the inhabitants rushed almost naked into the streets. A lady in Piccadilly, a collector of old porcelain, had many of her treasures broken, while the proprietor of a china shop in St. James' Street made capital out of his misfortunes by offering a pair of jars at an enhanced price because they had been cracked in the earthquake. On the whole, however, the material damage was slight, but the moral and intellectual damage was a much more serious matter. When the bishops averred that the earthquakes were judgments upon society for indulging in ridottos and masquerades, and a crazy soldier prophesied that there would be a third shock on April 4th, which would destroy the town, the people, high and low, fell easy victims to a most demoralising panic.

Horace Walpole gives an amusing account of the humours of the earthquake period in his letters to Sir Horace Mann, from which a passage or two may be quoted. Writing on April 2nd, he says: "You will not wonder so much at our earthquakes as at the effects they have had. All the women in town have taken them up upon the foot of *Judgments*: and the clergy, who have had no windfalls for a long time, have driven horse and foot into their opinion. There has been a shower of sermons and exhortations. Secker,[1] the Jesuitical Bishop of Oxford, began the mode. He heard the women were all going out of town to avoid the next shock, and so, for fear of losing his Easter offerings, he set himself to advise them to await God's pleasure in fear and trembling. . . . Several families are literally gone, and many more going to-day and to-morrow; for what adds to the absurdity is, that the second shock having happened exactly a month after the former, it prevails that there be a third on Thursday next, another month, which is to swallow up London. I am almost ready to burn my letter now that I

---

[1] Thomas Secker (1693–1768). Studied medicine in London, Paris, and at Leyden, but later took Orders, and was appointed chaplain to George II. He was successively Bishop of Bristol and of Oxford, but in 1750 he was made Dean of St. Paul's. He became Archbishop of Canterbury in 1758

have begun it, lest you should think I am laughing at you; but it is true that Arthur of White's told me last night that he should put off the last ridotto, because he hears nobody would come to it. I have advised several who are going to keep their next earthquake in the country, to take the bark for it, as it is periodic. Dick Leveson and Mr. Rigby,[1] who had supped and stayed late at Bedford House the other night, knocked at several doors, and in a watchman's voice cried, 'Past four o'clock and a dreadful earthquake.'"

On April 4th Walpole resumes his tale of the panic: "I return to the earthquake, which I had mistaken; it is to be to-day. This frantic terror prevails so much that within three days seven hundred and thirty coaches have been counted passing Hyde Park Corner, with families removing into the country. Here is a good advertisement that I cut out of the paper to-day: 'On Monday next will be published (price 6*d.*) A True and Exact List of all the Nobility and Gentry who have left, or shall leave, this place through fear of another Earthquake.' Several women have made earthquake gowns; that is, warm gowns to sit out of doors all night. These are of the more courageous. One woman, still more heroic, is come to town on purpose; she says all her friends are in London, and she will not survive them. But what will you think of Lady Catherine Pelham,[2] Lady Frances Arundel,[3] and Lord and Lady Galway,[4] who go this evening to an inn ten miles out of town, where they are to play at Brag till five in the morning, and then come back—I suppose to look for the bones of their husbands and families under the rubbish. The prophet of all this (next to the Bishop of London) is a trooper of Lord Delawarr's,[5] who was yesterday sent to Bedlam. His Colonel sent for the man's wife, and asked her if her husband had ever been disordered before. She cried 'Oh dear! my lord, he is not mad now; if your *lordship* would but get any *sensible* man to examine him, you would find he is quite in his right mind.'"

This account is briefly corroborated by a paragraph in the *Gentleman's Magazine*, which states that on the 4th of April, "incredible numbers of people being under strong apprehensions that London and Westminster would be visited with another and more fatal earthquake on this night, according to the predictions of a crazy Life-guardsman, left their houses and walked in the fields, or lay in boats all night; many people of fashion in the neighbouring villages sat in their coaches till daybreak; others went to a greater distance, so that the roads were never more thronged, and lodgings were hardly to be

---

[1] Richard Rigby (1722–88). A well-known, though not highly estimated politician. He began his career as M.P. for Castle Rising in 1745, and in 1758 became secretary to the Duke of Bedford. He was Paymaster of the Forces for a time, and held other lucrative offices, leaving at his death a large fortune, which was supposed to consist of public money.

[2] Lady Catherine Pelham was a daughter of the Duke of Rutland, and the wife of Henry Pelham (1695–1754), the well-known statesman, brother of the Duke of Newcastle.

[3] Lady Frances was sister of the Duke of Rutland, and wife of Richard Arundell, brother of Lord Arundell of Trerice. She was aunt to the second Viscount Galway, who assumed the name and arms of Arundell in 1769.

[4] This must have been John Monckton, the first Viscount Galway (1695–1751), and his second wife, Jane Westenra.

[5] John, first Earl Delawarr, who fought at Dettingen. He died in 1766.

ENGLISH CREDULITY, OR THE INVISIBLE GHOST

THE MILITARY PROPHET: OR A FLIGHT FROM PROVIDENCE

ADDRESSED TO THE FOOLISH AND GUILTY WHO TIMIDLY WITHDREW THEMSELVES ON THE ALARM OF ANOTHER EARTHQUAKE, APRIL 1750

procured at *Windsor:* so far, and even to their wits' ends, had their superstitious fears or their guilty consciences driven them."

This scene of panic is illustrated by a large engraving in the style of Boitard, called *The Military Prophet, or a Flight from Providence, addressed to the Foolish and Guilty, who timidly withdrew themselves on the alarm of another Earthquake, April, 1750* (Pl. CLVII.). Here we have the panic-stricken crowds hurrying along Piccadilly past the top of St. James' Street. Behind the coaches and chariots gallops the Life-guardsman brandishing the sword of prophecy. The bustling scene, the smart ladies in their carriages, the tradesman's family with their bundles and baskets, the gin-dealer and ballad-seller by the roadside, and the spectators in the windows—all these are portrayed by the artist with excellent spirit and effect.

The town was not left long without popular excitements. In January, 1753, all classes were thrown into a state of quite inexplicable ferment over the disappearance of Elizabeth Canning, an extremely uninteresting case, judged on its own merits, but possessing the mysterious power of setting people by the ears, and dividing society into Canningites and Anti-Canningites. Briefly stated, it concerned the sudden disappearance of the heroine, a servant of eighteen, who was missing from her home from January the 6th to the 29th. On returning to her family she declared that she had been carried off by two men who had beaten and robbed her. They dragged her to a house where she was received by an old gipsy and two younger women. Refusing to comply with the suggestion that she should lead an immoral life, she was imprisoned in a garret, where she was left without any food beyond bread and water until the 29th, when she broke out of a window and made her escape. On inquiry, it was supposed that the girl had been taken to the house of one Mother Wells, at Enfield Wash, and that the gipsy was a certain Mary Squires. Canning professed to identify these two persons, who were tried and condemned, the one to death, the other to be branded and imprisoned.

Some doubt having been thrown on the girl's evidence, a keen controversy arose, Henry Fielding leading the party in favour of Canning, and Sir Crisp Gascoygne,[1] the Lord Mayor, that in favour of the gipsy. Finally, the gipsy having succeeded in proving an alibi, the accused were released, and Canning was tried for perjury, found guilty of having fabricated the whole story, and sentenced to transportation for life. Her undaunted admirers, however, raised a handsome sum for her benefit, and Gascoygne rendered himself so unpopular by his action that his carriage was attacked in the street by an irate mob. A contemporary cartoon is called *A True Draught of Eliza Canning, with the House she was confined in, also the Gypsies' flight, and conversing with the Inspector-General of Great Britain* (Pl. CLVIII.). This contains five designs representing respectively Wells' house at Enfield (two views), a portrait of Canning, a witch on a broomstick, and a room in which the gipsy is conversing

---

[1] Sir Crisp Gascoygne (1700–61) was Lord Mayor of London 1752–3. He was the first Lord Mayor who occupied the Mansion House.

with "Sir" John Hill, who was an Anti-Canningite. Another print is called *The Gypsy's Triumph*, and shows the Lord Mayor hand in hand with Mary Squires, the pair being borne on the shoulders of four witches armed with besoms.

In January, 1762, came the famous imposture of the Cock Lane Ghost, which Dr. Johnson prided himself upon having helped to expose. A man named Kent, formerly a postmaster in Norfolk, came to town on the death of his wife to seek a situation. He was accompanied by his sister-in-law, generally alluded to as Miss Fanny, and the pair lodged at the house of the sexton of St. Sepulchre's, a man named Parsons, in Cock Lane, Smithfield. Having quarrelled with Parsons over money matters, Kent removed to another house in Cock Lane, where Miss Fanny died of small-pox, and was buried in St. John's, Clerkenwell. Shortly afterwards mysterious scratchings and rappings were heard in the bedroom occupied by the Parsons' eleven-year-old daughter. It was taken for granted that the sounds proceeded from a spirit, and by means of a system of raps the Parsons professed to have discovered that the spirit was that of Miss Fanny, who accused Kent of having poisoned her by means of arsenic put in her purl. In a short time the mystery became noised abroad and crowds of persons assembled every night, both within and without the house in Cock Lane, to hear the knockings and scratchings.

For a contemporary account of the scene we must again turn to Horace Walpole, who, always " in the movement," paid a midnight visit to Cock Lane, which he described in a letter to George Montagu, dated February 2nd, 1762. " I could tell you volumes on the ghost," he writes, " and I believe if I were to stay a little I might send you its *Life*, dedicated to my Lord Dartmouth by the Ordinary of Newgate, its two great patrons. A drunken parish clerk set it on foot out of revenge, the Methodists have adopted it, and the whole town of London think of nothing else. Elizabeth Canning and the Rabbit-woman were modest imposters in comparison with this, which goes on without saving the least appearances. . . . I went to hear it, for it is not an *apparition*, but an *audition*. We set out from the Opera, changed our clothes at Northumberland House, the Duke of York, Lady Northumberland, Lady Mary Coke, Lord Hertford, and I, all in one Hackney coach, and drove to the spot. It rained torrents, yet the lane was full of mob, and the house so full we could not get in; at last they discovered it was the Duke of York, and the company squeezed themselves into one another's pockets to make room for us. The house, which is borrowed, and to which the ghost has adjourned, is wretchedly small and miserable; when we opened the chamber in which were fifty people, with no light but one tallow candle, we tumbled over the bed of the child to whom the ghost comes, and whom they are murdering by inches in such insufferable heat and stench. At the top of the room are ropes to dry clothes. I asked if we were to have rope-dancing between the acts. We had nothing; they told us (as they would at a puppet-show) that it would not come that night till seven in the morning; that is, when there were only 'prentices and old women. We stayed, however, till half an hour after one."

A View of the Front and Back of S. Wells's House at Enfield Wash, where E. Canning deposed she was confined from ye 1st to ye 30th of January, 1753. R. R. the great Road to Hertford. L. a Lane. O. the Window thro' which she said she escaped. W. W. the Loft, her pretended Prison.

E. Canning vindicated, or M. S—s ye Gypsies Flight to Enfield Wash.

The Gypsey conversing with ye Inspector General of Great Britain.

Elizabeth Canning from the Life.

A TRUE DRAUGHT OF ELIZA CANNING

The child was afterwards removed to the house of the Rev. Stephen Aldrich, Rector of St. John's. Here many eminent gentlemen assembled, including Dr. Johnson and Sir John Fielding, and interrogated the spirit. Having received Miss Fanny's promise that, to prove the truth of her story, she would rap on her own coffin at one o'clock in the morning, they adjourned in a body to the vault.[1] Nothing was heard, however, and the learned committee came to the conclusion that " the child had some art of making or counterfeiting noises, and that there was no agency of any higher cause." Further examination led to the discovery that the child had been in the habit of taking a piece of board to bed with her, on which she made the scratchings and rappings that had mystified all London.

The end of the matter was, that the much-maligned Kent took action against his persecutors. Parsons, his wife, a clergyman named Moore, a tradesman named James, and Mary Frazer, the woman who had interpreted the raps, were tried before Lord Mansfield for conspiracy, and found guilty. Moore and James purchased their pardon with fines, amounting to £600, Parsons was condemned to stand in the pillory three times, and go to prison for two years, while his wife and Mary Frazer were condemned to shorter terms of imprisonment. That the mob was not ungrateful towards the man who had provided them with so much free entertainment is proved by the fact that when Parsons stood in the pillory, he was not only not pelted, but a considerable sum was collected for his benefit.

Among the pictorial satires called forth by this imposture is a wood-cut entitled *The true Portrait of the Ghost. Taken from the Li—, and In-graved by S. S. P. Sexton. Parsons Inv. Scratched by one, two, three and one more.* The print contains two designs, one of which shows the piece of board on which the child had performed, the other, " A Plan of the Room, and the Ghost's Representations." Below the plan are inscribed the words, " N.B. None but true Believers can make out the identical Figure of the Apparition in this picture. Infidels see in it a confused affair, signifying nothing." In a poor etching called *English Credulity ; or, the Invisible Ghost,* we see a bedroom with two children in bed, and a number of persons, including clergymen, examining the premises. The blind Sir John Fielding, who was instrumental in exposing the fraud, enters the room, exclaiming, " I should be glad to *see* the Spirit." A clergyman demands of his neighbour, Foote, the actor, " Now, thou Infidel, dost thou not believe ? " to which Foote replies, " Yes, if it had happened sooner it would have served me for a new character in the Lyar," alluding to the comedy in which he was then performing. On the head-cloth of the bed is the luminous figure of a woman holding a mallet, and on the walls are representations of Elizabeth Canning and the " Bottle Conjurer " (Pl. CLVI.).

The latter part of the century is not so rich in caricatures on popular delusions, though popular delusions were not wanting. The quack doctor

---

[1] An account of this appears in Churchill's poem, *The Ghost.*

was even more *en évidence* than he had been in the time of Hogarth, who introduced the notorious " Dr. Rock " into more than one of his engravings. Among Dr. Rock's more celebrated successors were Dr. Bossy, a famous charlatan, who made a large fortune, and used to arrive at his stage, erected opposite the colonnade of Covent Garden, in a splendid chariot, attended by a liveried servant ; Signor Dominecetti, commonly called " The Stewing Doctor," who lived in Cheyne Row, where he treated his patients with aromatic and vapour baths ; Dr. Graham, of the Temple of Health and the Celestial Bed ; and Dr. Manneduke, an early disciple of Mesmer. The mesmeric craze, though it attracted a good deal of ridicule, seems to have given rise to but little pictorial satire, but Dr. Graham's system of earth-baths is illustrated by a poor etching (*c.* 1780) representing a number of ill-drawn little women reposing in holes in the earth. The beautiful Goddess of Health, supposed to be none other than Emma Hart (afterwards Lady Hamilton) who attracted so many artists and sculptors to the Temple, does not appear in the design.

This subject may, perhaps, most appropriately be closed by a brief consideration of Hogarth's design, *Credulity, Superstition, and Fanaticism : a Medley*, published in March, 1762. The " first thought " for this engraving was entitled *Enthusiasm Delineated*, and was " Humbly dedicated to his Grace the Archbishop of Canterbury by his Grace's most obedient humble Servant, **Wm. Hogarth**." The intention of this print, so runs the advertisement, was to give a " lineal representation of the strange effects of literal and low conceptions of Sacred Beings, as also of the Idolatrous tendency of Pictures in Churches, and Prints in religious books, etc." After taking only two impressions from this plate, Hogarth erased the design, except for two figures, and " changed the point of his satire from the superstitious absurdities of popery and ridiculous personifications delineated by ancient painters, to the popular credulities of his own day." The motto for the engraving in its final state is taken from 1 John, chapter iv. : " Believe not every Spirit, but try the Spirits, whether they are of God, because many false prophets are gone out into the world." In both designs we have the interior of a church, with a clergyman preaching to an impressionable and hypocritical congregation. In the first, the preacher, who has a harlequin's dress under his gown, and a tonsure under his wig, holds a puppet in each hand as symbols of his discourse. Among the congregation are a group of excited devotees, who also clasp little figures of saints in pious fervour ; an amorous couple, who mingle love-making with religious exaltation ; a convict, apparently convinced of sin by means of a gin-bottle ; and the parish clerk, who is weeping hypocritical tears. Into the second design are introduced, as instances of popular credulity, Mary Tofts, the so-called Rabbit-Woman, the Tedworth Drummer (immortalised by Addison), the Boy of Bilston, and the Cock Lane Ghost.

ROYALTY

PART I

IN the early half of the eighteenth century non-political attacks upon royalty are by no means numerous, but this scarcity of a class of caricature that was afterwards extremely popular must be attributed rather to the absence of general interest in the domestic affairs of those Teutonic monarchs, George I. and George II., than to any feeling of respect on the part of the caricaturist for the domestic privacy of his sovereign. The marriage of Frederick, Prince of Wales, in 1736 to the Princess Augusta of Saxe-Gotha, and his consequent abandonment of his mistress, the Hon. Anne Vane, daughter of Lord Barnard, gave rise to lampoons, both poetical and pictorial, from among which one anonymous print may be chosen for reproduction.

Miss Vane, one of the Maids of Honour to Queen Caroline in 1732, became the mother of a boy, Cornwall Fitz-Frederick Vane, whom the Prince of Wales believed to be his son. Lord Hervey was another of Miss Vane's numerous admirers, and is reported to have quarrelled with the Prince about the lady, to whom Dr. Johnson referred in the *Vanity of Human Wishes* in the line :—

"Yet Vane can tell what ills from beauty spring."

The print in question shows a handsomely decorated room in which stands an empty throne (Pl. CLIX.). A young man has taken the hand of a lady, and is about to lead her to the throne, on the steps of which lounges a stout gentleman, probably meant for Sir Robert Walpole. In a window in the background sits a young lady, evidently in great distress of mind, with a little boy of about four years old, who wears a large hat and feathers. The boy, it may be added, died in this year, 1736, and his mother only survived him a few months.

The public discontent at George II.'s frequent and prolonged absences in Hanover occasionally found vent in contemporary caricature. Thus an engraving called *An actual Survey of the Electorate, or Face of the Country whereon Hanover stands, with a view of Herenhausen (sic) and the seats of Manufactures* (1743), represents, from one point of view, a landscape with

[April 25ᵗʰ 1736]

FREDERICK PRINCE OF WALES
AND
THE PRINCESS AUGUSTA OF SAXE-GOTHA

St JAMES'S IN OCTOBER. THE K<u>ING</u> AT H<u>ANOVER</u> MDCCL
(7 MONTHS ABSENT)

Publish'd by T. Fox in the Old Baily. Price 6<u>d</u> Col<u>d</u> 1<u>s</u>

mountains and a lake; but when held up by one end, the design transforms itself into a portrait of George II., wearing a large Kevenhüller hat. "Tho' this is not given as ye most regular, ye most varied, or ye most noble Prospect in the World," runs the legend engraved below, "it is not doubted it will pass for the most Pleasant. And if it be true as Butler sings :—

'The real Value of a Thing
Is as much money as 'twill bring,'

everybody must allow it to be the most valuable, because the most costly."

In April, 1750, the King left London for Hanover, and did not return until the beginning of November. In the course of the autumn a caricature appeared, called *St. James in October; the K—— at H——. MDCCL.* (Pl. CLX.). Here we have the gate of St. James' Palace, with two sentinels on guard. A funeral procession is passing with the coffin of Trade, while a group of tradesmen protest "Seven months in twelve is too hard indeed," and severally complain that not a suit is bespoke yet, nor a hat, nor a wig. The landlord of the Thatched House Tavern is trying to induce some of the bystanders to subscribe to the Birthday Dinner, but they refuse on the plea that Trade is dead. In one corner is a Savoyard with a hurdy-gurdy and dancing-girl. The man complains "A Long-don dare be nutting at all to be got here—Begar."

The Rebellion of 1745 called forth one or two caricatures of social rather than political interest, among them a curious little print called *Scotch Female Gallantry*, designed and engraved by Canot.[1] This represents the Young Pretender in an adaptation of Highland costume, surrounded by Scotch lasses who are jostling each other in their anxiety to press kisses upon his hands, his coat-sleeve, and his ribbon of knighthood. In an anteroom are yet more women eagerly awaiting their turn to be admitted to the royal presence. The design is accompanied by some derisive verses, which conclude with the lines :—

"No base-born wretch! Let William stand
The Pride and Darling of our Land.
William on Earth the young Nassau,
Born to defend the World below."

The William alluded to in these flattering terms was the "Butcher" Duke of Cumberland, who became the butt of the satirist a few years later, in consequence of his infatuation for a Savoyard girl. According to Horace Walpole, who sent a caricature on this subject to George Montagu, the girl refused the Duke's advances and his offer of a hundred pounds, on the ground that he was a heretic. A print called *John of Gant in Love, or Mars on his knees* (1749), shows the fat Duke kneeling at the feet of the Savoyard girl, and imploring her to accompany him to "Windsor's shady kind retreat." In another cartoon, *Mars on his Journey*, we see the Duke

---

[1] Peter Canot, a French engraver, who settled in London about 1740. He became a member of the Society of Artists, and in 1770 was elected an associate of the Royal Academy.

Publish'd according to Act of Parliament

Aug. 1747. Price 6ᵈ

JOHN OF GANT MOUNTED OR MARS ON HIS JOURNEY

IF MUSIC BE THE FOOD OF LOVE PLAY ON

Gay

1762

THE KITCHEN METAMORPHOSED

on horseback, riding at full gallop with the girl behind his saddle, while her brother runs after the pair, vainly shouting to them to stop. The motto chosen for this design is the line (in allusion to the hurdy-gurdy of the Savoyards) :—

"If music be the food of love, play on,"

which, oddly enough, is attributed to the poet Gay (Pl. CLXI.).

With the accession of George III. a veritable war of political satire was waged over the supposed influence of the Princess of Wales and Lord Bute with the young King. The non-political caricatures deal for the most part with the economical methods of the royal household. A little etching called *The Christening*, dated September, 1762, shows the Archbishop of Canterbury, Thomas Secker, holding the infant Prince of Wales (afterwards George IV.) at the font, and exclaiming, " More water, nurse, here's hardly enough to make the child a Christian." Other members of the group comment upon the absence of cake and wine, while the Queen says apologetically, " Consider, we are but a young couple," and the King adds, " And likely to have many more," a prophecy which was certainly fulfilled.

One or two caricatures for the same year deal with the shortcomings of the royal kitchen. In March, 1761, Lord Talbot[1] had been made Lord Steward of the Household, a most unpopular appointment. " As neither gravity, rank, interest, abilities, nor morals could be adduced to countenance this strange exaltation," writes Walpole, " no wonder it caused very unfavourable comments. . . . As the Court knew that the measures it had in contemplation could only be carried by money, every stratagem was invented to curtail the common expenses of the palace. As these fell into the province of the Lord Steward, nothing was heard of but cooks cashiered and kitchens shut up. Even the Maids of Honour, who did not expect rigours from a great officer of Lord Talbot's complexion, were reduced to complain of the abridgment of their allowance for breakfast. The public joined in the cry, and the shops teemed with scandalous prints against the reformer and his patroness."

This account of the squabbles in the household is corroborated in an unpublished letter addressed by Mrs. Daniel Fox to a friend in December, 1762. The writer relates that " the two German women who attend the Queen fall out with their Bread and Butter. They dine by themselves, and their Dinner being sent up in silver, they sent it down to be put into the King's gilt Plate, or they would not eat it. The Officers of the Kitchen returned for answer that they would keep the Dinner hot till they chose to eat, but the King's gilt Plate could be used by nobody but the King and Queen without the King's express order. The next day the Ladies sent down that the King had ordered them the gilt Plate, and they expected to have it, but the Officers of the Kitchen refused, alleging that the order must come to them thro' Lord Talbot, and the day after they apply'd to Lord Talbot to

[1] This was William, second Baron Talbot, who was created Earl Talbot in 1762. He died in 1782.

know if the Ladies were to have the gilt Plate. 'No,' says he, 'nor the silver neither—let them have the Pewter, it is quite as good as they have been used to.' So the poor Ladies were reduced to Pewter."

A rare print, said to have been suppressed, is called *The Kitchen Metamorphosed*, and represents a large empty kitchen, with shrubs in one of the grates, while in another a tiny fire burns under a cauldron. In the foreground Lord Talbot superintends the proceedings of a cook, who is weighing a herring and a half on a steelyard. Another cook is yawning drearily because he has nothing to do, and a lean dog and cat prowl about in the vain search for scraps (Pl. CLXII.). A caricature of the same date is called *A Catalogue of the Household Furniture of John Bull, Esq., leaving off Housekeeping, now selling by Auction*. In this we see Lord Talbot giving instructions to an auctioneer's clerk about the sale of the now superfluous kitchen utensils, while the Princess of Wales and Lord Bute look on approvingly. It may be noted that the publisher of this print, J. Williams, "near the Mitre Tavern, Fleet Street," was condemned to stand in the pillory on January 23rd, 1765, for having reprinted No. 45 of the *North Briton* after the House of Commons had ordered it to be burnt by the common hangman. In No. 12 of the same publication (August 22nd, 1762) Wilkes had expressed ironical satisfaction with the changes in the household. "I much admire," he writes, "many of his Lordship's new regulations, especially those for the royal kitchen. I approve the discharge of so many turnspits and cooks, who were grown of very little use. It was high time to put an end to that too great indulgence in eating and drinking, which went by the name of *Old English Hospitality*, when the House of Commons had granted a poor niggardly Civil List of only £800,000."

It says much for the character of the royal couple that the economical ways of Queen Charlotte and the homely tastes of George III. were the only (non-political) points of attack open to the caricaturist at Court until the young princes came to man's estate. Mention may be made of a print, *Farmer George studying the Wind and Weather*, which appeared in the *Oxford Magazine* in 1771. The King is here represented looking out of a window through a telescope, evidently with a view to ascertaining the prospect for his crops. The little princes are amusing themselves with a rocking-horse, and a dog and cat play with *A Remonstrance* and the *Art of Mechanick Government*, which lie on the floor. A portrait of the unpopular favourite, Lord Bute, hangs in a conspicuous position on the wall. The King had already made his appearance in the *Oxford Magazine* (1770) as one of the *Remarkable Characters at Mrs. Cornely's Masquerade*. In this plate he is depicted as a baby in a leading-string, one end of which is held by Lord Bute. A satyr holds up the Mirror of Truth to His Majesty, who observes, "'Tis a fine mirror, but I do not like anything that reflects."

Contemporaneous with the coming of age of the Prince of Wales, and the earliest of his amours, is the beginning of a long series of royal satires from the etching needle of James Gillray, of whose career a brief summary may here be given. Born in 1757, a year later than Rowlandson, he was the son of a Scottish out-pensioner of Chelsea Hospital, who, having lost an arm at Fontenoy, passed his later years in the inglorious post of sexton to the Moravian burial-ground. After giving his son as good an education as he could afford, he apprenticed him to a letter-engraver. The boy worked at the occupation chosen for him long enough to acquire considerable facility with the graving tools; then, tiring suddenly of the monotony of his 'prentice life, he ran away and joined a troupe of strolling players. Though he must have gained a good deal of material for the future in this new calling, the experiment was not a success, and, wearying of irregularity as he had wearied of routine, he returned to London, where he contrived to get admitted to the Academy Schools.

While working from the life, and pursuing other legitimate studies at the Academy, Gillray found time to perfect his knowledge of the graver's craft, and published some precocious specimens of his humour, which are now difficult to identify, since he commonly signed them with initials other than his own. "His improvement," to quote the words of one of his biographers, "was rapid and extraordinary, and he soon obtained a marvellous freedom, both of design and in the management of the etching needle. It is believed that he frequently etched his ideas at once upon the copper, without any previous drawing, his only guides being sketches of the distinguished characters he intended to introduce, on small pieces of card, which he always carried about with him."

The long series of political and social caricatures by which Gillray gained notoriety, not always of an enviable kind, began in 1779 and were continued down to 1811, when he sank into a state of imbecility, brought on, it is said, by his habits of intemperance. He seems to have led a retired and uneventful life, the chief incident of his middle age being a visit to France and Holland with de Loutherbourg, who was collecting materials for his picture, *The Siege of Valenciennes*. During this tour Gillray made several sketches of Flemish life and character, and on the travellers' return they were invited to submit their drawings to the King's inspection. George III. warmly admired de Loutherbourg's work, but dismissed Gillray's sketches with a contemptuous "I don't understand these caricatures." The King's attitude will be readily understood and condoned by those who are acquainted with Gillray's attacks upon royalty up to this period; indeed, the marvel is that the caricaturist should have dared to set foot within the palace. Later, when the excesses of the French Revolution, together with the fear of prosecution for a blasphemous print, had transformed Gillray into an outwardly loyal supporter of the monarch and the constitution, George III. regarded his caricatures in quite a different light, particularly those which contrasted Buonaparte with the King of England, greatly to the advantage of the latter. Even the etching produced by Gillray in revenge for the snub administered to his Flemish sketches, *A Connoisseur Examining a Cooper*, is said to have been taken in good part by His Majesty, though it represented him in the act of studying a miniature of Oliver Cromwell, with the query, " Does he understand that ? " a significant hint considering the state of public feeling at that period.

Though many of Gillray's productions were published by Fores, Holland, and other print-sellers, Humphrey, who began business in the Strand, and afterwards migrated in turn to Bond Street and St. James' Street, was his chief employer, obtaining in the course of time the practical monopoly of his work. The latter part of his life was spent at "Mistress Humphrey's" establishment in St. James' Street, where he had a room over the shop, and boarded with his employer. Gillray is reported to have proposed marriage to Miss Humphrey more than once, and on one occasion he even accompanied her as far as the church door, but at the last moment he thought better of the matrimonial project, and whispering, " This is a very foolish affair, Miss Humphrey ; we live very comfortably together, we had better let well alone," he returned to the shop and set to work on a new plate. Although he was guilty of artistic infidelities towards Miss Humphrey, in that he secretly etched plates for Fores, disguising his own style ; and although he caricatured her and her maid Betty in *Twopenny Whist*, Gillray continued under her roof until the end of his days. During his last years Miss Humphrey ministered to him with disinterested devotion, and buried him at her own expense in St. James' Churchyard, where the following inscription marks his resting-place :—

" In Memory of Mr. James Gillray
The Caricaturist
Who departed this life 1st June, 1815
Aged 58 Years."

Although princes and politicians winced under the lash of Gillray, whose satires are stated to have " moved the unimpassioned Pitt, troubled not a little the mind of Fox, exasperated Sheridan, and stung the feelings of Canning so sharply that he called on the caricaturist to complain and remonstrate," it is certain that his productions added to the gaiety of the nation during the closing years of the century, and gave a powerful stimulus to satiric art. " England is altogether von libel," declared an old general of the German Legion, and foreign visitors generally expressed their astonishment at the extraordinary audacity of the English caricaturists, and the impunity with which they pursued their calling. " I can well remember," observes a writer of the period, "when the daily lounger at the eastern side of Bond Street and St. James' Street, upon approaching Humphrey's shop, had to quit the pavement for the carriage-way, so great was the crowd which obstructed the footpath to look at Gillray's caricatures."

The most personal as well as the most "topical" of all the eighteenth-century caricaturists, Gillray's inexhaustible imagination, joined to a keen power of observation, an amazing technique, and, it must be added, a

[1772]

THE BIRD OF PARADISE

Printed for & sold by Carington Bowles at his Map & Print Warehouse, No 69 in St Paul's Churchyard, London.   Publish'd as the Act directs

Mᴿ JAMES GILLRAY

[FROM A PORTRAIT BY HIMSELF]

complete absence of remorse or scruple, rendered him the most dangerous as well as the most pitiless of all antagonists. Unlike Hogarth, he never hesitated to hit below the belt, and too often sought to make his points by exposing the infirmities of the body instead of attacking the deformities of the mind. While Hogarth came before the world in the guise of a reformer, Gillray appeared in that of an executioner, and his favourite mode of punishment was the torture. No satirist has ever attacked with such concentrated malignity, combined with such skill in touching the raw, persons in private life who had done him no wrong—with whom, in all probability, he had never exchanged a word. Gillray, silent and saturnine as he seemed to his fellows, possessed a curious faculty for working himself up into a cold fury of personal resentment against some obscure offender who was quite unworthy his powder and shot. An instance of this will be found in his elaborate etching of that cantankerous person, Philip Thicknesse, Governor of Landguard Fort, who was always at loggerheads either with the military authorities or with members of his own family. It cannot be supposed that Thicknesse was a personage of much interest to the public in general, or to Gillray in particular; yet the most diabolical ingenuity has been employed upon the portrait of Thicknesse[1] as *Lieutenant-Governor Gallstone inspired by Alecto*. In the same way, it is extremely unlikely that the caricaturist had any personal knowledge of his favourite social butts, Lady Cecilia Johnstone and Mrs. Hobart, or that he should have received any injury from them; yet they are honoured with as minute attention, as detailed a treatment, as is vouchsafed to the most important public characters, even to Buonaparte himself.

In spite of the blots and blemishes which disfigure much of his work, the outcome probably of a brain warped by intemperance, it would be impossible to deny the important services that Gillray has rendered to students of the history, whether social or political, of the last years of the century. There is scarcely an incident, a fashion, or a folly that he has not illustrated, scarcely a public personage that he has not portrayed, and all with such power, such originality, and such remorseless cruelty, that we hesitate whether to marvel or to shudder at his genius. Gillray had a giant's strength, and he never scrupled to use it like a giant—frequently like an ogre; yet it is impossible to dissent from the tribute paid to him by his loyal friend, John Landseer, who after commenting upon the merits of Gillray's finest etchings, notably *Sin, Death, and the Devil*, and *The Sacrifice to Avarice*, concludes, " There are passages in these so luminous, so energetic, so vivid, and so far elevated above the tenour of caricature that they well deserve to be classed with the higher works of art " (Pl. CLXIV.).

Turning from Gillray as an artist to Gillray as a man, we find him

---

[1] Philip Thicknesse (1719–92). Governor of Landguard Fort, Suffolk. He quarrelled with Colonel Vernon, who commanded the regiment, and was imprisoned three months for libelling him. He claimed to have " discovered " Gainsborough, with whom he also quarrelled. He had a bitter feud with his eldest son, upon whom devolved the barony of Audley through his mother (Thicknesse's second wife), a daughter of Lord Castlehaven. Philip Thicknesse published his *Memoirs, Travels*, and some other works.

described by one who wrote apparently from personal knowledge as "silent, shy, inexplicable, yet a lover of low company and gross mirth." The professional humorist, according to Harry Angelo, who knew many of that class, was generally a dull dog, Peter Pindar being described as witless even over his bottle, while Anthony Pasquin was sour, and Churchill a sulky sot. "Poor Gillray was always hipped, but he was a careless sort of cynic who neither loved nor hated society, and further was an unaffected wight, free from all professional jealousy and assumption of superiority." John Landseer, defending his friend from the charge of being a lover of low society and gross mirth, explains that he was only silent and saturnine until he made sure that his companions were frank and liberal, when he "discovered no deficiency either of good sense, benevolent feeling or gentlemanly propriety of conduct; yet there was an eccentricity about him, which, being no unusual concomitant of genius, was felt to be agreeable." On one such occasion, a meeting held to institute a society for the benefit of decayed artists, "After business and supper were concluded we drank toasts," relates Mr. Landseer; "and when it came to Gillray's turn to name a public character, the Juvenal of caricature surprised those who knew him but superficially, by proposing that we should drink David, the French painter! He was by this time a little elated, having become pleased with his associates, and drowned his reserve in the flow of soul; and kneeling reverentially on a chair as he pronounced the name of the (*supposed*) first painter and patriot in Europe, he expressed a wish that the rest of the company would do the same."

Another sketch of the caricaturist, this time in lower life, has been drawn for us by his friend and contemporary, Harry Angelo. "For years," he narrates, "Gillray occasionally smoked his pipe at the Bell, the Coal-hole, or the Coach and Horses; and although the *convives* whom he met at such dingy rendezvous knew that he was *that* Gillray who fabricated those comical cuts, the very *moral* of Farmer George and Bony-party, of Billy Pitt and Black Charley, he never sought, like that low coxcomb, Morland, to become the king of the company. He neither exacted, nor were they inclined to pay him any particular homage. In truth, with his associates, neighbouring shop-keepers and manufacturers, he passed for no greater wit than his fellows. Rowlandson and he sometimes met. They would perhaps exchange half a dozen questions and answers upon the affairs of copper and acquafortis; swear all the world was one masquerade; and then enter into the common chat of the room, smoke their cigars, drink their punch, and, sometimes early, sometimes late, shake hands at the door, look up at the stars, say it is a frosty night, and depart, one to the Adelphi, the other to St. James' Street."

ROYALTY

PART II

IN 1779 a nine days' wonder was created in society by a romantic amour of the eighteen-year-old Prince of Wales, who had hitherto led a secluded life under the strict supervision of parents and tutors. The object of this early passion was the young actress, Mrs. Mary Robinson,[1] better known as "Perdita," from the rôle in which she first attracted the attention of her Florizel. Mrs. Robinson was a *protégée* and pupil of Garrick, and made her first appearance at Drury Lane in 1776, at the early age of eighteen, but did not then make much impression on the public. The Prince saw her in the *Winter's Tale* on December 3rd, 1779, when her conquest seems to have been immediate and, for the time being, complete. A correspondence was begun between the pair, some stolen interviews took place at Kew, and at the end of the season Mrs. Robinson retired from the stage, relying for her future provision upon a bond for £20,000, sent her by the Prince, to be paid when he came of age and received a separate establishment.

Perdita settled down in a little house in Cork Street, and for a brief season she was the most admired, the most fêted, and the most conspicuous of all the beauties of the period. "To-day she was a *paysanne* with her straw hat tied at the back of her head. Yesterday, perhaps, she had been the belle of Hyde Park, trimmed, powdered, patched, painted to the extreme power of rouge and white lead; to-morrow she would be the cravated Amazon of the riding house; but be she what she might, the hats of the fashionable promenaders swept the ground as she passed." A caricature of a lady in a huge pleated cap, called *A Bird of Paradise*, was supposed to be aimed at Mrs. Robinson, though in the Burney Collection it is stated to be the portrait of another and an earlier actress, Mrs. Maton (Pl. CLXIII.).

By the time that the Prince was fully emancipated, and the master of £60,000 a year, the charms of his first love had been eclipsed by those of several other ladies. Florizel gave his Perdita the cut direct when he met her in the Park, and repudiated his bond for £20,000, though, thanks to

---

[1] Mary Robinson, *née* Darby (1758–1800). She married Thomas Robinson secretly in 1774, but the marriage turned out badly. In later life she wrote sentimental stories and verses. Her portraits by Reynolds and Romney are well known.

the good offices of Charles Fox, one of the lady's numerous admirers, an annuity of five hundred pounds was granted her. Among Mrs. Robinson's successful rivals was the sporting Lady Salisbury,[1] and this amourette was commemorated by Gillray in July, 1782, by a caricature called *Monuments lately discovered on Salisbury Plain* (Pl. CLXV.). To quote from the explanation appended, "The figures numbered 1 and 2 [Lady Salisbury and the Prince] are judged by connoisseurs to have been lately animated by celestial fire. No. 3 [Lord Salisbury] is an unfinished resemblance of the human form ; from the vacancy of countenance and roughness of workmanship, this figure cannot be supposed to have ever been intended as a companion for No. 1. No. 4 [Mrs. Robinson ?] from the attitude is supposed to represent some forlorn Dido or Ariadne of quality."

Three years later, in 1785, the Prince played the leading rôle in a much more serious romance, a romance which was to have far-reaching consequences, and to affect his whole after-life. This, it need scarcely be said, was his amour with Mrs. Fitzherbert,[2] a twice-widowed lady, eight years older than himself. The widow's uncompromising rejection of his early advances and her flight to the Continent inflamed the Prince's passion to matrimony point, and although the lady was a Catholic and thus legally debarred from marriage with the heir-apparent, he proposed formally to make her his wife. After prolonged hesitation, and an attempt (real or feigned) at suicide on the part of the Prince, Mrs. Fitzherbert consented to a private marriage, which took place at her own house on December 31st, 1785. By the Roman Church the ceremony seems to have been considered valid, and Mrs. Fitzherbert, though her position must always have been anomalous, was received into society, and treated with every consideration by the royal family.

The subject under various aspects is treated by Gillray and other caricaturists. Wicksteed[3] produced a clever design, called *The Marriage of Figaro*, which was imitated or adapted by most of his fellow-satirists. Gillray published *The Follies of a day ; or, the Marriage of Figaro*, as well as a companion plate, *The April Fool ; or, the Follies of a Night*. The first shows the Prince being married to Mrs. Fitzherbert by a priest who bears a strong resemblance to Burke, and who reads the service from the section on Matrimony in Hoyle's *Games*. The bride is given away by Colonel " Georgy " Hanger (afterwards Lord Coleraine), the Prince's *âme damnée*, who is armed with the knotted bludgeon that was his favourite weapon. Another imaginary sketch of the marriage by the same artist, but more elaborately worked out, is *Wife or no Wife ; or, a Trip to the Continent* (Pl. CLXVI.).

---

[1] Mary Amelia, daughter of the first Marquis of Downshire. She married James, seventh Earl and first Marquis of Salisbury in 1773. She was burnt to death at Hatfield in 1835.

[2] Maria Anne Fitzherbert, *née* Smythe (1756–1837). She was first married to Mr. Weld of Lulworth Castle in 1775, and secondly to Thomas Fitzherbert of Swynnerton in 1778. He died in 1781. Mrs. Fitzherbert's relations with the Prince continued till 1803.

[3] This was presumably James Wicksteed (1729–91), a stipple engraver.

In *The April Fool; or, the Follies of a Night*, the Prince and Mrs. Fitzherbert are seen dancing a reel, while Burke plays on the gridiron with a pair of tongs, and Colonel Hanger is drubbing on the salt-box (Pl. CLXVII.). That some pressure was put upon the Prince to induce him to go through the marriage ceremony is suggested by another plate, *The Padlock; or, To be or not to be a Queen is the Question*, which shows Mrs. Fitzherbert, armed with a large padlock, resolutely conducting her royal lover towards a church door. The Prince's confidential associates, Fox, Burke, and Hanger, are scattered about the churchyard, eagerly watching the movements of the pair, while Lord North is sound asleep upon a tombstone. That the satirists were by no means unanimous on the subject of Mrs. Fitzherbert and her charms may be gathered from a pair of anonymous designs which appeared about this time. The first, *Fair, Fat, and Forty*, is a libellous representation of the lady's age and appearance; but the second, *Tender, Trim, and Thirty*, was evidently the work of an admirer, and published as an antidote to the ill-nature of the earlier design.

The Prince's reckless extravagance, his dissipated mode of life, and his dissensions with the King were creating much unfavourable comment at this period, and matters were not mended by the incident of his private marriage, which seems to have been an open secret. In 1786 his difficulties seem to have reached a climax, and finding that no help was forthcoming from the King, he sold off his race-horses, invested part of his income for his creditors, and temporarily retired into private life. This apparently laudable behaviour was not regarded with favour by the Court, since it was believed to be an attempt to enlist the sympathy of the public, and to put the King and his ministers in the wrong. This topic is treated by Gillray in one of his most successful designs, a parody of the auction scene in *The School for Scandal* (Pl. CLXVIII.). Here the Prince, in the character of Charles Surface, is offering the portraits of his ancestors for sale. Colonel Hanger as Careless, the amateur auctioneer, is holding up a picture of the King and Queen, and crying, "Going for no more than one Crown," while the Prince says, "Careless, knock down the Farmer." Lots two and three are portraits of Mrs. Fitzherbert and Perdita. Through an open door is a view of Tattersall's, where the prodigal's horses and carriages are being sold.

The Colonel Hanger who plays so prominent a part in the above designs was a younger son of the first Lord Coleraine, who obtained his title by a judicious bribe to one of George II.'s mistresses. Young George began his career as an ensign in the Foot-guards, and for a time lived splendidly on credit, his pay of four shillings a day being insufficient to defray the stitching of a single button-hole, or the embroidery of the gold clocks on his stockings. His chief extravagance at this time lay in the direction of clothes, and he tells us that he always had two suits for the Birthday, the morning one costing him £80 and the evening one £180. In spite of the respect thus displayed towards his sovereign, the King, he plaintively records, never once thought proper to address a single word to him.

After making the American campaign with a regiment of Hessians, Hanger, on his return to England, was appointed equerry to the Prince of Wales, and spent several seasons with him at Brighton. This, he says, was the happiest time of his life, and he further protests that had he been an ensign or a curate, he would have chosen the Prince for his companion and friend, and have been guided by his judgment in the most weighty and intricate affairs of life. Georgy's chief accomplishments seem to have consisted of a talent for "spotting the winner," and so great a skill with the pistol that he is reported to have been able to kill a flea once in eight shots at eight yards, so long as the flea was not allowed to hop. When the Prince's household was reduced after his marriage Colonel Hanger's services were dispensed with, and he was glad to accept a small post under the East India Company.

It was about this time, 1796, that the Colonel was accustomed to ride down Grosvenor Street every day on a small Scotch pony, and alight at a then famous tavern, "The Mount," in Lower Grosvenor Street. Gillray has etched his portrait in a plate called *Georgy a' Cock Horse*, which shows him astride his tiny steed, his feet nearly touching the ground (Pl. CLXXIV.). Colonel Hanger was accustomed to declare that in Scotland he had seen as many as thirteen dead calves carried by a little cock-horse like his own. In a second plate Gillray sketched him perched on the top of a pile of dead calves, which are loaded on the back of a small rough pony. In the last part of his career Colonel Hanger saw many vicissitudes, as he informs us in the memoirs which he compiled with the help of William Coombe. In 1798 he found his way into the King's Bench, but by 1800 he was at liberty again, and had "commenced coal merchant," much to the amusement of his friends. He succeeded to the title late in life, and died in 1724, aged about seventy-three.

The contrast between the extreme frugality and simplicity of the life led by the Court at Windsor, and the riotous extravagance of the heir-apparent, naturally gave an opening to the caricaturist. Many are the designs that deal with the "Farm" at Windsor, and Farmer George feeding his pigs and poultry in the company of his homely wife. In *The Constant Couple* (1786), by Metz,[1] we see the King and Queen mounted on an old rough horse, and travelling towards Windsor, having just reached the twentieth milestone from St. James' (Pl. CLXIX.). In somewhat similar style is Gillray's etching, *Going to Market*, which represents the King driving a market-cart, with the Queen and her hencoop at his side, and the escort carrying great bundles of vegetables on their drawn swords. His Majesty is observing to his too parsimonious spouse, "You should have given a shilling with the bunch of turnips to the old soldier you relieved just now; turnips, Charley, are very insipid without a bit of mutton," and then he breaks into a stanza from his

---

[1] Conrad Martin Metz (1755–1827), a German engraver and a pupil of Bartolozzi, was working in London during the later years of the eighteenth century.

Jn Gd

Pub'd June 15th 1782 by H Humphrey
New Bond Street

MONUMENTS LATELY DISCOVERED ON SALISBURY PLAIN

Design'd by Carlo Khan

Publish'd by Wm Holland
No 66, Drury Lane

WIFE & NO WIFE—OR—A TRIP TO THE CONTINENT

March 27 1786]

THE APRIL FOOL OR THE FOLLIES OF A NIGHT

AS PERFORMED AT THE THEATRE ROYAL, C—— HOUSE, FOR THE BENEFIT OF THE WIDOW WADMAN

Published 1st April, 1786, by S. W. Fores at the Caricature Warehouse. No. 3, Piccadilly

A SCENE IN THE SCHOOL FOR SCANDAL

London. Published July 18, 1786, by S. W. Fores, No 3, Piccadilly

favourite poet, Tom D'Urfey. In *Summer Amusements at Windsor* (1791), by Isaac Cruikshank[1] the scene is laid in a large dairy, where the King is diligently churning, while the Queen is receiving money from her market-woman and scolding her for selling as many as six eggs for a groat. Through the open door we have a view of Billy Pitt milking a cow; and Lord Thurlow, in the guise of a carter, seems to be trying to crack a whip (Pl. CLXX.). These royal avocations are illustrated by Peter Pindar in the stanzas :—

> " The modern bard (quoth Tom) sublimely sings
> Of sharp and prudent economic Kings,
> Who rams and ewes and lambs and bullocks feed,
> And pigs of every sort of breed :
>
> " Of Kings who pride themselves on fruitful sows,
> Who sell skim milk, and keep a guard so stout
> To drive the geese, the thievish rascals, out,
> That ev'ry morning used to suck the cows :
>
> " Of Kings who cabbages and carrots plant
> For such as wholesome vegetables want ;
> Who feed, too, poultry for the people's sake,
> Then send it through the villages in carts,
> To cheer (how wondrous kind !) the hungry hearts
> Of such as *only pay* for what they take."

In 1789 the King's recovery from his first attack of mental malady gave rise to general rejoicings, and the leaders of society appeared in hats and dresses decorated with ribbons bearing loyal mottoes, such as *God Save the King* and *The King Restored*. This fashion was illustrated by the indefatigable Gillray in his *Restoration Dresses*. The royal procession to St. Paul's for the thanksgiving has been sketched by an anonymous artist in a design called *City Horsemanship* which gives us an opportunity for comparing the show with similar functions in our own day. The procession is apparently passing along the Strand, and the City magnates, being in considerable trouble with their steeds, are parting company with their hats and even their boots. The artist has sketched the crowds of spectators on the pavements and at the windows. The decorations consist chiefly of banners and mottoes, and it appears that as much as three guineas was charged for the smallest peepholes along the route (Pl. CLXXI.).

In a pair of etchings published by Gillray in 1792, *A Voluptuary under the Horrors of Digestion* and *Temperance Enjoying a Frugal Meal*, the difference between the arrangements at Carlton House and Windsor Castle is sharply emphasised. In the first, we have the Prince of Wales reposing, toothpick in hand, after the labours of a Gargantuan meal. Several empty bottles lie beneath the table, and some well-picked bones have overflowed from the plate on to the table-cloth. A dice-box, a Newmarket Calendar, and a list of " Debts of Honour "—unpaid—are scattered about the

---

[1] Isaac Cruikshank, the father and teacher of George and Robert, was born *circa* 1756, and died about 1811. The son of a Scotchman, who held a place in the Customs, he was left an orphan at an early age. He became fairly well known as a caricaturist and illustrator of books. He belonged to the school of Gillray, whose style he imitated, and, like Gillray, his death was hastened by his habits of intemperance.

floor. The Prince, though he wears an expression of dull repletion, is distinguished by that sensual, full-blown beauty which even Gillray never denied him. (Pl. CLXXIII.). In the companion picture the King and Queen are represented as dining frugally off boiled eggs, sauerkraut, and cold water. There is a vase of flowers in the grate, the furniture is swathed in holland covers, and in the foreground stands a strong iron chest, securely padlocked, which presumably contains the royal savings. On the chest lie some books with such appropriate titles as "Dr. Cheyne[1] on the Benefits of a Spare Diet" and an "Essay on the Dearness of Provisions."

Among the many other satires on the same subject executed by Gillray are *Frying Sprats, vide Royal Supper* (1791), in which Queen Charlotte is depicted cooking the humble fish over a small fire, while her savings fall out of her heavily laden pockets, and *Toasting Muffins, vide Royal Breakfast*, in which royal George toasts one of the three muffins intended for the breakfast of himself and his wife. The following year, 1792, appeared a more ambitious plate called *Anti-Saccharites ; or, John Bull and his Family Leaving off the Use of Sugar. To the Masters and Mistresses of Families in Great Britain this Noble Example of Economy is Respectfully Submitted.* The five blonde princesses are here portrayed sulkily stirring their sugarless tea, while the Queen, in the ogress guise in which Gillray always represents her, exclaims, "Oh, dear creatures, do but taste it! You can't think how nice it is without sugar! And then consider how much work you'll save the poor Blackamoors by leaving off the use of it. And above all, remember how much expense it will save your poor Papa! Oh, it's a delicious cooling drink." The King with his cup to his lips obediently echoes, "Oh, delicious, delicious!" A prettier and more good-humoured design, *The Milliner's Shop*, shows the royal family cheapening goods in a shop at Windsor (Pl. CLXXII.). This is obviously suggested by Pindar's verses :—

> "The modern bard, says Tom, divinely sings
> Of virtuous, gracious, good, uxorious Kings,
> Who love their wives so constant from their heart ;
> Who down at Windsor daily go a-shopping,
> Their heads, right royal, into houses popping,
> And doing wonders in the haggling art.

> "And why, in God's name, should not Queens and Kings
> Purchase a comb or corkscrew, lace for cloaks,
> Edging for caps, or tape for apron-strings,
> Or pins, or bobbin, cheap as other folks?"

In 1789, the Duke of York's duel with Colonel Lennox,[2] in consequence of a military squabble, gave rise to a number of caricatures. Gillray took the Duke's side, and published an etching called *A Prince and a Poltroon*, which represents the Duke firing in the air, while his adversary aims straight

---

[1] Dr. John Cheyne (1777–1836). An army surgeon, who published some medical works. In the latter part of his career he had a large practice at Dublin, and in 1820 he was appointed physician-general to the forces in Ireland.

[2] Colonel Charles Lennox (1764–1819), nephew of the third Duke of Richmond. He succeeded as fourth Duke in 1806. He gave the famous ball at Brussels on the eve of Quatre-Bras. His quarrel with the Prince was about some military detail.

W.M 1786

Published Feb 24th 1786, by J. Phillips
No 13, Piccadilly

THE CONSTANT COUPLE

SUMMER AMUSEMENT AT FARMER G——'S NEAR WINDSOR

Sold by W. Moore, No 308 Oxford Street April 28th 1789

CITY HORSEMANSHIP OR PROCESSION TO ST PAUL'S

CLXXII

A MILLINER'S SHOP

London, Publish'd March 24th 1787 by S. W. Fores, No 3, Piccadilly

at his head. Lord Rawdon,[1] the Prince's second, and Lord Winchilsea,[2] Colonel Lennox's second, also figure in the design (Pl. CLXXVI.). In September, 1791, the marriage of the Duke of York to the eldest daughter of the King of Prussia was the subject of much rejoicing, not only in the simple household at Windsor, but in the country at large. The Duke was the first of the royal princes to submit himself to the marriage yoke, if we except the unofficial union of the Prince of Wales with Mrs. Fitzherbert, and the match was regarded as a brilliant one. The bride was young and pretty, and brought with her a dowry sufficiently substantial to ensure her welcome at the English Court. She became, for a time at least, an immense favourite with the public, and her pretty face, her tiny foot, and her charming manners were celebrated on all sides. Even Gillray softens his pencil when he deals with the little Duchess. In *The Introduction* he depicts the presentation of the bride to her parents-in-law by her husband. The attention of the King and Queen is exclusively fixed upon the gold pieces which the Duchess carries in her apron, and upon the sacks of specie borne by her attendant, a gigantic member of the Prussian Guard. In *The York Minuet* the Duke and Duchess are dancing at the state ball which was given in honour of their return; while in *The York Reverence* the bride and bridegroom are receiving a congratulatory address from the Mayor and Corporation of London. The City Fathers appear in the guise of bulls, and their spokesman is an ass. To show the affability and condescension of the royal pair, the Duke bows down to the ground, and the Duchess makes so low a courtesy—of the type that children call a " cheese "—that only her head is visible above the swirl of her robes (Pl. CLXXV.).

The Duke of Clarence came in for his share of public attention about the same period, in consequence of his notorious connection with Mrs. Jordan.[3] The lady, who was born in 1762, had made her first appearance on the London stage as Peggy in *The Country Girl* in 1785, and found instant favour with the public. Although she bore the Duke no fewer than ten children, she continued in the exercise of her profession down to the year 1809. As her royal protector was only able to allow her a thousand a year, her salary of thirty pounds a week was necessary to the comfort of the *ménage*. Gillray, who published a blubber-lipped portrait of the Duke as *Nauticus*, with the motto, "Those lips were made for kissing, ladies," also etched a plate called *La Promenade en Famille—A Sketch from Life* (1796). The Sailor Prince is dragging a small selection of his family in a go-cart from Richmond to Bushey. It is a hot day, and the Duke mops his face, while the ugly children scream in chorus. In a modifi-

---

[1] Francis, Lord Rawdon (1754–1826). Distinguished himself in the American War. Created Baron Rawdon in 1783, succeeded as Earl Moira in 1793, and was created Marquis of Hastings in 1817. His brilliant career in India is a matter of history.

[2] George, eighth Earl of Winchilsea and fourth Earl of Nottingham. He died unmarried in 1826.

[3] Dorothea Jordan, *née* Bland (1762–1816). She played a long series of comedy parts with the greatest success down to 1809. When the Duke broke with her she was granted a modest pension. She retired to France in 1815, and died at St. Cloud in somewhat mysterious circumstances.

cation of her favourite masculine attire, Mrs. Jordan walks beside the go-cart, absorbed in the study of her part from a play-book inscribed " Act III., enter Little Pickle."

The Prince of Wales could never complain of neglect at the hands of the caricaturists ; indeed, he might have adapted Peter Pindar's *mot*, and said that he was a better subject to Gillray than Gillray was to the King. In 1787 the Prince had won a temporary relief from his financial difficulties by authorising Fox to deny in the House of Commons his marriage to Mrs. Fitzherbert. Reassured by this denial, Ministers had sanctioned fresh grants to the prodigal, who is accordingly depicted (June 2nd, 1787) as *The Prince in Clover*. The only drawback to this comfortable state of things was the natural indignation of Mrs. Fitzherbert when she discovered that her reputation had been sacrificed in order to smooth over her lover's difficulties. Her distress was maliciously illustrated by Gillray in the plate *Dido Forsaken. Sic transit gloria Reginae*. Seated on her sacrificial pile, the poor lady bewails her fate, while the plumed coronet is blown off her head by a blast raised by Pitt and Dundas. The faithless Prince is sailing away to Windsor Castle in a boat labelled " Honour," with Burke, North, and Fox for his crew. He looks back contemptuously at the forsaken lady, and declares roundly, " I never saw her before in my life."

The quarrel seems to have been speedily made up, for the couple lived together in more or less harmony until the Prince's admiration for Lady Jersey[1] led to further trouble in 1795. Another crisis was approaching in the Prince's financial affairs, but it was felt that a second application to Parliament for a grant towards payment of the ever-accumulating debts would hardly be entertained, unless the heir-apparent was prepared to make certain sacrifices in return for the relief he craved, and give some guarantee of future reformation. The King had long been anxious that his eldest son should choose a wife from among the princesses of Europe ; while the fact that Lady Jersey was in favour of the royal marriage, thinking that a larger establishment for her lover would add to her own importance, probably strengthened the Prince's resolution to take the plunge. When it became known that Caroline of Brunswick was the chosen bride, and actually on her way to England, the hopes of the nation rose high, for it was believed that now at last the royal prodigal would mend his ways and settle down into a respectable member of society. The popular feeling was well illustrated by Gillray in his *Lover's Dream* (January 4th, 1795), in which the Prince is seen dreaming of his bride, a vision of whom floats towards him through the air, while the darker powers, including Fox, Sheridan, Mrs. Fitzherbert, Bacchus with his barrel, and the race-horses, are hastening away, unable to face the radiant presence of the young Princess.

---

[1] Frances, wife of George Bussy, fourth Earl of Jersey, and daughter of Dr. Twysden, Bishop of Raphoe. She married Lord Jersey in 1770, and died in 1821.

Jo Gy design et fecit

Pubd July 2nd 1792 by H. Humphrey
No 18, Old Bond Street

A VOLUPTUARY UNDER THE HORRORS OF DIGESTION

Pub.d Nov. 23, 1796
by H. Humphrey, New Bond Street

GEORGEY A' COCKHORSE

The YORK-REVERENCE; _ or _ City-Loyalty, amply rewarded.

Pub.d Dec.r 27th 1791, by H. Humphrey, N.o 18, Old Bond Street

The public inquiry into the Prince's difficulties, which proved even more serious than had been imagined, his undisguised indifference to his bride, the baleful influence of Lady Jersey, and Caroline's natural jealousy, were elements out of which no happy *ménage* could be formed. In an etching for July, 1795, by Isaac Cruikshank, called *Washing the Blackamoor* after a comic opera of that name, the Prince and two attendants are seen hard at work trying to scrub Lady Jersey's face clean. The Princess, looking in at the door, says, "It won't do; she must put on another face" (Pl. CLXXVII.). Mrs. Fitzherbert also came to the fore again, with permission from her confessor to rejoin her husband, and with claims which could only be satisfied by a large pension and a house in Park Lane. "His Royal Highness," observes one of the Prince's biographers, "had thus the delight of being hampered with three women at a time, two of them prodigal, and totally past the day of attraction, if attraction could have been an excuse, and the third complaining of neglect, which brought upon him, and even his two old women, a storm of censure and ridicule."

Even the birth of the little Princess Charlotte in February, 1796, had not the hoped-for effect of bringing the unhappy couple together. A partial separation was followed by a temporary reconciliation in the summer of 1796, which was commemorated by Gillray in a design called *Enchantments Lately Seen upon the Mountains of Wales; or, Shon ap Morgan's Reconcilement to the Fairy Princess*. But a final rupture took place only a few months later, owing to fresh follies on the part of the Prince. The Princess and her ladies were established in a house at Blackheath, and for a brief period the domestic affairs of the heir-apparent ceased to occupy the attention of the caricaturists.

MISCELLANEOUS

PART I

DOMESTIC INTERIORS, STREET SCENES, SHOPPING, ETC.

IN this chapter it is proposed to give a few scenes from the life of the middle and lower classes, whether at home or abroad, a subject which is not easy to deal with in face of the ferocious candour with which the caricaturist sketched the ugliness, the squalor, the brutalisation of the trading and labouring classes. John Collet is the chief exponent of middle-class and professional life between the years 1765 and 1778, and later Rowlandson drew a certain amount of his material from the same source, as did Bunbury, Woodward, and Collings, all working between 1780 and 1800. Previous to the middle of the century comparatively few designs were based upon scenes in private life; or even, strange to say, upon the humours of the streets. The professional man, the shopkeeper, and the labourer could not compete for popular interest with the dramatic artist and the charlatan.

Nevertheless some half-dozen pictorial satires, dealing with commonplace everyday existence, may be singled out for notice among those published between 1730 and 1760. The best and most characteristic specimens are to be found, it need hardly be said, amongst the works of William Hogarth—in his series of *Industry and Idleness* and *Four Times of the Day*, or in detached plates such as *The Stage Coach* or *The Sleeping Congregation*. In *Southwark Fair*, "invented, painted, and engraved" by Hogarth in 1733, we are shown the humours of the populace assembled in the open space in front of Newington Church, and of the performers on the platforms of theatrical booths, the rope-dancers, conjurers, and quack doctors (Pl. CLXXVIII.). In *A Sleeping Congregation*, published in 1736, the interior of a country church is depicted, where the congregation has taken only too literally the preacher's text, " Come unto me all ye that labour and are heavy laden, and I will give you rest," for all are sound asleep except the clerk, who is kept up by a sense of the responsibility of his position, and also by the attractions of a young woman who has dozed off with her Prayer-book open at the service for Holy

A PRINCE AND A POLTROON

*Pub.d May 27.th 1789
by J. Aitken, Castle St
Leicester Field*

s

Price 1/6 plain

I. Cruikshanks

WASHING THE BLACKAMOOR

Pub.ᵈ July 24, 1795 by S. W. Fores, Piccadilly

THE VIEW AND HUMOURS OF BILLINGSGATE.

THE
Wonders of y.° Deep,
often attempted and
never performed, but by
Arndt Vanhuesten
1736.

Here Great Belinus held his Court of Old
Takes are now obstreperously Sold
There Bows were made to Ministers of State
The Populace now purchase Ling and Skate

And where the Courtier's smiling Face portended,
Deceit to those who thought they were befriended:
You may, if Prudence is your courteous guide
Procure the produce of the oceans Pride

But Ah! beware, when you your Beard would grace:
To rouse the Elevation of that place
For else while bargaining for Prawns & Shrimps,
You'll hear your self proclaimed a thous and Pimps

Consider likewise when you are resort:
To this fam'd Market that was once a Court:
Our gracious Court with a propitious hand
Diffuses plenteous Markets through the Land.

Painted, Engraved & Published
by Wm Hogarth March 25th 1738

MORNING

[FOUR TIMES OF THE DAY]

Invented, Painted & Engraved by Wm Hogarth, 1733

SOUTHWARK FAIR

H. Gravelot inv. et sculp 1741

FORE-WARNED, FORE-ARMED

Published by John Osborn in Paternoster Row

A PARISH FEAST

HUMBLY INSCRIBED TO THE CHURCH-WARDENS, VESTRYMEN, QUESTMEN, AND PARISH OFFICERS, BY Sᴙ GUZZLEDOWN TEARFOWL

Publish'd Decʳ 26, 1741.   Price 6ᵈ   Sold by Samuel Lyne, Print Seller at the Globe in Newgate Street

Price one shilling

Design'd and Engrav'd by W. Hogarth—Publish'd according to Act of Parliament 1747

THE STAGE COACH;
OR COUNTRY INN YARD

MISCELLANEOUS

Matrimony. The clergyman has been identified as the Rev. J. Theophilus Desaguiliers, chaplain to the Prince of Wales and author of *A Course of Mechanical and Experimental Philosophy.*

In the same year, 1736, appeared an interesting design by Arnold Vanhaecken called *The View and Humours of Billingsgate—The Wonders of the Deep*—"Often attempted and never performed, but by Arnold Vanhaecken" (Pl. CLXXIX.). This is a representation of Billingsgate Market, a large open space, bounded on one side by shops and booths, with the quay, along which several fishing-boats are moored, in the background. Scattered about the market are groups of persons engaged in buying or selling fish, a quack doctor on horseback, a party of ladies alarmed at a dog with a flask tied to his tail who has upset a hawker, and a boy who fastens a fish to the wig of an old gentleman eating oysters at a stall. The lines below refer to the days when "Great Belinus held his Court of old" on the spot where "Oisters are now obstreperously sold," and warns the purchaser to beware when he his board would grace, lest he "rouse the Elocution of that place."

In 1738 came Hogarth's series *Four Times of the Day*, which throws such a vivid light upon the street life of London at that period. The prints are so familiar that a few words will be sufficient to recall each subject to the reader. The scene of the first, *Morning*, is laid in Covent Garden at 7.55 a.m. by the clock on St. Paul's Church. A tall, thin old maid is on her way home from early service with a shivering footboy behind her. This lady is apparently sketched from the same original as the spinster who is seen rushing into a building inscribed "Lottery for Husbands" in Hogarth's early satire on *The South Sea Scheme*. Tradition has it that the model was an elderly relation of the artist's, who, for some unknown reason, had cut him out of her will. To the right of the spectator is Tom King's too notorious coffee-house, whence issue some roystering blades, who force their attentions upon the more comely of the young market-women, much to the scandal of the old maid (Pl. CLXXX.).

In *Noon* the scene changes to Hog Lane, Soho, just outside the French Chapel. Although the district was more fashionable then than it is now, it was already occupied by a large number of French refugees, to which class belong, we may suppose, the effeminate-looking man and the fashionably dressed lady, who are the most striking figures among the congregation that issues from the chapel. A little boy is crying bitterly over a broken dish in which he was carrying home a pudding for dinner, while a small girl, with the practicality of her sex, gathers up scraps of the scattered dainty and eagerly devours them. It will be noted that there is no footway to the roughly paved street, and that a dead cat is among the contents of the overflowing gutter. In the third plate of the series, *Evening*, we are taken to a lane near Sadler's Wells, along which strolls a bourgeois family on its way home from a rural expedition. The father of the family carries a little girl and walks meekly beside his stout wife, while the pair are followed by another girl who scolds a small brother because he lags behind. It is made painfully evident that each member of the family is hot, tired, and cross, a not uncommon result of a party of pleasure. With the last scene, *Night*, we are back again in town, in a street near Charing Cross. The Salisbury Flying Coach has just been upset in consequence of the horses taking fright at a bonfire in the street. A squib has been thrown into the coach, which adds to the terrors of the travellers who are struggling at the windows. The bonfire and the squibs are in honour of Restoration Day, May 29th, and the anniversary has evidently been celebrated by a drunken man who is being escorted home by a small youth.

Parochial officials and their methods of conducting public business have always been considered fair game by the satirist, so that it is not surprising to find an early attack upon Bumbledom in a caricature (*circa* 1740) called *A Parish Feast, humbly inscribed to Churchwardens, Vestrymen, and Parish Officers, by Sir Guzzleton Tearefowl* (Pl. CLXXXII.). A party of men, including two clergymen, a churchwarden, and a parish clerk, are feasting in a vestry room. The churchwarden is sending a chicken and some wine to his own house, while a beadle, who is in attendance, steals a bottle from an ice-pail. Over the fireplace is the churchwarden's account, which proves that one dinner has cost £30, and that £80 has been spent on Sacramental wine, most of which has been drunk in the vestry. In the background are two little figures representing a charity-school boy and girl, and on a ribbon between the pair is their complaint: "Our Churchwardens spends the silver, and gives us the farthins."

An elaborate domestic satire was published by H. Gravelot[1] in 1741 under the title of *Fore-warned, Fore-armed; or, the Bachelor's Monitor—being a modest Estimate of the Expenses attending the Married Life* (Pl. CLXXXI.). The design represents the Temple of Hymen, in front of which stands the presiding deity, holding his torch and a set of manacles, and attended by the symbolical figures of Discord and Poverty. He is introducing a lady with a small bag of money to a youth who offers her a paper inscribed "Joynture." A satyr points to a screed headed "Estimate," while Liberty is deserting the would-be bridegroom. Below is engraved a long list of the probable expenses of a married man, which is in painful contrast to a very short list setting forth the cost of living to a bachelor. With the passing of time this bit of pictorial cynicism has acquired the value of an historical document, since it gives us an insight into the domestic arrangements of an upper-middle-class household in the reign of George II. A few of the more important items in the estimate may here be quoted, but in dealing with prices it must be remembered that the purchasing power of money was about double then what it is now.

---

[1] Hubert François Gravelot (1699–1773). A French engraver, whose real name was Bourguignon. He was a pupil of Restout, and came to London in 1732, where he found plenty of employment as a book-illustrator. He executed designs for Sir T. Hamner's *Shakespeare*, the *Dunciad*, Gay's *Fables*, and many other works. He was also responsible for caricatures, costume plates, and architectural drawings. He kept a school of art in the Strand, where Gainsborough is said to have been among the pupils. In 1745 Gravelot returned to Paris, and in the following years illustrated the works of Voltaire, Racine, and Marmontel.

CHRISTMAS GAMBOLLS
BOXING DAY
Publish'd Dec y* 26, 1747 by P. Griffin Fleet Street, price 6¹*

STAND COACHMAN, OR THE HAUGHTY LADY WELL FITTED
Taken from Fact, and Publish'd for J. Wakelin in Flower de Luce Court, Fleet Street. Pr.ce 6ᵈ 1750

CLXXVII

J. Collett pinxit   *Rennoldson Sculpsit*

GROWN LADIES TAUGHT TO DANCE

ENGRAVED AFTER AN ORIGINAL PICTURE OF MR. JOHN COLLETT IN THE POSSESSION OF MR. SMITH

London. Printed for Robt Sayer, No 53, in Fleet Street & John Smith, No 35, in Cheapside

CLXXVI

[c 1770]

A PLEASING METHOD OF ROUZING THE DOCTOR—

OR A TYTHE PIG NO BAD SIGHT

Printed for Carington Bowles at his Map & Print Warehouse No 69 in St Paul's Churchyard. London

MISCELLANEOUS

We are given to understand that the couple in question enjoy an income of £600 or £700 a year (the lady brought a dowry of £2,000), equal to £1,000 or £1,200 at the present time. During the first fifteen years of their union eight children are born to them, of whom four die in infancy. The average annual expenses of these fifteen years are calculated, with allowance for interest on the money sunk in furniture, repairs, and so forth. The house-rent amounted to £40 a year, with £9 for rates, taxes, and pew-rent. This sum represents barely a tenth of the income, while in these days the rent of a London house has to be reckoned at one-eighth or even one-sixth of the income. The couple kept three servants (including a man in livery) whose united wages came to £22 a year. The butcher's bill amounted to £60 a year, and the grocer's to £20, but there is a heavy separate entry of £20 for tea, coffee, and chocolate. The bread and the coal bills come to £15 each, and fruit, vegetables, and butter run away with another £20. The doctor's little account is £12, a rather high yearly average, even though four children had to be helped out of the world during the period under consideration. The expenses attendant on the arrival of eight are considered under another heading. Clothes for the mother and the young people cost £90 a year, but there is another £30 for Madam's pocket money, which is spent in coach-hire, chair-hire, waterage, balls, plays, concerts, and visits to Vauxhall. There is also the money lost at cards, "an amusement that has banished the needle out of modern education for Ladies."

But the most extraordinary items in the whole estimate, according to modern ideas, are those which relate severally to education and drink. One year with another £30 was spent on the schooling of the four surviving children, while no less than £50 annually went in wine, beer, and spirits. Taking the modern equivalents of these sums, we should have a couple with £1,200 a year spending a hundred annually on their cellar and £60 on their children's education.

Turning to the reverse of the medal, the happy bachelor is represented as living in elegant comfort on £87 a year, his income being divided between rent (£30), board (£30), laundress (£10), tea and sugar (£10), firing and candles (£7). Clothing and amusements are omitted, as being the same in both states of life. The moral drawn from the two budgets is, that "the Ladies ought, in justice and gratitude, to think themselves under great obligations to the gentlemen who will marry them under all these apparent disadvantages, and to be kind, frugal, and obedient wives."

Hogarth's delightful *Stage Coach; or, Country Inn Yard at Election Time*, appeared in 1747 (Pl. CLXXXIII.). The design throws an interesting light upon the discomforts suffered by outside travellers, who sat in a precarious position upon the roof, with no seats or rails. Nothing could well be more characteristic than the back of the old lady who is being assisted into the interior of the coach, and who obviously belongs to the class of female that insists on having the windows shut, and eats peppermint steadily throughout a long journey. The manners of the London populace are sketched in a couple of prints for Christmas of the same year, *Christmass Gambolls: Boxing Day* and *The Covent Garden Morning Frolic*. The scene of the first is laid in a street, apparently intended for Cheapside, where a motley crowd is assembled, including the famous quack, "Dr. Rock," a woman singing carols, a street preacher, a crossing-sweeper, and representatives of "Captain Flash" and "Fribble," characters in Garrick's farce *The Modern Duel* (Pl. CLXXXIII.). The second subject is more distinctly jovial in tone (as joviality was then understood), the principal personages being a pair of drunken revellers—male and female—who are returning from a masquerade through Covent Garden, the man on the roof of a sedan-chair and his companion inside. The watch has been assaulted by the masqueraders, and the market-people seem to be jeering impartially at the revellers and the guardians of the peace.

That the mob did not allow itself to be unduly oppressed by the superior classes may be gathered from a design for the year 1750, called *Stand, Coachman; or, the Haughty Lady well fitted*, and described as "taken from the Fact" (Pl. CLXXXV.). A fine gilt chariot has been drawn up across the footway in front of a toy-shop situated at the bottom of the Haymarket, and a gentleman is in the act of passing through the interior of the vehicle, much to the annoyance of the lady within. A chimney-sweeper and a porter are preparing to take advantage of the right of way thus established, while several passers-by look on in amusement. According to the rhymed explanation, a gentleman had civilly requested the coachman to draw out of the way, but the fine-lady occupant of the chariot having responded with the order, "Stand, coachman," the doors were forcibly opened, and the mob began to make its way through, whereupon

> "The Lady, much ruffled, soon altered her tone,
> And called to her coachman in haste to move on."

Between 1760 and 1770 a large number of crudely coloured mezzotints dealing with the foibles of professional men were issued by Carington Bowles, of St. Paul's Churchyard. These rough satires, many of which were designed by John Collet, include such subjects as *A Master Parson with a Good Living* (a prosperous cleric at dinner with his family, waited on by a servant in livery) and *A Journeyman Parson with a Bare Existence* (a poor curate hungrily gnawing a bone, surrounded by his half-starved children); *Dr. Gallipot and his Wig of Knowledge* (a physician weighing the fee which he has just received from a patient); *A Sharp between two Flats* (a lawyer between two litigants); and *A Flat between two Sharps* (a countryman between two lawyers). This rather obvious type of caricature may be illustrated by an example called *A Pleasing Method of Rousing the Parson; or, A Tythe Pig no bad Sight* (Pl. CLXXXVI.). A country parson is here seen sound asleep in his study, with a table by his side, on which are a bottle of wine, a book on "Tythe Laws fully considered," and a paper inscribed "Banns of Marriage." A maid-servant has just brought in a plump sucking-pig, and is rousing her master by tickling his nose with the animal's tail. The boy who has brought the pig waits in the doorway. In one variation of this design, the offering consists of a baby, presumably the tenth of the farmer's family.

A pair of companion prints after pictures by John Collet, *Grown Gentlemen taught to Dance* and *Grown Ladies taught to Dance*, were among the most popular caricatures of the sixties. The designs were probably suggested by the advertisement of Le Roque's famous dancing academy, where adults were taught to thread the mazes of a minuet. In the first, an awkward elderly man is being instructed by a well-formed, supple young professor, while another unpromising pupil awaits his turn. A blind fiddler is playing on a violin with a broken string, and on the wall is a placard announcing that " Grown Gentlemen are taught to Dance, and qualified to appear in the most brilliant assemblies at the Easy Expense of £1 11s. 6d." (Pl. CLXXXVIII.). In the companion subject, *Grown Ladies taught to Dance*, a stiff lady of mature years is taking a lesson from a young instructor, while two little girls look on and giggle at her mistakes (Pl. CLXXXVII.). The popularity of these subjects may be gauged by the fact that they were copied or adapted in innumerable forms, and introduced in the shape of tableaux into a contemporary pantomime.

Two or three pictures from a lower stratum of social life were executed by Collet about the beginning of the seventies, of which it may be sufficient to mention *The Bold Attempt* (engraved by Caldwall),[1] a scene in what may be called the Hogarth "school," representing a young man trying to snatch a kiss from a girl in a churchyard, much to the horror of the parson and of the congregation of old ladies who are issuing from the church; *The Recruiting Sergeant* (engraved by Golder),[2] a conventional design, in which we see a young man on the point of taking the shilling from a wily sergeant, in spite of the persuasions of his sweetheart and the grief of his aged mother; and *High Life Below Stairs* (engraved by Caldwall), a rather pretty drawing of a party of servants in a kitchen. A valet dresses the hair of a comely maid, and another girl sings to a guitar, to the delight of an admirer and the distress of a dog. An elderly woman stands at a wash-tub, and pays no attention to the vagaries of her fellows (Pl. CXCI.).

A pair of hand-coloured mezzotints after drawings by J. H. Grimm, which found favour with the public about this time (*circa* 1770), illustrate the consternation with which the dress and frivolities of certain up-to-date young people filled the breasts of their old-fashioned provincial parents. "Well-a-day, is this my son Tom?" exclaims a respectable old John Bull of a farmer, in blue coat, top boots, and flat beaver hat, who, during a visit to town, has run against his son, a full-blown Maccaroni, in the regulation club wig, little cocked hat, scarlet coat, green waistcoat, yellow breeches, two watches,

---

[1] John Caldwall (1739–89). A pupil of Sherwin. He engraved a number of portraits.
[2] John Golder (1729–95).

and long cane (Pl. CLXXXIX.). In the companion design the scene is laid in the neighbourhood of a farmhouse. The farmer's wife, in her black hat and mantle and neat muslin apron, stands aghast at the sight of her daughter, who has just returned from town, wearing the fashionable high-frizzured head, a low-cut gown, and shepherdess hat. "Be not amazed, dear mother," exclaims the young woman, "it is indeed your daughter Anne" (Pl. CXC.).

A group of street scenes may conveniently be discussed together, though they are spread over a period of some twenty years. One of the earliest is an engraving by Rennoldson, after a picture of John Collet, called *The Female Orators* (1768). Here we have two coster-women engaged in a violent altercation, while a boy steals the cherries of the one and a dog steals the fish of the other (Pl. CXCII.). A man points significantly to a poster on the wall, inscribed "Epicœne, or the Silent Woman," and a gentleman steps out of a sedan-chair, holding his hands to his ears. In *The Lady's Disaster*, also from a design by Collet, the scene is laid in a London street on a windy morning. A lady's hat, cap, and wig have been blown off her head, and are being brought back to her by a passer-by, while others look on and laugh at her confusion. On the wall is one of Collet's favourite posters, this time an advertisement of the popular "Lecture on Heads" by G. A. Stevens [1] (Pl. CXCIII.). Rowlandson's graceful *Street Cries* gives rather an idealised representation of some of the London costers, male and female; and in *The East End of the Town* we have a picturesque group of young sailors flirting with their sweethearts in the shadow of the Tower. Lastly, the costume and general appearance of a London crowd in 1785 may be studied in Bunbury's clever sketch, *A Dancing Bear* (Pl. CXCIV.).

Turning next to shopping scenes we find that milliners' shops provide the majority of the subjects, and that the customers were most frequently men, whose stock of lace frills and ruffles required constant replenishment. It is curious how small a part the occupation of shopping seems to have played in the life of the fashionable ladies of the eighteenth century; at least, if we may judge from contemporary letters and journals. There are occasional references to visits to a toy or china shop, but a great lady seems to have been "waited upon" by mercers and tailors at her own house. The smart young shopman, however, appears to have been quite a recognised type of the period. As early as 1709 Steele had sketched his portrait in the *Tatler*. "This afternoon," he relates, "some ladies, having an opinion of my fancy in clothes, desired me to accompany them to Ludgate Hill, which I take to be as agreeable an amusement as a lady can pass away three or four hours in. The shops are perfect gilded theatres, the variety of wrought silks, so many changes of fine scenes, and the Mercers are the performers in the Opera. They are the sweetest, fairest, nicest dished-out creatures; and by their elegant address and

---

[1] George Alexander Stevens (1710–84). Author of *The History of Tom Fool* (1760), *A Lecture on Heads*, first delivered at the Haymarket in 1764, and *A Trip to Portsmouth*, a successful farce acted in 1773.

B. Clowes fecit

GROWN GENTLEMEN TAUGHT TO DANCE

ENGRAVED AFTER AN ORIGINAL PICTURE OF Mʀ JOHN COLLETT, IN THE POSSESSION OF Mʀ SMITH

London.   Printed for Robᵗ Sayer, No 53, in Fleet Street, 30ᵗʰ Sept 1768

From an original drawing by Grimm [c. 1770]

BE NOT AMAZ'D DEAR MOTHER—IT IS INDEED YOUR DAUGHTER ANNE

Published for Carington Bowles at his Map & Print Warehouse, No 69, in S! Paul's Churchyard, London

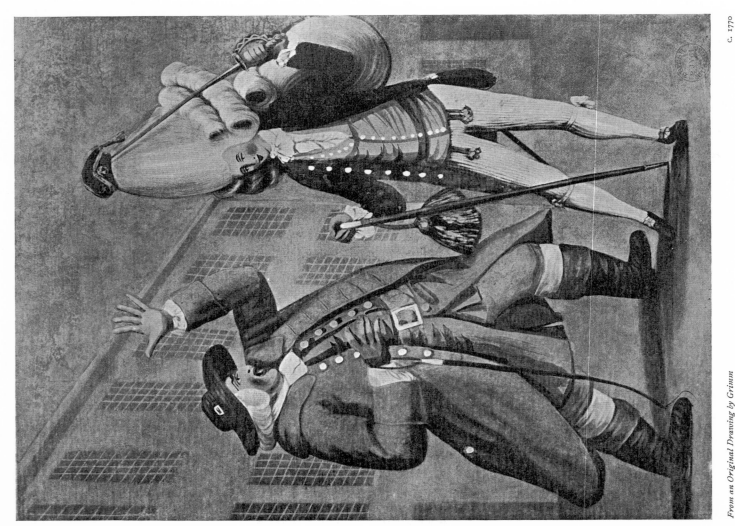

From an Original Drawing by Grimm

WELL-A-DAY! IS THIS MY SON TOM!

Pub. by Carington Bowles, No 60, in S! Paul's Churchyard, London

c. 1770

Collett pinx.

Caldwell Sculpt

HIGH LIFE BELOW STAIRS

London.   Printed for R. Sayer, No 53, Fleet Street, & I. Smith, No 35, Cheapside

Pub. 20th May 1772

M. Rennoldson sculp

THE FEMALE ORATORS
ENGRAVED FROM AN ORIGINAL PICTURE PAINTED BY Mʀ JOHN COLLET

Printed for Jnᵒ Smith, No, 35, Cheapside & Robᵗ Sayer, No 53 Fleet Street. Nov 20, 1768

THE LADIES DISASTER

Jᵃ Caldwell Sculp

ENGRAVED FROM AN ORIGINAL PICTURE PAINTED BY Mᴿ JNᵒ COLLET

London. Printed for J. Smith, No 35, Cheapside, & R. Sayer, No 53 in Fleet S. 2ⁿᵈ April 1771

H. Bunbury Delinᵗ

A DANCING BEAR

Engrav'd by C. Knight
[1785]

Brandoin pinxt.   *Caldwell Sculp*

THE CHARMING MILLENER OF —— STREET

London, Printed for J. Smith, No 35, Cheapside, &
Robt Sayer No 53, Fleet Street 6th Decr 1771

A MAN MILLENER.   The MUFF

Pub. Feby 16 1787 by S.W. Fores at the Caracature Warehouse No 3 Piccadilly   *th Feb. 1787*

J. Collett pinx^t   THE RIVAL MILLINERS   [C. 1770]

CXCVIII

A MILLENER'S SHOP

MRS. MONOPOLIZE, THE BUTCHER'S WIFE, PURCHASING A MODERN HEAD DRESS

Publish'd April 9th 1772, by W. Humphrey, St Martin's Lane

Painted by H. Wigstead

Engraved by E. Williams
1781

THE COUNTRY VICAR'S FIRE SIDE

CC

J. Collet pinxt

J. Caldwell sculp

THE UNWELCOME CUSTOMER

Printed for J. Smith, No 35 Cheapside & R. Sayer, No 53, Fleet Street   17 August 1772

soft speeches, you would guess them to be Italians. . . . We saw abundance of gay fancies, fit for Sea-captains' wives, Sheriff's Feast and Taunton-deane ladies. 'This, Madam, is so diverting a silk. This, Madam, is wonderfully charming. This, Madam, my stars! how cool it looks! But this, Madam—ye gods! would I had ten thousand yards of it.' . . . When we had pleased ourselves, and bid him 10s. a yard for what he asked 15s.; 'Fan me, ye winds, your Ladyship rallies me! Should I part with it at such a price, the Weavers would rise upon the very shop. Was you at the Park last night, Madam? Your Ladyship shall abate me sixpence,'" etc. etc.

It is just such a "pert young particle" that we see three-quarters of a century later in *The Man Milliner*, a sketch of a pretty youth in a scarlet coat with yellow facings, who carries a bandbox and a bundle. He reappears in *The Man Milliner and the Muff*, with a female companion who is almost hidden behind one of the huge fur muffs then in fashion (Pl. CXCVI.).

In a mezzotint called *The Milliner's Shop*, which appeared about 1772, we have a butcher's wife trying on one of the high-frilled caps that were then considered extremely chic. The shopwoman, who wears a cap in the same style, is showing her customer some lace, which she evidently recommends as a suitable trimming for the headdress (Pl. CXCVIII.). In another mezzotint of the same period, *The Unwelcome Customer*, a mad bull is depicted in the act of forcing its way into a milliner's shop. A drover is beating the animal about the head, and a couple of little dogs are barking at it, while the customers, male and female, scatter in terror. Two elderly men climb upon the counter, but a valiant youth draws the sword of an old gentleman, who is too frightened to use it (Pl. CC.).

From two more designs of the same decade we learn how popular a resort for gilded youth was a fashionable milliner's shop. In *The Rival Milliners*, by Collet, a couple of coquettish young shopgirls are seen dancing attendance upon a Maccaroni, one measuring his wrist for ruffles, and the other taking the size of his shoulders for epaulettes. On the counter are a box of lace and a mannequin, upon which the youth has placed his cocked hat (Pl. CXCVII.). The same subject is illustrated by a print called *The Morning Ramble*, in which two young men are lounging on the counter of a milliner's establishment and flirting with the shopgirls. Lace lappets and a petticoat are exhibited in the window, and on the shelves are bandboxes labelled "Coxcomb," "Mode," "Love," etc. The youths might well be forgiven for their infatuation if all the girls behind the counter were as pretty as *The Charming Milliner of ———— Street*, who was sketched by Brandoin in 1771, as she tripped along with her big bandbox on her arm (Pl. CXCV.).

A popular etching of Gillray's was *Heroes Recruiting at Kelsey's; or, Guard Day at St. James'*, which appeared in 1797. Kelsey was a well-known fruiterer in St. James' Street, and Gillray, from his room over Miss Humphrey's shop, must often have seen the officers of the Household troops refreshing themselves after the fatigues of parade. In the above-mentioned design he has drawn a tall, lanky, and extremely ugly officer, said to be a portrait of a Colonel Burch, who is devouring ice-creams at Kelsey's counter. A short, plump captain, perched on a high stool, is greedily eating sweets out of a bag; while a third warrior stands in the doorway, his cocked hat very much on one side, watching the carriages going to the " Drawing-room Levee."

MISCELLANEOUS

PART II

BEFORE entering upon the consideration of a small group of "domestic interiors" and satires upon foreigners in England, of which the best examples are drawn from Rowlandson's works, it may be well to give a brief summary of the career of Gillray's greatest rival. Born in the Old Jewry in 1756, Thomas Rowlandson was the son of fairly well-to-do parents, his father belonging to that large class which is vaguely described as "something in the City." Owing, however, to a dangerous habit of "experimenting in various branches of manufacture," with insufficient capital, the elder Rowlandson became involved in difficulties before his son had finished his education. But Thomas had, throughout his life, a happy knack of landing on his feet; and at this crisis in the family affairs his path was smoothed for him by a generous uncle, Thomas Rowlandson the elder, who had married a French lady with property of her own. The boy received his early education at Dr. Barrow's school in Soho Square, where among his schoolfellows were John Bannister,[1] the future comedian, and Harry Angelo, son of the famous fencing-master, a pair of kindred spirits with whom he kept up a friendship which only ended with his life.

On leaving Dr. Barrow's, Thomas was entered at the Academy Schools, but his training here was interrupted by a long visit to his French aunt, then (1771) a widow, and living in Paris. His stay in France lasted nearly two years, and during this period he studied painting at one of the academies, learnt to talk French like a native, and was transformed into a "complete beau." During the last part of the time his studies suffered somewhat from his taste for Parisian gaiety, which, at eighteen, he was old enough to appreciate; but on his return to London he continued his training at the Academy Schools, where he was regarded as a pupil of exceptional promise, more especially as regarded his drawings from the life. His first contribution to the Royal Academy exhibition appeared in 1775, a drawing called *Delilah payeth Samson a visit while in prison at Gaza*, which attracted little attention. After further travels in France and Holland, he seems to have settled down in

---

[1] John Bannister (1760–1836). He made his début at the Haymarket in 1778, and in the same year was engaged as a permanent member of the company at Drury Lane. He created several Sheridan parts, including Charles Surface, Bob Acres, and Tony Lumpkin. Bannister retired in 1815.

Wardour Street in 1777 as a portrait painter, and up to 1784 his pictures exhibited at the Academy were of a serious nature.

The natural gaiety of his disposition, which had been fostered by his experience of Parisian life, the almost fatal facility of his style, and his intimacy with Bunbury, Woodward, Collings, and the "facetious" Nixon, all helped to turn Rowlandson's attention in the direction of caricature, for which there was an ever-increasing demand on the part of the public. It was extremely difficult for a "serious" artist to succeed in England, but a clever caricaturist had the ball at his feet. In 1784 he was represented at the Academy by two of his best humorous subjects—not as yet over-exaggerated—*Vauxhall Gardens* and *An Italian Family*, and these were followed during the next two or three years by *The Introduction*, *A French Coffee-house*, *A French Family*, *Grog on Board*, and *Tea on Shore*, to note only a few of his most popular productions.

The sudden success of his drawings in this new style, and a legacy of seven thousand pounds from his French aunt, had a disturbing effect upon Rowlandson's mental equilibrium. He plunged into the wildest dissipation, haunting the gambling clubs of both London and Paris, and playing sometimes for a day and a night without interruption except for refreshment. At the same time he prided himself upon being a man not only of honour, but of honesty; he had a horror of debt, and his I.O.U. was as safe as hard cash. He lost more than one fortune over the dice, but his losses troubled him little, since he was superbly conscious of the Fortunatus' purse which he possessed in his pen.

"I have played the fool," he was accustomed to say when he came home with empty pockets, "but," holding up his famous reed pen, "here is my resource." And in his best days, before he had exhausted his imagination and deteriorated his talent by the incessant production of hasty sketches, his boast was more than fulfilled. It was believed by even the more critical of his contemporaries that had he chosen to take himself seriously he might have become one of the first historical painters of the day. Reynolds and West declared that many of his drawings would have done honour to Rubens himself.

Of the events of Rowlandson's life but little has been recorded, though we get brief glimpses of him in the rambling pages of Angelo, Pyne,[1] or J. T. Smith,[2] and it seems probable that his mode of existence was as desultory as these records. We glean a vague impression that when he was not at work he was eating huge dinners and drinking unlimited punch in the company of Bannister, Wigstead, and Peter Pindar, sitting long hours at the gaming-tables, or roving about the Continent with his friend and patron,

---

[1] William Henry Pyne (1749–1843). Artist and author. He exhibited at the Academy, but his best work is to be found in his *Microcosm, or Picturesque Delineation of the Arts, Sciences, and Manufactures of Great Britain* (1802). In later life he published some volumes of desultory reminiscence under the pen-name of Ephraim Hardcastle.

[2] John Thomas Smith (1766–1853). Topographical draughtsman and antiquary. In 1816 he was appointed Keeper of Prints and Drawings at the British Museum. His *Book for a Rainy Day*, which contains curious anecdotes of the "characters" of his time, was published after his death.

MISCELLANEOUS

Henry Mitchell, a jovial ex-banker. We learn from Angelo that on one occasion the artist was knocked down and robbed, and that he got a man hanged in consequence; not his own assailant, but a hardened villain whom, by a lucky guess, he convicted of having robbed another victim.

A deeper note is struck in Angelo's account of the visit which he paid to Portsmouth with Rowlandson in 1794, at the time of Lord Howe's return with his wounded after the victory of June 1st. The pair witnessed the landing of the French prisoners, and visited Forton Prison, where " in one of the sick-wards we saw one of the prisoners, who, an officer told us, had been a tall handsome man previous to the battle; but having received a shot that had lacerated his side, a mortification had taken place. He was then making his will; his comrades were standing by, consoling him, some grasping his hand, shedding tears. This scene was too much for me, and made such an impression on my mind that I hastened away; but I could not persuade Rowlandson to follow me, his inclination to make a sketch of the dying moment getting the better of his feelings. After waiting some time below for my friend, he produced a rough sketch of what he had seen; a ghastly figure sitting up in bed, a priest holding a crucifix before him, with a group standing around."

As time passed on Rowlandson's facility of production began to have an ill effect upon his market. His admirers were numerous and his patrons were liberal, but still the demand failed to keep pace with the extraordinary rapidity of the supply. His friend and employer, Rudolf Ackermann,[1] who kept the Repository of Fine Arts at 101, Strand, and who was to Rowlandson what the Humphreys were to Gillray, saw that something must be done to stimulate the public taste, already nearly satiated with his *protégé's* work. He finally hit upon the idea of issuing a series of periodical publications, elaborately illustrated by Rowlandson, but brought out at a price and in a form that put them within the reach of the larger public. The idea proved a happy one, as evidenced by the brilliant success of *The Poetical Magazine*, *The Dance of Death*, *The Military Adventures of Johnny Newcome*, and the various *Tours of Dr. Syntax*.

During his later years Rowlandson was too indolent to seek fresh employment, and his once prolific fancy seemed almost incapable of originating fresh designs. It was left for Ackermann to suggest promising subjects, and to keep his talent in constant exercise. In 1825 Rowlandson was attacked by illness, and remained an invalid until his death on April 27th, 1827. It is stated in the obituary notice contributed to the *Gentleman's Magazine* by an old friend of the artist, that Rowlandson's reputation did not reach its zenith in the lifetime of his friendly publisher, who survived him just seven years. Nevertheless, Ackermann's collection of water-colour drawings by Rowlandson were highly appreciated by connoisseurs, and his folios were

---

[1] Rudolf Ackermann (1764–1834). A German art publisher, who settled in London as a coach-designer, and later opened what he called a Fine Art Repository in the Strand. He found employment for many of the French *émigrés* at the time of the Revolution, and also aided the sufferers after the war (1814). He introduced art-lithography into England, and his many art publications are among the best of his period.

viewed with admiration and delight by the many artists and amateurs who frequented the famous conversazioni at the house in the Strand.

The same biographer gives a brief account of the method in which Rowlandson worked, at least in his later years, an account which has been amplified by Mr. Grego.[1] He describes how the artist used to saunter round to the Repository of Arts from his lodgings in the Adelphi, call for reed pens, drawing paper, and saucers of Indian ink and vermilion. He would then combine his inks in his own inimitable style; "in the flesh-tints vermillion predominated, in the draperies Indian ink, shadows were a warm mixture of the two, and distant objects were faintly rendered in Indian ink alone. For the octavo book illustrations, with which especial care was taken, a finished drawing was first made, and then the artist etched the outline firmly and sharply on the copper-plate, an impression from the bitten-in outline was printed on drawing paper, and the artist put in his shadows, modelling of forms, and sketchy distance, in the most delicate handling possible; the shadows were then copied in acquatint on the outlined plate, sometimes by the designer, but in most cases by an engraver. Rowlandson next completed the colouring of his own Indian-ink-shaded impression in delicate tints, harmoniously selected." This tinted impression served as a copy for Ackermann's famous staff of colourists, who, having worked under his supervision for many years, attained a degree of perfection and neatness never arrived at before, and almost beyond belief in the present day when this system has fallen into comparative disuse.[2]

Rowlandson's versatility and his powers of imagination have been almost equally praised; yet that his fancy often wearied may be guessed from the frequency with which he executed the designs of others, and also from the fact that in his later years it became necessary for his publisher to supply him with subjects as well as drawing materials. The least personal of the caricaturists in his social work, he dealt as a rule with general types and abstract topics, while he especially affected any subject which gave him the opportunity of executing a pair or a series of etchings wherein the point lay in strongly marked contrast. It is difficult to point to any artist who has ever expressed so much with so little apparent effort, and to his supple genius no type or topic came amiss. Horses, dogs, ships, landscapes, seascapes, Cockneys, soldiers, peasants, foreigners, pretty girls, and sinister rascals—he made each his *spécialité*, and excelled in all. One exception, however, must be made. Rowlandson, unlike Gillray, seldom drew a veritable *grande dame*, and though his studies in *beauté du diable* are sometimes adorable, his pretty girls tend too often to the Blowsalinda type. It may further be noted that he endows the majority of his models, male and female, with the sensual mouth that was his own most characteristic feature.

[1] In *Rowlandson the Caricaturist.*

[2] The curious resemblance between Rowlandson's style and that of certain Japanese artists of the "Popular" school, has been noted by Huysmans, who observes: "Négligeant aussi les ridicules scènes de la Vie Intime de Gavarni, les libertinages de Deverie, et les vignettes étrignées du doux Tassaert, je ne ferai halte que devant Rowlandson et les Japonais."

MISCELLANEOUS

It is scarcely surprising, when we consider his style and the general tendency of his work, that Rowlandson should have found more favour with the French than any other English caricaturist. Gillray they feared and hated, but Rowlandson had perfected his art in Paris, and assimilated no small portion of the Gallic spirit. He is, we are assured by French critics, more artistic than Gillray, more observant, and not less inventive. Though he, too, is a *débordant*, he has a caressing touch; and, even in his enormities, there is an unexpected coquetry that reminds the critic of those "jolis clowns Anglais" who perform their acrobatic feats in white kid gloves. The influence of Watteau and Boucher is apparent in his work, and certain of his designs, it is admitted, are not unworthy of one of the "little masters" of eighteenth-century France. His *morale*, as M. Filon has pointed out, was that of the ancient Gallic comedy. Ruthless towards old age, ugliness, or squalor, he showed a spirit of universal indulgence to all that was young, graceful, and charming. He was on the side of the servants against the mistresses, of the children against the parents, of debtors against their creditors, and of all rebels against established authority. He had none of the reforming spirit that animated the majority of the British caricaturists; where Hogarth frowned and Gillray struck, Rowlandson merely shrugged his shoulders and passed on with a smile.[1]

In appearance Rowlandson was tall and powerfully built, with regular features and dark, piercing eyes, deep-set under heavy brows. In the portrait of himself which he introduced into his *Countrymen and Sharpers* exhibited in 1787, he wears an expression of good-humoured rascality, but this may have been assumed for pictorial purposes. Sensuality early set its mark upon his features, and we are not surprised to read that in the course of his travels on the Continent he astonished the inn-keepers' wives, who, on his arrival, looked at the larder, and then again at the guest. "All regarded him as that reported being, of whom they had heard, the veritable Mr. Bull. His orders for the supplies of the table, ever his first concern, strengthened this opinion, and his operations at his meals confirmed the fact." In middle and later life the artist comes before us under a somewhat different aspect. There is a highly respectable, almost bourgeois, presentment of him at the age of fifty or thereabouts, and a drawing by J. T. Smith, taken at the age of seventy, shows a venerable gentleman examining an engraving through his spectacles.[2]

A rather numerous group of caricatures belonging to the last thirty or forty years of the century deals with foreigners and foreign parts, these being treated from the John Bull point of view. Hogarth's well-known *Calais Gate* was followed, especially during the periods that we were at war with France,

---

[1] In M. Filon's interesting and suggestive notes on Rowlandson, he dwells with especial admiration on the artist's studies of equine life, from the high-mettled racer down to the worn-out cart-horse with hanging head and trembling knees. The French critic inclines to the opinion that it was Rowlandson who revealed the psychology of the horse to the animal painters of the succeeding generation.

[2] This was sketched during one of Rowlandson's visits to the Print Room at the British Museum. J. T. Smith was then Keeper of the Print Department.

by many other designs of the same *genre*. A couple of pictures by John Collet (*circa* 1770) represent *The Frenchman in London* and *The Englishman in Paris*. In the first, the scene is laid in a London street, where a terrified Frenchman is being urged to fight a butcher, much to the amusement of the onlookers; in the second, we are transported to a Parisian barber's shop, where an Englishman is having his hair powdered. On the wall is a picture of a bear being adorned by monkeys, and on the floor lies a book called "A Six Weeks' Tour to Paris." Less familiar are two drawings by Charles Brandoin, *The English Lady in Paris* and *A French Petit Maître and his Valet* (1771). The first, engraved by B. Godfrey, shows a stout, elderly lady in a very gorgeous costume, standing before a looking-glass, while her maid puts the finishing touches to her toilette. A male visitor looks on in apparent admiration, and a servant brings in a tray of chocolate and a letter addressed to " Her Grace "[1] (Pl. CCI.). In *The French Petit Maître*, engraved by C. Grignion, we have a young exquisite, wearing a coat covered with a pattern of hearts, a tall bouquet in his button-hole, and a wig tied with an immense bow. He is walking in the Rue d'Enfer, followed by his valet, who seems to be bringing him a bill (Pl. CCII.).

With a passing mention of a design by S. H. Grimm[2] called *The French Lady in London ; or, the Headdress for the year 1771* (Pl. CCIII.), and of Bunbury's early etchings of French types, we may proceed to a consideration of Rowlandson's drawings—executed during his best period—of *A French Family* and *An Italian Family*. In the first are portrayed with admirable effect the mingled squalor and tawdry finery of a family of professional dancers practising their steps (Pl. CCV.); in the second, we have the squalor, without much attempt at finery, of a family of Italian musicians, engaged in playing, amid many interruptions, a piece of concerted music. In the same *genre*, and by the same artist, are *The French Coffee-house* (Frontispiece), and three pairs of contrasted designs, a *French Valet* and an *English Valet; French Barracks* and *English Barracks; French Travelling; or, the First Stage from Calais* (Pl. CCVI.), and *English Travelling; or, the First Stage from Dover* (Pl. CCVII.). Although Rowlandson was himself no bigoted patriot, he was working for a public that was prejudiced against our neighbours, and as often as he contrasts French with English institutions, the advantage is with those of his native land.

Turning to scenes from domestic life during the last decades of the century, we find an *embarras de richesses* in the works of Rowlandson alone. For 1785 we have the companion designs, *Filial Affection ; or, a Trip to Gretna Green*, and *Reconciliation; or, the Return from Scotland*. In the first, a runaway couple are seen galloping towards Gretna Green in a chaise and four, hotly pursued by several horsemen, the foremost of whom flourishes

---

[1] This may have been intended for the pseudo-Duchess of Kingston.
[2] Samuel Hieronymus Grimm (1734–94). A Swiss water-colour painter, who produced a few caricatures. He settled in London in 1778, and exhibited occasionally at the Royal Academy.

C. Brandoin   1771

THE ENGLISH LADY AT PARIS

Brandoin pinxt

C. Grignion
sculp.

A FRENCH PETIT MAITRE AND HIS VALET

LA FRANCOISE A LONDRES

THE FRENCH LADY IN LONDON
OR THE HEAD DRESS FOR THE YEAR 1771

DONE FROM THE ORIGINAL DRAWING BY J. H. GRIMM

Printed for S. Sledge, Printseller in Henrietta Street, Covent Garden 2 Ap. 1771

RECONCILIATION or the RETURN from SCOTLAND.

T. Rowlandson del.

S. Alken fecit

A FRENCH FAMILY

[Published Dec. 1785 by S. Alken, Dufour's Street, Soho
and republished in 1790 by S. W. Fores, No 3, Piccadilly]

Design'd by T. Rowlandson

Acquatinta by F. Jukes

FRENCH TRAVELLING, OR THE FIRST STAGE FROM CALAIS

Publish'd Novr 5 1792 by S. W. Fores. No 3 Piccadilly

Design'd by T. Rowlandson

ENGLISH TRAVELLING OR THE FIRST STAGE FROM DOVER

London published Oct:r 25 1785 by T. Smith, No 6 Wardour Street, Scho

his whip at the eloping lovers. The bridegroom points a pistol at the pursuers out of one window, and the bride levels a second pistol, presumably at her father, out of the other. In the sequel, the newly-married pair have returned home to plead for forgiveness, which, judging from the attitude of the offended father and the old servants, has not been withheld (Pl. CCIV.).

In 1789 appeared *The Dull Husband*, a sketch of a rather prosaic-looking gentleman who has fallen asleep while his graceful young wife is making music upon the harp; and *Domestic Shaving*, in which we see an elderly man shaving himself before a mirror held by his pretty wife, while his little girl watches the gambols of a cat and a kitten. In *A Visit to the Uncle* and *A Visit to the Aunt* (1786 and 1794), the not too disinterested attentions of some nephews and nieces to their well-to-do relations are humorously portrayed. Other subjects by the same artist which may be mentioned in this connection are *A Hen and Chickens*, a pretty woman surrounded by a group of chubby children, *The Sailor's Family*, *A Rustic Courtship*, *She would be a Soldier*, and a charming sketch (without a title) of a young husband examining in consternation a document, which is obviously his wife's dressmaker's bill. The indifference of the lady and the pious horror of an old lawyer are excellently suggested.

Turning from Rowlandson to his friends and contemporaries, a specimen of Henry Wigstead's[1] work may be given in the *The Country Vicar's Fireside*, engraved by E. Wilkins in 1788 (Pl. CXCIX.). In front of a roaring fire sits a stout old cleric in a powdered wig, with a clay pipe in his mouth and a pot of hot toddy on the trivet. On the other side of the hearth sits his old wife, and between the two is a pretty daughter with a book on her lap, to which she pays more attention than to the curate or schoolmaster, who is making love to her in the intervals of using the bellows. In another domestic interior by an anonymous artist, called *Politics*, we are introduced into an evening party, where the male guests are busily engaged in discussing politics, while at each end of the room sits a group of ladies, obviously very much bored. One elderly dame has gone to sleep, and a young one is yawning unaffectedly.

Another popular caricaturist of the day was George Moutard Woodward,[2] commonly called "Mustard George." Woodward, according to his friend Angelo, was the son of a land agent and spent his youth in a country town, where nothing was less known than everything pertaining to the arts. "A caricaturist in a country town," said Mustard George, "like a bull in a china shop, cannot live without noise; so, having made a little noise in my native place, I persuaded my father to let me seek my fortune in town." Thanks to a small allowance from his father, supplemented by his own earnings, George

---

[1] Little seems to be known of Wigstead except that he exhibited at the Academy from 1784 to 1788, and died in Greek Street, Soho, in 1793. One of his most popular plates was called *Traffic*, a representation of a few old-clothes dealers. Rowlandson etched some of his designs.

[2] G. M. Woodward (*c.* 1760–1809). Besides his *Eccentric Excursion*, he produced the *Caricature Magazine*, *Le Brun Travestied*, and other volumes of comic sketches.

was able to enjoy life in his own Bohemian fashion, and ultimately took up his quarters at the "Brown Bear," Bow Street, where he was able to study the inhabitants of the roundhouse and the regular attendants at the police-court. At the "Brown Bear" he died suddenly, departing in character with a glass of brandy in his hand, and was long mourned by his tavern associates.

In his *Eccentric Excursion*, which appeared in volume form in 1796 (the designs engraved by Isaac Cruikshank), there are several domestic subjects, such as *The Polite Congregation, Showing Family Pictures*, and *The Formal Introduction*. Among other popular designs by Woodward are *Raffling for a Coffin, The Club of Quidnuncs, Babes in the Wood, A Goldfinch and his Mistress* (Pl. CCVIII.), and a series called *Six Ways of Carrying a Stick*. The majority are marred by extravagant hideousness, but Angelo was of opinion that "had this low humourist studied drawing and been temperate in his habits, such was the fecundity of his imagination and perception of character that he might have rivalled even Hogarth."

Another member of this school of minor caricaturists was Samuel Collings, whose designs for *The Picturesque Beauties of Boswell* have already been noticed. Collings, sometime editor of *The Public Ledger*, was a lively satirist both with pen and pencil, and, like the rest of the fraternity, a regular frequenter of taverns and green-rooms. He was found dead late one night on the steps of an hotel, and "great was the surprise of his *convives* on discovering that he, scribbler and caricaturist, should die with sixty pounds in his purse, which was found in his pocket." Several of Collings' designs were engraved for the *Wit's Magazine* (1784-5), among the best known being *The Citizens at Vauxhall, The Battle of the Umbrellas*, and *The Park Shower*. More ambitious are a pair of companion plates published under the title of *The Heir Disinherited* and *The Disinherited Heir*. The first scene is laid in a drawing-room, where an old lawyer is reading a will aloud to an assembled family. The eldest son, who has been cut off with a shilling, spills his glass of wine in his agitation, while his dog looks up at him in uncomprehending sympathy. His mother and sisters are evidently distressed at his misfortune, but the younger brothers find it impossible to conceal their triumph (Pl. CCX.). In the companion design the heir is being turned out of doors by his younger brother's orders. His mother is too much absorbed by the attentions of a fortune-hunting youth to notice his departure; the lawyer and the sisters are apparently indifferent, and even the dog growls at the disgraced youth (Pl. CCXI.).

John Kay, the Edinburgh caricaturist (1742-1826), has already been represented in his sketch of a golf-player, but so prolific a worker deserves further mention. The son of a mason near Dalkeith, Kay was early apprenticed to an Edinburgh barber, and in 1771 started in business on his own account. In his leisure moments he executed portrait sketches in the caricature *genre*. Although self-taught, he showed considerable talent, and was encouraged to persevere in his art by many of his clients, notably by

CCIX

Here's amusement for married Gentlemen or a Specific for a Scolding Wife; Who buys of me.

Oh Murder!Murder!Oh Cruel Barbarian.

Cruel he has according to Law you Jezabel.

Pub. By I.Cook e.Temple Bar,Nov.2,1782

Judge Buller

JUDGE THUMB

OR—STICKS OF A LAWFUL SIZE FOR FAMILY DISCIPLINE

CCVIII

Woodward del

Cruikshank sculp

A GOLDFINCH AND HIS MISTRESS

Published by Allen & West, 15 Paternoster Row. Sep' 24, 1796

Drawn by Collings

Eng^d by R. F. Jukes
[C. 1786]

THE HEIR DISINHERITED

Pub^d by R. Pollard, Printseller, Spa fields, London

Drawn by Collings

Eng. by R. F. Juke.
[C. 1786]

THE DISINHERITED HEIR

Pub.d by R. Pollard, Printseller, S/afields, London

JOHN KAY
DRAWN AND ENGRAVED BY HIMSELF, 1786

THE SOCIAL PINCH

[BY JOHN KAY]

MISCELLANEOUS

Mr. Nisbet, of Dirleton, who treated him as a friend and equal, and at his death in 1784 left him an annuity of twenty pounds. The following year Kay gave up his barber's business and devoted himself to his etching. In all, he etched nearly nine hundred plates, producing caricature portraits of nearly every celebrated Scotchman of his time. One of the earliest of his published plates was a portrait of himself (dated 1786), in which he is represented with a favourite cat, and his tastes are indicated by a palette, a brush, and a manuscript (Pl. CCXII.). He sketched Mrs. Siddons as the heroine of *Douglas*, Lunardi with his balloon, Captain Grose examining an ancient inscription, and the elder Angelo on his favourite *manège* steed. Among the best of his social subjects are *A Military Promenade, Modern Nursing*, a lady in fashionable costume carrying a baby in a most uncomfortable attitude, and *The Social Pinch*, a capital sketch of a gentleman taking a pinch of snuff out of the horn of a sedan-chair man (Pl. CCXIII.). Kay's etchings, though somewhat stiff and angular, are distinguished by a certain quaintness and individuality, while his portraits were reputed to be excellent likenesses.

This hasty survey of domestic life as viewed by the later caricaturists may be concluded by an illustration that throws a somewhat lurid light upon the whole subject. In 1782 a good deal of sensation was caused in family circles by Judge Buller's[1] public pronouncement that a man might lawfully beat his wife with a stick no thicker than his thumb. The caricaturists seized with delight upon so promising a subject, and Gillray, among others, etched a plate called *Judge Thumb, or Patent Sticks for Family Correction : Warranted Lawful*. The Judge is hawking bundles of sticks surmounted with thumbs, and in the background a husband is thrashing his wife. In a print with the same title, which seems to have been adapted from Gillray's design, the Judge is shouting, "Here's Amusement for Married Gentlemen, or a Specific for a Scolding Wife." The husband, who is administering chastisement, replies to his wife's complaints and reproaches, " Cruel, ha ! 'tis according to Law " (Pl. CCIX.).

---

[1] Sir Francis Buller (1746–1800). Justice of the King's Bench in 1778, and Justice of the Common Pleas from 1794 to 1800.

INDEX

INDEX

INDEX